GUIDE TO TEACHING STRINGS

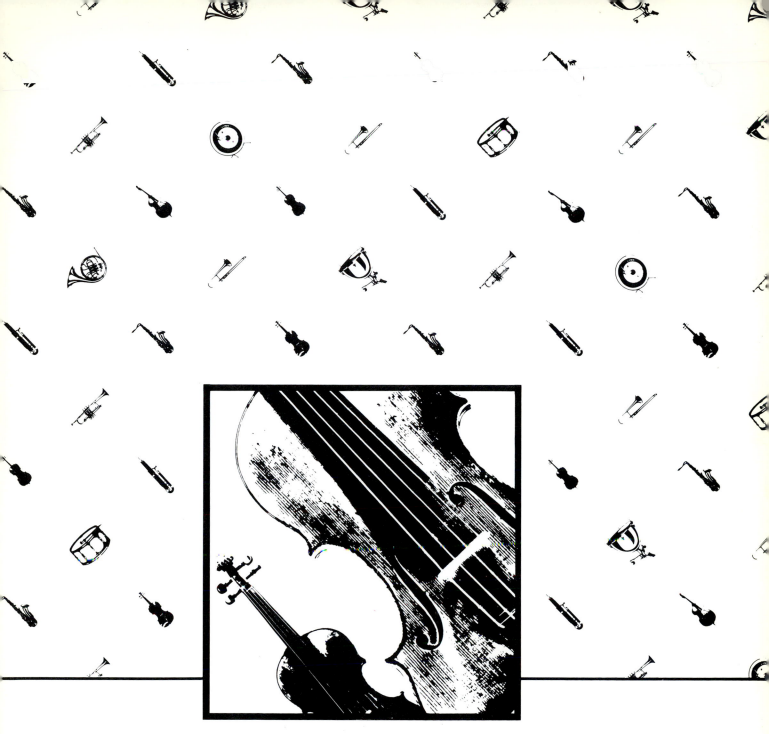

GUIDE TO TEACHING STRINGS

NORMAN LAMB

RETIRED
CALIFORNIA STATE UNIVERSITY, SACRAMENTO

FIFTH EDITION

Wm. C. Brown Publishers

Book Team

Editor *Meredith M. Morgan*
Developmental Editor *Cindy Kuhrasch*
Production Coordinator *Peggy Selle*
Permissions Editor *Mavis M. Oeth*

 Wm. C. Brown Publishers

President *G. Franklin Lewis*
Vice President, Editor-in-Chief *George Wm. Bergquist*
Vice President, Director of Production *Beverly Kolz*
Vice President, National Sales Manager *Bob McLaughlin*
Director of Marketing *Thomas E. Doran*
Marketing Communications Manager *Edward Bartell*
Marketing Manager *Kathleen Nietzke*
Production Editorial Manager *Colleen A. Yonda*
Production Editorial Manager *Julie A. Kennedy*
Publishing Services Manager *Karen J. Slaght*
Manager of Visuals and Design *Faye M. Schilling*

College Instrumental Technique Series
Consulting Editor: Frederick W. Westphal

Library of Congress Catalog Card Number: 88-63657

ISBN 0-697-05861-1

Printed in the United States of America by Wm. C. Brown Publishers,
2460 Kerper Boulevard, Dubuque, IA 52001

10 9 8 7 6 5 4 3

Contents

Part IV

Preface

Since its original publication, *Guide to Teaching Strings* has gained wider use each year in college and university string pedagogy classes. Many teachers and students have found that *Guide to Teaching Strings* picks up where the average method book leaves off. It supplies the category of practical information and know-how that can mean the difference between success and failure or satisfaction and frustration for the starting teacher. While the book focuses primarily on the needs of the school instrumental music teacher, private teachers will also find it a valuable resource.

Guide to Teaching Strings is not a substitute for a good step-by-step method of instruction on a string instrument. Learning through playing an instrument is essential to the adequate preparation of the future school orchestra director. *Guide to Teaching Strings* supplements that kind of instruction with vital information that most methods do not cover. This body of knowledge includes information about the physical aspects of the instruments themselves—bows, strings, cases, and accessories, their selection and maintenance. It also includes information about the kinds of problems a teacher will have to deal with in teaching strings, plus suggested solutions to these problems. Coverage of this almost totally neglected facet of string teaching receives major emphasis in this book.

Guide to Teaching Strings presents in understandable language, reinforced with clear illustrations, an approach to playing and teaching the string instruments, which is based upon the author's many years of experience as a teacher, music supervisor, and professional musician. But I want to stress that it does not pretend to be *the only way*. For if my experience has taught me anything, it is that there is more than one satisfactory way to hold the bow, shape the left hand, produce a vibrato, and execute a shift. To deny this would demonstrate a narrow view, a closed mind, and the height of conceit. But if it is thought that this admission in some way decreases the useableness of the book, the reader is reminded that such great teachers and players as Leopold Auer, Carl Flesch, D. C. Dounis, Ivan Galamian, Leonard Rose, Janos Starker, and Pablo Casals—to name a few—have demonstrated rather pronounced differences of opinion in their approaches to various aspects of teaching and playing.

Each college and university string teacher will have personal views and convictions about how the instruments and bows should be held and manipulated, and in what order certain skills should be taught. The author looks upon this kind of thing as the natural and inevitable modification and adaptation of ideas in a discipline which is given to very personal and individual concepts and practices. He would caution only that departures from what is presented here should be defended with something stronger than "this is how I do it."

Guide to Teaching Strings is unique in that it contains under one cover practical information which heretofore, if it was available at all, had to be searched for extensively or learned through experience. In addition to the information about each of the instruments and how to teach them, this book discusses ways to organize and schedule classes, techniques for recruiting students, as well as motivation and evaluation.

This revision contains a new chapter that explores the use in the string instruction program of some of the new technology, including computer programs that can help students improve in the areas of note reading, rhythmic comprehension, and pitch discernment. *Strolling Strings* is discussed as an interesting new concept of performance for school groups and as a way to inject new life into a program that might be in need of reenergizing. And *Music Medicine* is given a brief introduction for the benefit of those who may not be aware of this rapidly growing field of medical specialization. There are study questions, an appendix listing terms and symbols pertaining to string music, illustrations of new products, an updated and enlarged list of teaching materials for string classes as well as for each of the instruments, and a new appendix that furnishes names and addresses of music, instrument, and equipment suppliers.

Where possible and warranted, the author has incorporated minor changes in terminology that have shown up in the recently published (1988) *The Complete String Guide: Standards, Programs, Purchase, and Maintenance* (written jointly by ASTA, MENC, and NSOA) in the belief that this *Complete String Guide* will be the authoritative resource book for the school string instruction program for the forseeable future. It is my sincere wish that these and other changes will add to the value and usefulness of the book.

My gratitude again goes to all of those who provided assistance and guidance in the preparation of the first edition and this revision of *Guide to Teaching Strings*.

Readers are advised to make inquiries through their local music dealer regarding any of the products discussed in this book.

Prologue

The four instruments which will be discussed in this book are the violin, the viola, the cello, and the bass. These four instruments make up the string section of the orchestra. Collectively they are referred to in any of the following ways:

The String Family
The String Section
The String Orchestra
The String Choir
The String Quartet
The String Instruments
The Strings

In the orchestra, as in the string quartet, the violins are divided into two sections—firsts and seconds. Since the full string section of a symphony orchestra comprises nearly two-thirds of the total membership of the orchestra—and hopefully the school orchestra aspires to these proportions—it is extremely important that anyone who contemplates the possibility of directing an orchestra become as knowledgeable as possible of the problems and possibilities of these instruments.

Part I

The simplicity of the design and function of the string instruments tends to be somewhat misleading. The absence of keys, corks, springs, valves, and pads creates the impression that there is little that one needs to know about the workings of these simple wooden boxes with the strings stretched across them.

While it is true that a well constructed, correctly outfitted and adjusted string instrument can give months or even years of relatively carefree service, the details that go into putting an instrument in this condition originally are of the utmost significance and importance.

One of the major deterrents to a string program is poor equipment or good equipment in poor condition. Frequently the reason poor equipment is tolerated is that the teacher is not aware of the problems. The aim of chapters 1 through 5 is to provide an understanding and appreciation of the details that must be considered in equipping and adjusting a string instrument properly. If the teacher is aware of what is required for string instruments to function well, and is diligent about keeping them in prime condition, he or she will have eliminated a prevalent cause of frustration and failure. Chapter 5, Care and Maintenance of the String Instruments, will be very helpful also in indicating the kind of maintenance program needed to keep equipment in good order.

1 Chapter

Introduction to the String Instruments

Before beginning the study of the practical aspects of string instruction, the student will benefit from this brief history and overview of the instruments of the string family.[1]

1. This history is not intended to be complete or exhaustive. Any student who is especially interested in this aspect of study need only consult the standard reference books and books on the history of music, or books such as David Boyden's *History of Violin Playing* and Wechsberg's *The Glory of the Violin.*

2. However, E. Van der Straeton in *History of the Violin* (New York: Da Capo Press, 1968) quotes material from Kathleen Schlesinger's *Precursors of the Violin Family* that claims the violin descended from the 7th century Egyptian kithara, and charts the lineage.

HISTORY

Early Ancestors

It is probably not too farfetched to say that each of the very early string instruments played with a bow had some part in the development of the violin, even though, in some cases, the part played may have been small, remote and may not be well documented. Some of these early instruments are the Arabian *rebab,* the oriental *rebec,* the French *vielle* and *gigue,* the English *crwth,* and the Italian *viola.* Historians and scholars agree that these instruments existed, but they do not agree on any sort of evolutionary lineage leading through them to the violin.[2] Contributing to the confusion

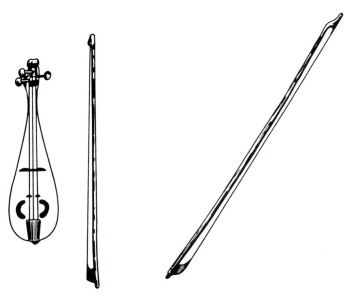
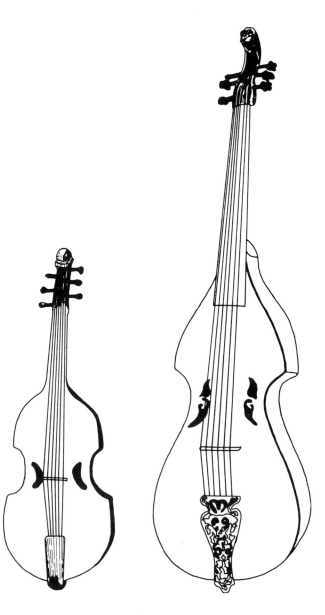

Figure 1.1. Left to right: Rebec (14th–16th centuries); Viol (1632); Viola da Gamba (1550).

Figure 1.2. Bowed and plucked instruments of the Baroque Period. (Ferris / music, The Art of Listening, 2 ed)

surrounding the ancestry of the violin is the absence of reliable historical records and the tendency of writers and keepers of diaries in those days to apply a variety of names to the same instrument. For instance, it appears that the Roman *cithara* was also called *fidicula, fidula, fidel; fiddle* in Anglo-Saxon and German countries; *viguela* and *vihuela* in Spain; *vielle* and *viole* in France, and *viola* in Italy.[3]

There is also lack of agreement about whether members of the important viol family were forerunners of the violin. Some writers have claimed that the viols were the immediate predecessors of the violin. On the other hand, David Boyden, in *The History of Violin Playing from Its Origins to 1761,* states that no one has yet made a thorough study of the viols. He says further, "The viol and violin families represent two separate and distinct entities with respect to their structure, ideals of sound, and corresponding musical and social context." It seems to be fairly well agreed that the viols (treble, alto, tenor, bass) were in existence in the 15th century and that they continued to be used for nearly two centuries after the development of the violin.[4] Boyden concludes that the viol and violin families were not related.

Most writers on the subject of the origin of the violin agree that its exact beginnings are "clouded in mystery." That being the case, it would appear that each writer has collected the best possible information through research and has then devised theories based upon that information. These theories vary according to prior beliefs on the part of the writer, strength of the evidence collected, and the degree of objectivity of the writer.

Agreement on broad generalizations is probably more important to most of us than agreement on specifics. And for our purposes it is sufficient to know that for hundreds of years prior to the appearance of the violin, as we know it, there were string instruments played with a bow in existence in a number of countries. These early instruments were played at court functions, at fairs, festivals, and in taverns, for entertainment and dancing. There was no need for a big tone because rooms and audiences were limited in size. Performances were usually adjunct to a court function or festive celebration rather than being self-motivated entities. And from early paintings it would appear that such distractions as eating, playing cards, or simply conversing were acceptable conduct while music was played.

In the 15th century there were instruments resembling the violin; some had three strings, some had five. In Europe these instruments were called fiddle, violino, violon, and lira da braccio. It was only a matter of time until Amati, Gasparo da Salo, Maggini, and others came to a common agreement on the shape and construction of the violin, and a new and glorious period of music was born. For the violin was such a marvelous instrument, capable of such a range of expression and technique, that men devoted their lives to its mastery. The violin inspired composers to write for it to the limits of their creative and technical capability, and a whole new body of great music was born.

---

3. op. cit.

4. William Sandys in *The History of the Violin* (London: John Russell Smith, 1864) says there is evidence of viols dating back to the 12th and 13th centuries, and cites Potier in "Monumens Français" as saying there are frequent cases of representations of viols dating from the 11th century.

16th Century Italian Violin Makers

There is absolutely no doubt that the violins crafted in northern Italy beginning in the 16th century were the finest ever made. We can be sure of this because instruments from that period are still in existence, and in use, today, and are still capable of producing tone the beauty of which has never been equalled. What is not clear is who should be credited with the "invention" of the violin. The names of two prominent Italian makers are most often mentioned when the subject of the "invention" of the violin is discussed. They are Andrea Amati (1520–1580) and Gaspar da Salo (1540–1609). Some historians have given credit for invention to lesser known makers such as Testator, Kerlino, and Duiffopruggar. These names are only important to historians, whereas Amati and Gaspar da Salo are important because examples of their work and their artistry are not limited to museum cases, but are still producing the beautiful sounds they first made more than four hundred years ago.

The first great violins were made in Brescia and Cremona in northern Italy between 1500 and 1550, probably closer to the middle of the century. Later Cremona became the main center of activity, primarily because the city of Cremona was the home of one of the greatest violin makers of all time, Antonio Stradivari (c. 1644–1737). Following in Stradivari's footsteps was a long line of Italian makers who created marvelous instruments: Guarneri, Ruggieri, Bergonzi, Storioni, Grancino, and Gagliano. Sons learned the craft from their fathers and in turn taught their sons, and the glorious period of great violin making continued for two hundred years, ending with the Ceruti family.

Two points should be clarified here. First, the term violin, as used here, refers to the other members of the string family as well, that is the viola, violoncello, and bass. Almost without exception the great violin makers made violas, cellos, and basses too, even though they did not make as many of these instruments as they did violins. The primary reason for this was because the demand for violins was greater, secondarily because from the same amount of wood required for one cello a maker could get possibly three violins, and also the time involved in making the larger instrument was greater.

The second point is that while there was a significant concentration of great violin makers in Italy, other countries, mainly France and Germany, can rightfully claim some great makers and some fine instruments. In Germany the Klotz family and Jacob Stainer became famous for fine instruments. The name Klotz was closely associated with the city of Mittenwald as a center of violin making. (It is interesting to note that it was in Mittenwald that mass production of violins began.) The most famous French maker was J. B. Vuillaume; others were Gand and Lupot. Not a long list. But to give credit where it is due, it should be noted that it was the French who perfected the modern bow, the most famous name in bow makers being François Tourte.

The fine old instruments by such makers as Stradivari, Guarneri, Guadagnini, and others are regarded as masterpieces. They are breathtaking to look at and to hear. The design of these instruments is a thing of beauty in itself. The curve of the ribs, the slope of the top and back, the elegance

Figure 1.3. A fine old Italian violin.

of the scroll—each is beautiful in form and shape. Add to this the natural beauty of the woods used, enhanced by varnish of unsurpassed luster, and one can understand one of the compelling reasons people of wealth seek to acquire the instruments of the masters as they do fine paintings and precious jewels. For from the standpoint of intrinsic value, these instruments are works of art comparable to a painting by da Vinci or a statue by Michelangelo.

These instruments inspire a cult of near worship. The worshipers divide themselves into three groups—the players, the dealers, and the collectors. The players know the instruments in terms of their playing quality; the dealers and the collectors are conversant with the physical characteristics such as model, grain of wood, color of varnish, blemishes, if any, and last but not least, value.

The large majority of these fine instruments are catalogued, their location and ownership is known, and their condition, value, and line of ownership is a matter of record.[5] Many of these fine instruments have taken on as nicknames the name of an early prominent owner. A few examples of the names given to certain Strads are "The Hellier," "Betts," "Sarasate," "Rode," to name a few.

---

5. Hill and Sons of London, one of the largest dealers in string instruments in the world, claim that Stradivari made 1116 instruments between 1666 and 1737. Of these, 540 violins, 12 violas, and 50 cellos are known and catalogued.

Modern Instruments

Fine handmade instruments are produced today in Italy, Germany, France, England, the United States, and some other countries. Some of these instruments are exquisitely made and rival the old masters in tone quality.

Mass Production of Violins

Burgeoning string programs in the public schools in the last thirty years have placed heavy demands upon string instrument suppliers. The need for large numbers of instruments of various sizes at minimal cost has brought about mass production techniques in the manufacture of string instruments—particularly violins.

In mass production techniques much of the work is done by machine. Parts are stamped out or sawed out in quantity; care is not given to graduation or consideration of the grain of the wood. In the factory-made instruments the wood is not always carefully selected or matched; parts do not always fit as they should; and symmetry is often lacking.

These remarks are not meant to imply that all quantity-produced instruments are cheap and tawdry. To the contrary, many production-line instruments are carefully made; good wood is used, and many of the finish details are done by hand by competent craftsmen.

Labels

The maker(s) or manufacturers of a string instrument identify themselves by means of a label, which is glued inside the instrument. The label is glued to the back and is visible through the *f* holes.

In the case of a handmade instrument the label usually contains the following information:

The maker's name.
The year the instrument was made.
The city or town in which the instrument was made.
In the case of modern instruments a serial number is not uncommon.

Labels in mass-produced instruments generally show the following information:

The name of the shop or firm for which the instrument was made.
The name of the maker whose instruments were used as a model.
The year the instrument was made.
A serial number or model number.

The name Stradivari is placed on the label of many factory or production-line instruments. These labels simply indicate that the instrument is a copy of a model made by Stradivari. People often become excited when they discover that a violin which has been in their house for many years (passed along to them by a relative or brought from Europe by someone who used to play), has a label bearing the name Stradivari. If it were a true Strad, they would surely have an insrument of considerable value. But there is little likelihood that the instrument is a Stradivari, since no unaccounted-for Strads have shown up for many years.

PRINCIPLE OF TONE PRODUCTION

Modern string instruments have four strings. These strings are stretched between the tailpiece and the tuning pegs, and each string is tightened to the tension that produces a given pitch. The hairs of the bow are drawn across the string setting the string into motion. The vibration of the string is carried through the bridge to the top of the instrument and to the back via the sound post. These two members in vibration cause the air contained within and without the instrument to vibrate.

In order for the various parts of the instrument to react and respond as needed to produce an even quality throughout its more than four octave possible range, these parts must be measured and carved to exact proportions. Careful attention must be given to the graduation of the thickness of the wood from side to center and from top and bottom to the center. Careful selection of wood is also important.

Maple is usually used for the back and ribs and pine or spruce for the top. The wood must be properly aged and have the kind of grain needed for the various parts. The varnish must give a luster to the wood and must be able to withstand the effects of constant handling, perspiration, and rosin.

When the bow is drawn across a string or strings which the fingers of the left hand are not touching, the result is known as playing on the "open string" or "open strings." When a finger is pressed down on a string, it is said to be "stopping" the string. This process raises the pitch of the string by reducing the length of the string. When one string is played in this manner, the term "single stop" is used to describe the effect. When two strings are played simultaneously, the effect is described as a "double-stop."

USE OF STRINGS IN THE ORCHESTRA

The string choir has an enormous range. Extending from the lowest notes on the bass to the highest notes on the violin, this range spans more than six octaves.

This extensive range, plus the great variety of tonal effects of which the strings are capable, and the nearly limitless number of ways in which they can be divided and combined, has interested and intrigued composers through the centuries. There are many beautiful and varied works for string orchestra. In the full orchestra context the strings form the basic foundation of sound to which the woodwinds, brasses, and percussion add color and reinforcement.

In the symphonies of Haydn and Mozart the strings were treated much as if they were a quartet. Their technical limitations were determined by the extent of musical and technical exploration of that period. The romanticists extended the playing range of each of the instruments and suited the treatment of the string choir and its members to the more advanced demands made by the richer, more opulent texture of their kind of music. Wagner, Strauss, Berlioz, and later Ravel and Debussy, expanded and extended the technical demands made upon the strings. These composers discovered new vistas of color and required the ultimate in technical dexterity from each section of the string choir.

In string writing the violin plays the dominant role to a great extent. It carries the lead, the soprano, the melody. An examination of the symphonies and quartets of Haydn and Mozart will bear this out. Beethoven and Brahms gave increased importance to the viola and cello, and more recent composers have placed increasing demands on all of the strings. However, even today the greatest technical and musical demands lie with the violins. These demands include speed, variety of techniques, and range.

Ranges

In writing for strings the high range limits must be used with care, knowledge, and skill. The extremes should only be used in music intended for performance by accomplished players. For school musicians ranges must be somewhat limited. Beginning, intermediate, and advanced ranges are shown below.

PARTS OF THE STRING INSTRUMENTS

The violin, viola, cello, and bass are much alike except for size and a few minor details such as tuning mechanisms and end pins. Each is made of wood, is played with a bow, and employs four strings.

Of the four instruments, the bass differs most in that it retains the sloped shoulders of the viol family. In addition, the back of some basses has an angular rather than a curved construction. It is literally the bass viol.

On the other hand, the violin, viola, and cello look like small and large versions of one another. If seen from a distance, without the benefit of perspective or relationship, they

can be mistaken for each other in appearance. This is particularly true of full-size violins and small violas, which are nearly identical in size.

The most important parts of the instruments are described below. The parts are identified in Figures 1.5, 1.6, 1.7, 1.8, and 1.9.

Body

The body consists of the top, back, and ribs. Note the points at which body length is measured. The body is the resonating chamber of the instrument. It is this resonating chamber that receives and amplifies the vibrations set up by the strings. Each part of the body vibrates in the tone-producing process. It is for this reason that the selection of wood, the manner in which it is graduated; the final design of the instruments; the correct setting and alignment of bridge, soundpost, and strings; and the varnish, which is used to preserve the wood and give it beauty, are so important.

It should be pointed out here that with the exception of some basses and cellos which are made of plywood, the wood used in the making of the string instruments is generally maple and spruce. These woods are carefully selected for their grain, strength, and beauty.

Top (Belly, Table)

The top is made of a softwood such as spruce. It is usually made of two pieces joined in the center. The center of the top is its highest point. It then dips to the outer edges at the top, bottom, and sides.

Just below the center and to each side of the middle, *f* holes are cut. These holes permit the flow of the vibrations from the instrument. The design of the *f* holes has undergone some modification up until the period of the great Italian masters, at which time it became fairly stereotyped. The *f* holes are both beautiful and practical. In addition to acting as air vents, they give access to the interior of the instrument.

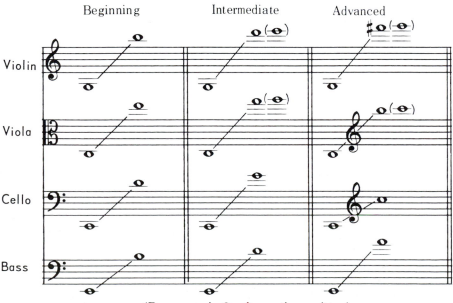

(Bass sounds *8va* lower than written)

Figure 1.4. Bass, cello, viola, violin. Scale is in feet.

It is through the *f* holes that the sound post is inserted and set, and the bass bar and other parts of the interior may be examined.

Bass Bar

The bass bar is a long, narrow piece of spruce cut to conform to the curve of the top. It is glued lengthwise to the top, left of center, in line with the left foot of the bridge. Its purpose is to reinforce the top of the instrument. It strongly influences the tone quality of the instrument.

Back

The back is made of a hardwood such as maple. Most often two pieces of wood are glued together to form a two-piece back. When the two pieces have been joined, they are then treated like one piece of wood as it is shaped into the back. Occasionally a back is made of one piece of wood.

Purfling

The purfling is a decorative line of inlaid wood, which runs around the outline of the instrument, close to the edge, on the top and the back. It is made of three very narrow strips of wood, the two outer strips being dyed black. The purfling is laid in a channel. In addition to adding beauty to the instrument, the purfling will prevent cracks from reaching the outer edge of the top or back. In some inexpensive instruments a painted line replaces the inlaid purfling.

Ribs

The ribs are also made of hardwood, usually matching the grain of the back. The ribs are made in six pieces, each about 3/64 inch thick, in the case of the violin.

Blocks and Linings

The top, back, and ribs are glued together with the help of blocks at the four corners of the middle bouts and at the center of the top and bottom of the body. The linings are long,

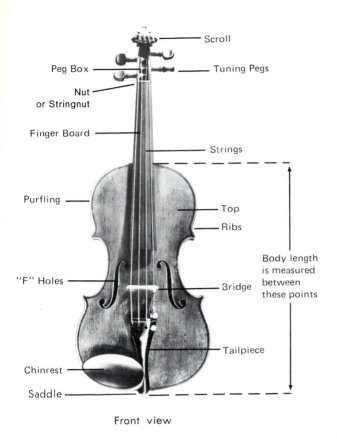

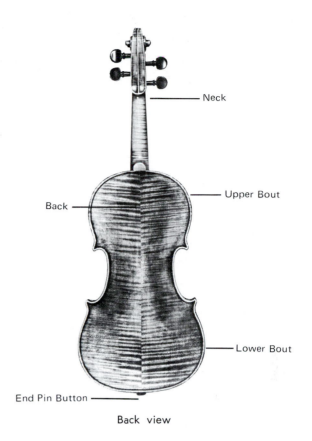

Scroll

Peg Box — Tuning Pegs

Nut
or Stringnut

Neck

Finger Board

Strings

Purfling

Top

Ribs

Back

Upper Bout

Body length
is measured
between
these points

"F" Holes

Bridge

Lower Bout

Tailpiece

Chinrest

Saddle

End Pin Button

Front view

Back view

Figure 1.5. Parts of the violin and viola. (Courtesy Scherl & Roth, Elkhart, Indiana)

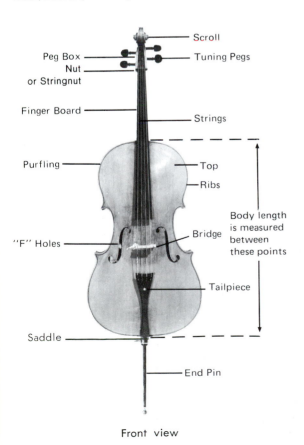

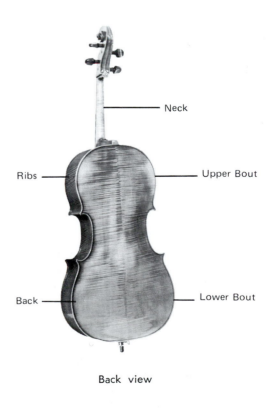

Scroll

Peg Box — Tuning Pegs
Nut
or Stringnut

Neck

Finger Board

Strings

Purfling

Top

Ribs

Ribs

Upper Bout

Body length
is measured
between
these points

"F" Holes

Bridge

Tailpiece

Back

Lower Bout

Saddle

End Pin

Front view

Back view

Figure 1.6. Parts of the cello. (Courtesy Scherl & Roth, Elkhart, Indiana)

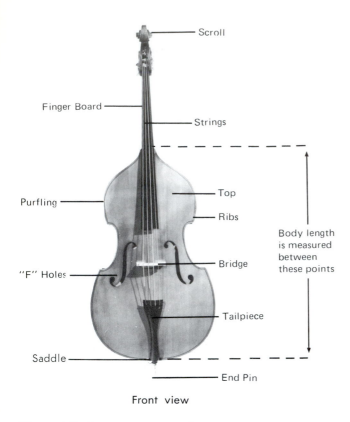

Scroll

Finger Board

Strings

Purfling

Top

Ribs

Body length
is measured
between
these points

"F" Holes

Bridge

Tailpiece

Saddle

End Pin

Front view

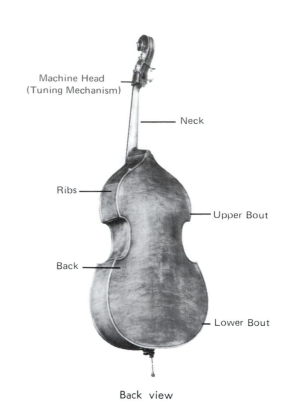

Machine Head
(Tuning Mechanism)

Neck

Ribs

Upper Bout

Back

Lower Bout

Back view

Figure 1.7. Parts of the bass. (Courtesy Scherl & Roth, Elkhart, Indiana)

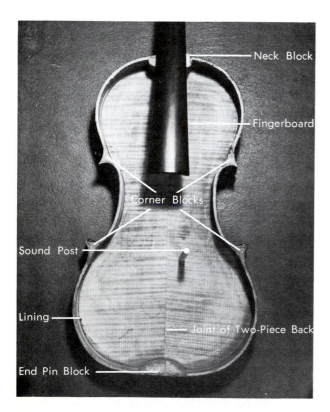

Neck Block

Fingerboard

Corner Blocks

Sound Post

Lining

Joint of Two-Piece Back

End Pin Block

Figure 1.8. Interior view of the body and back of a violin.

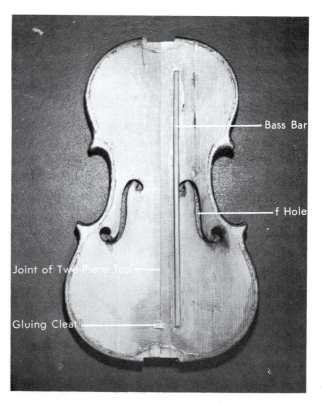

Bass Bar

f Hole

Joint of Two-Piece Top

Gluing Cleat

Figure 1.9. Interior view of the top of a violin.

wedge-shaped pieces of softwood, which are glued to the top and bottom edges of the ribs. They provide added gluing surface for the joint between the ribs and the top and back.

Sound Post

The sound post is a dowel made of softwood, which fits vertically between the top and the back of the instrument. It is generally positioned just to the rear of the right foot of the bridge, although the exact location is determined by trial and error. The position of the post has a great deal to do with the tone quality and playing properties of the instrument. The ultimate objective of "adjusting" the sound post is to find the exact spot that produces the optimum tone and response from the instrument. This process requires skill, patience, and a discerning ear.

Neck

The neck is made of maple. It is fastened into the top of the body with the help of a gluing block. Its shape and smoothness are important to the player; it is the neck upon which the important thumb of the left hand moves about.

Fingerboard

The fingerboard is made of ebony, an extremely hard wood. The fingerboard is fitted and glued to the top of the neck. It provides the surface upon which the strings are pressed down by the fingers of the left hand in the process described as "stopping" the strings.

Nut or String Nut

This is a small piece of ebony, which fits across the top end of the fingerboard. It is slightly higher than the fingerboard and is notched for the strings. Its purpose is to position the strings at the correct height above the fingerboard and provide the correct spacing of the strings.

Pegs and Peg Box

The pegs are fitted into holes in the peg box. They are made of ebony or box wood. The strings are inserted into holes in the pegs and are tuned by turning the pegs.

Machine Head

This is the metal, screw-type tuning mechanism, which is used almost exclusively on the bass. At one time this type of tuning mechanism was used on the other instruments, but it is unusual to find such instances today.

Scroll

This is the only part of the instrument that is almost completely ornamental. The only practical use which can be attributed to it is that it balances the instrument and helps when fitting an instrument to a small child. (See Figures 7.1 and 7.2.) The scroll adds to the artistic appearance of the instrument and is a point of great interest and importance to the dealer in fine old instruments. Each maker carves the scroll in his own, personal style; so the scroll becomes a source of valuable information when attempting to identify the maker of an instrument that has no label and has, perhaps, undergone some transformations.

Bridge

The bridge is maple and is cut with a traditionally elaborate design. The feet of the bridge are carved to conform to the top of the instrument. The top is cut to match the curvature of the fingerboard and to position the strings at the desired height above the fingerboard. Notches are made in the top of the bridge to space the strings at the desired distance.

The bridge serves the very important function of carrying the vibrations from the strings to the top of the instrument.

Tailpiece

The tailpiece is made of ebony. The lower ends of the strings are held in the slotted holes in the tailpiece. The tailpiece is fastened to the end pin by a strong loop of gut, nylon, or wire. This anchors the strings to the bottom of the instrument. Metal tailpieces such as the Wittner, with built in adjusters, are made for some of the small-sized instruments.

Saddle

This is a small piece of ebony centered along the top edge of the lower bout. Its purpose is to support the tailgut or tailhanger, which loops around the end pin.

End Pin, End Button

VIOLIN AND VIOLA

The end pin or end button is a small peg that is inserted into a hole at the base of the instrument. The loop from the tailpiece goes over the end pin, thus anchoring the strings to the bottom of the instrument.

CELLO AND BASS

The cello and bass end pins serve the same purpose as described above, and, in addition, they contain a slot for an adjustable peg. This peg has the capability of regulating the height of the instrument from the floor.

Chinrest

The chinrest is, in the truest sense, an accessory to the violin and viola since it is not an integral part of the instrument's construction. But it is as important to the player as the neck and fingerboard. The chinrest can be made in many shapes and sizes. Its function is to provide a surface that the player can hold firmly with the forward part of the jaw. The chinrest is fastened to the bottom of the instrument to the left of the tailpiece, or on each side of the tailpiece, by means of a screw-type clamp.

VIOLIN

Violino (Italian)   *Violon* (French)
Geige (German)

The violin is the smallest member of the string family. Being the highest pitched of the four string instruments, it is referred to as the soprano. The violin has four strings, which are tuned as follows:

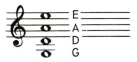

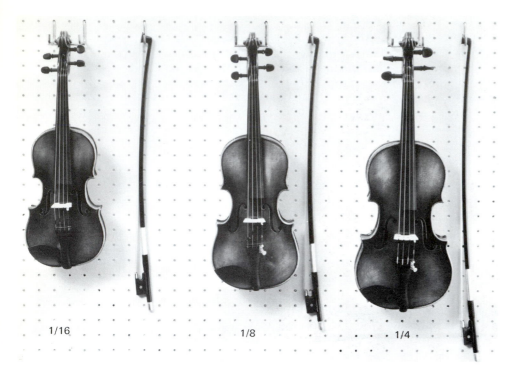

Figure 1.10. Violins: 1/16, 1/8, 1/4 sizes. (Courtesy Scherl & Roth, Elkhart, Indiana)

The violin is made in 4/4, 3/4, 1/2, 1/8, and 1/16 sizes. The 1/4, 1/8, and 1/16 sizes are becoming increasingly common and will be found in music stores and in schools where Suzuki programs are functioning. The body lengths of each of these sizes is shown in Table 1.1 as well as the age span when each size is most commonly used. It should be understood that the age indications are approximations only, since children grow at different rates.[6]

The small instruments have been developed in order that children can begin instruction when they are young. In the case of the child who starts instruction on one of the smaller instruments, the teacher and parents should be aware of the need for successive changes to progressively larger instruments until the full size is reached.

It is extremely important that each instrument be carefully "shop adjusted"[7] to ensure maximum ease of performance and optimum tone quality.

For the player, the length of the string between the nut and bridge is an extremely important factor; since it is this distance which determines where the fingers must be placed on the strings to produce desired pitches. A string length 1/4 inch longer than normal means the fingers will have to be placed proportionately farther apart to produce accurate intervals.

TABLE 1.1[8]

Violin Measurements

Size	Over-all Length	Body Length	String Length	Typical Age
4/4	23 1/4″	14″	12 3/4″	9–adult
3/4	21 2/3″	13 1/8″	11 7/8″–12″	8–11
1/2	20 1/2″	12 3/8″	11 1/8″–11 1/2″	6–10
1/4	18 1/8″	11″	9 1/2″–10″	4–7
1/8	16 1/2″	10″+	9″+	3–5
1/16	15″	10″–	8 1/4″	3–5

String length is measured from the nut to the bridge. The bridge should be centered on the inside notches of the *f* holes. The bridge setting and degree of tilt of the bridge are variables in determining string length.

String length becomes a factor of paramount importance if a player uses two instruments interchangeably. If circumstances compel one to use different instruments on occasion, then it is incumbent upon the player to see that the string length of the instruments is identical; for only then can he or she expect to be able to execute acceptable intonation. This is important even for the experienced player who can compensate for slight differences in instrument size and string length. For the young student it is absolutely vital. Satisfactory intonation is enough of a problem for the young student without the presence of added obstacles.

---

6. A method of determining the right size instrument for a child is explained in Chapter 7.

7. See page 000 for details of shop adjustment.

8. Suggestions for selecting the correct sized violin, viola, cello, and bass are dealt with in Part III.

Figure 1.11. Violins: 4/4, 3/4, 1/2 sizes. (Courtesy Scherl & Roth, Elkhart, Indiana)

VIOLA

Viola (Italian)   *Alto* (French)
Bratsche (German)

The viola is the alto of the string family. It is pitched a fifth lower than the violin. The basic construction of the viola is identical to that of the violin. The viola is larger than the violin, which accounts for its deeper, richer, more somber tone quality. The viola has four strings which are tuned as follows:

For school purposes violas can be considered to be made in three basic sizes (Table 1.2). These are Junior, Intermediate, and Standard. Junior size has a body length of 13 1/4–14 inches, which is about the size of a 4/4 violin. Intermediate size is 14 inches. Standard sizes range from 15 to 16 1/2 inches and larger.[9]

In the artist-model line the design of violas has been subjected to considerable experimentation. The object of this experimentation has been to develop an instrument with the much desired "big" viola sound but which is not uncomfortably large for the player to hold and play. Lionel Tertis, the famous English violist, has been a prime mover on this front. He was responsible for a viola model which was named after

TABLE 1.2

Viola Measurements

Size	Over-all Length	Body Length	String Length	Age When Used
Standard	26 1/4″+	15″–16 1/2″	14 1/2″±	12–Adult
Intermediate	25 1/4″+	14″	13 3/4″+	11–13
Junior	25″	13 1/4″	13 1/2″	9–11 (or under)

him. With the collaboration of an English maker, Richardson, Tertis designed a viola with narrow shoulders to facilitate playing in the higher register, and with greater width in the lower bouts to compensate for the loss of internal air space in the upper section. To gain yet greater inside volume, the ribs were made wider than normal, creating a "thick" appearance.

VIOLONCELLO (CELLO)

Violoncello (Italian)   *Violoncelle* (French)
Violoncell (German)

The cello is the tenor of the string family. Its basic construction is identical to that of the violin and the viola except that the cello has an adjustable end pin. The end pin is a rod that may be extended to a desired length from the bottom end of the cello. It is usually made of steel and has a sharp point. It is adjusted to place the cello at the correct height for the player. The end pin is held in place by a thumbscrew.

---

9. Violas are made as large as 17½ inches, but the larger sizes are not recommended for public school use.

Standard   Intermediate   Junior

Figure 1.12. Standard, intermediate and junior violas.
(Courtesy Scherl & Roth, Elkhart, Indiana)

Figure 1.13. Cellos: 4/4, 3/4, 1/2 sizes. (Courtesy Scherl &
Roth, Elkhart, Indiana)

Figure 1.14. Bass. (Courtesy Scherl & Roth, Elkhart, Indiana)

The pointed end then is placed in a hole in the floor, or in a cello board, or some other device that will prevent the cello from slipping forward.[10]

Cellos are made in several sizes ranging from 4/4 to 1/8. Sizes found most frequently in schools are 4/4, 3/4 and 1/2. Dimensions of these three sizes are given below in Table 1.3.

TABLE 1.3

Cello Measurements

Size	Over-all Length	Body Length	String Length	Age When Used
4/4	48 3/4″	30″ ±	27″ ±	12–adult
3/4	44 1/2″	27″ +	24 1/2″	10–13
1/2	41 3/4″	25 1/2″	23″	9–11

The cello has four strings, which are tuned as follows:

A
D
G
C

---

10. See Figures 3.30 and 3.33 for cello end pins. See Figures 3.31, 3.32, and 3.34 for devices to hold end pins in place.

Figure 1.15. Bass mechanical extension.

STRING BASS, DOUBLE BASS, BASS

Contrabasso (Italian)   *Contre basse* (French)

Kontrabass (German)

The bass is, as its name implies, the bass of the string family. Its design is different from the other string instruments, but its basic construction and component parts are comparable to those of the cello.

The unique features of the bass are its size (Table 1.4) and its machine-screw tuning mechanism. This mechanical tuning system makes raising and lowering the pitch of the weighty and large-diameter bass strings a relatively easy matter. Furthermore, when this device is in good condition, it virtually guarantees against string slippage.

The bass, like the cello, has an end pin. The purpose of the end pin is to elevate the instrument above the floor to suit the height of the player. The bass is held in a nearly vertical position, but it is still necessary for the end pin to rest securely in a hole in the floor or in a holding device of some kind to prevent slippage.

TABLE 1.4

Bass Measurements

Size	Over-all Length	Body Length	String Length	Age When Used
3/4	71 3/4″	43 3/4″	41 5/16″	11–adult
1/2	65 3/4″	40 1/8″	38″	9–13

Note: 4/4 and 7/8 sizes exist but are rarely seen in schools.

The bass has four strings, which are tuned as follows:

These strings sound one octave lower than where they are written.

At one time the bass had only three strings. Around the start of the 19th century the three-string bass was discarded for the four-string bass, which is commonly used in schools today. Five-string basses are to be found occasionally, the fifth string allowing the player to reach notes lower than the bottom E, which is normally the lowest note on the bass. A more common method of accomplishing this is to install a mechanical device on the E string, which elongates that string and makes it possible to reach the extra low notes via mechanical fingers. With the mechanical device shown in Figure 1.15, the levers make it possible to play E♭, D, D♭, and C.

STUDY QUESTIONS

1. Name two 14th–17th century ancestors of the violin.
2. Name and describe two types of viols.
3. What links the names Amati, Stradivari, Guarneri, and Guadagnini?
4. How is tone produced on a string instrument?
5. Name ten parts of a string instrument.
6. List the string instruments from smallest to largest.
7. Supply the French and German terms for the four-string instruments.
8. What is the "machine head"?
9. Name the pitches to which the strings of each of the instruments is tuned.
10. What is the overall range of the string instruments?

2 Chapter

The Bow

Bow
Arco (Italian)   *Archet* (French)
Bogen (German)

EARLY BOWS

The bow, like the instruments with which it is used, has undergone a number of changes in reaching its present shape. The bow used with the early viols had an outward curvature in contrast to the inward curvature of the modern bow. These early bows resembled the hunting bow after which they were probably designed.

Because of the straight or outward curvature of the stick, the hair of the viol bow was under less tension than the hair in the modern bow. Being under less tension, it was not able to withstand a great amount of downward pressure upon the string, and consequently was not capable of producing a loud or brilliant tone. In fact, the dynamic range of the viol was limited quite as much by the shape of the bow as by the design of the instrument itself.

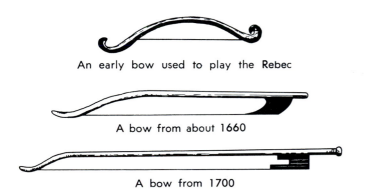

An early bow used to play the Rebec

A bow from about 1660

A bow from 1700

Figure 2.1.

THE MODERN BOW

As the instruments changed and the demands placed upon them changed, the design of the bow had to change too. In its present design the bow has much more strength and spring than its forerunner. It is capable of producing more tone and a wider range of dynamics, although the ability to sustain tone on more than two strings simultaneously has been sacrificed. The present design of the bow was perfected by the French bow maker, François Tourte, toward the end of the 18th century.

Violin, viola, and cello bows are similar in appearance. The viola bow is slightly larger in diameter and is slightly longer than the violin bow. The cello bow is larger in diameter and shorter in length than the violin and viola bows.

Bass bows are made in two models—the Butler or German model, and the French model. Each of these models is shown in Figure 2.2. The German model bow is held differently than the other bows as seen in Figure 10.7. The French model is similar in appearance to the violin, viola, and cello bows and is held in much the same way as the cello bow. The French model is presently used more extensively than the German model. However, some teachers prefer to start beginning students with the German bow.

BOW SIZES

Bows come in various lengths to match the size of the instrument they are to be used with. A 3/4 violin bow should be used with a 3/4 violin; a 1/2 size cello bow should be used with a 1/2 size cello; other sizes should match accordingly. The lengths of the various bows are shown below in Table 2.1. Measurements are from the tip to the end of the screw button. Measurements may vary slightly from those given.

TABLE 2.1

Bow Length

Violin	Inches
4/4	29 1/4
3/4	27
1/2	24 9/16
Viola	
Standard	29 5/8
Intermediate	29 3/16
Junior	27 1/4
Cello	
4/4	28 1/8
3/4	26 7/16
1/2	24 1/4
Bass	
French Model	28 1/16
German Model	30 3/8

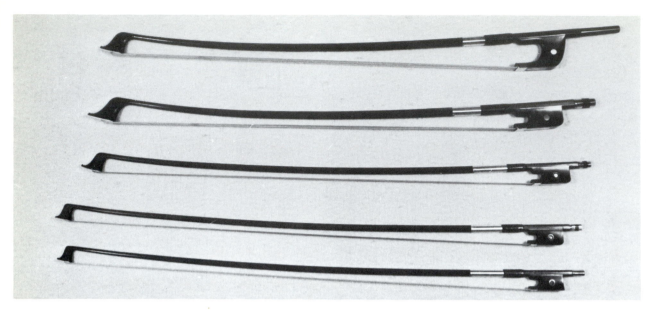

Figure 2.2. From top to bottom: German model bass bow,
French model bass bow, cello bow, viola bow, violin bow.

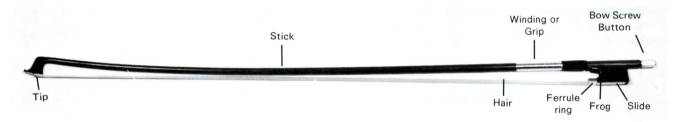

Figure 2.3. Parts of the bow. (Courtesy Scherl & Roth,
Elkhart, Indiana)

PARTS OF THE BOW

The main parts of the bow are pointed out above. These are the parts that are referred to in everyday use.

The Stick

Fine bows are made of pernambuco, a very hard, dense wood, which comes from South America. Lesser quality bows are made of rosewood and brazilwood. A few years ago a number of student bows were made of metal. These bows produced a very unpleasant tone quality. Fortunately, they have almost completely disappeared from use. Recently experiments have resulted in a promising bow constructed of fiberglass. This bow has many of the qualities of a conventional wooden bow and is less susceptible to breakage. The fiberglass bow is said to return to its original curvature even after being subjected to exaggerated tension over a long period of time.

The Hair

The best bow hair comes from Siberian horses. Some say the hair is taken from the mane; others say it is taken from the tail. The hair is cut to the correct length and is fitted into the tip and the frog. It can then be tightened and loosened by turning the screw in the frog.

Rosin is applied to the bow hair so that the hair will cause the strings to vibrate when it is drawn across them. Microscopic irregularities on the hair hold the rosin and activate the string. The quality of the hair is measured by the smoothness and steadiness with which it functions on the string, and how long it continues to function effectively, that is, before it loses its ability to "grip" the string.

As in the case of the attempt to find substitutes for wood for the stick, recent experiments have been made to find a suitable substitute for horse hair, which is becoming hard to acquire and very costly. Some synthetics have been tried and have been discarded as unsatisfactory. Others are on the market and appear to be comparable to horse hair in their performance.

The Frog

Frogs are made of ebony or other hardwoods, ivory, or tortoise shell. The function of the frog is to hold the hair and, with the help of the screw, tighten and loosen the hair. It also serves as a point against which to brace the thumb of the right hand. The frog must fit snugly onto the bow and must slide freely as the hair is tightened or loosened.

The Grip

The grip provides a slightly raised surface upon which to place the first and second fingers when holding the bow. Some grips are made only of leather, which is wrapped around the stick. Other grips begin at the frog with a leather wrapping and then continue with a silver wire or herring bone winding. The thickly wrapped part of the grip provides a secure place for the thumb and second finger to hold the bow. The wire wrapping, which extends toward the middle of the bow, provides a surface for the first finger to rest upon and protects the wood from wear. The Rolland Bow Grip was developed to assist young beginners in positioning the thumb correctly. (See Figure 3.28.)

The Screw Button

The screw button is made of metal and ebony or other matching wood in better bows, and of wood or plastic in cheaper bows. Turning the screw button tightens and loosens the hair.

Other Parts

Other parts which are essential to the bow, but which are not necessarily part of the vocabulary of the player are:

The metal bottom slide on which the frog moves.
The eyelet into which the screw fits.
The wedges that hold the hair in at the tip and frog.
The metal sleeve (ferrule) that holds the wedge in at the frog.
The mother-of-pearl slide that covers the opening in the frog into which the tied end of the hair and the wedge are placed.
The ivory tip that covers the plug, or wedge, and protects the point.

TIGHTENING THE BOW

To tighten the hair (or to tighten the bow, as is more frequently said), the frog is grasped between the thumb and fingers of the left hand, and the screw is turned with the thumb and first finger of the right hand.

There is no prescribed tension to which the bow should be tightened. Each bow has its own peculiarities. The tension of the bow must be suited to the player and the instrument. For young players, the general rule may be applied that the bow should be tightened until the hair is about one-half inch from the wood at its closest point. This may require from three to five turns of the screw, depending upon the bow. Unless guided, young students will often overtighten the bow to the point that the stick is straight or even attains an outward curvature. (See Figure 2.5.)

If the bow is in satisfactory condition—that is, if the stick has its initial curvature—it is never necessary to tighten it to the extent shown in (B) above. In fact, doing so completely removes any semblance of flexibility from the bow and produces what is slurringly referred to as a "club." The hair should always be loosened when the bow is returned to the case. Failure to do this can result in the bow becoming warped or losing its curve.

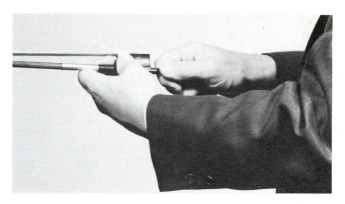

Figure 2.4. Correct way to hold the bow when tightening the hair.

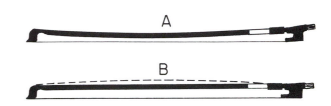

Figure 2.5. A. Bow correctly tightened; B. Bow that has been overtightened.

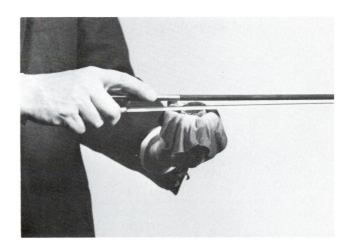

Figure 2.6. Correct way to hold the bow when applying rosin.

ROSINING THE BOW

Rosining the bow properly is a technique which is usually learned by trial and error. Some guidelines for the beginner are quite in order. Professionals know that rosin must be applied carefully and in the right amount. Children frequently apply too much rosin or apply rosin too infrequently, or not at all. Too much rosin on the bow is counterproductive in the effort to produce a good tone.

In rosining the bow, the rosin should be held in the left hand, the bow in the right. The first finger of the right hand rests on top of the stick; the remaining fingers grasp the frog. The hair is placed on top of the rosin cake, and the bow is drawn across the rosin from frog to tip and back.

A few back and forth strokes at both the frog and the point produce a small quantity of rosin dust, which is distributed the length of the hair as the bow is drawn across the cake. The bow should not be pressed down on the rosin too heavily; this causes excessive friction and will result in too much rosin or in the rosin melting and forming a glaze on the hair. Care should be taken to avoid touching the hair with the fingers; since oil from the skin removes the rosin and leaves a smooth spot on the hair that will not grip the string. The violin, viola, and cello bows are moved in both directions on the rosin, but because the bass rosin is so sticky, the bass bow is drawn across the rosin from the frog to the point only.

How often the bow should be rosined is a question that cannot be answered specifically because of the variables that apply. These variables are: the type of rosin used, the condition of the hair, the way the person plays, and the amount of use the bow is given. A general rule, which is fairly reliable, is that one rosining is good for approximately one to two hours of playing.

STUDY QUESTIONS

1. Supply the Italian, French, and German terms for the bow.
2. What was the principle difference between the ancient bow and the modern bow?
3. Who was the French bow maker who brought the bow to its present design?
4. What are the names of the two styles of bass bow?
5. Name the kind of wood of which the better bows are made.
6. List four parts of the bow.
7. Explain the purpose of rosin.
8. When tightened, the hair should be about how far from the stick at the middle of the bow?
9. What substance has been used in place of wood in making bows?
10. Why is it important to loosen the bow hair after use?

3 Chapter

Accessories

To compensate for the physical problems inherent in playing the string instruments, players, over the years, have invented numerous devices whose aim is to help the player. In time many of these accessories have become accepted as necessities. Included in this category are such items as shoulder pads, tuners, bow grips, and cello end pins. There are few players today who do not regard some of these accessories, in one form or another, as essential.

Of the accessories that will be discussed, only one, the mute, was designed deliberately to affect the tone of the instrument. All other accessories have to do with the mechanics of holding or playing the instrument, or with some aspect of the physical makeup of the instrument itself.

Some players argue that the type of shoulder pad used affects the tone of the violin and that the kind of end pin used influences the tone of the cello. The point made in regard to the shoulder pad is that if the shoulder or the pad is allowed to come into contact with the back of the violin or viola, the vibration of the back of the instrument may be somewhat reduced. For this reason a number of shoulder pads have been invented that keep the back of the violin completely clear of any contact, the feet of the pad, or rest, bearing only on the extreme edges of the instrument. The point made in the case of the end pin is that some of the vibrations set up by the instrument are carried through the end pin to the floor, or stand, upon which the player is seated, thus enhancing the quality and quantity of sound produced by the instrument.

It must be kept in mind that accessories come and go, and that new devices are continually appearing. Many are an improvement over their predecessor and may offer increased playing ease to the player, but each must be examined with an eye to utility, quality, and cost.

CHINRESTS

Purpose

Chinrests are used on violins and violas. The purpose of the chinrest is to provide an elevated, concave area, which the player can grasp firmly with his chin and/or jaw. Chinrests are made in a great variety of shapes and sizes to accommodate the many shapes and sizes of chins.

Before the invention of the chinrest, players simply grasped the violin between the shoulder and the chin, without the aid of a chinrest. This was unsatisfactory for two reasons. First, there is only the slightest rise at the outer edge of the violin and viola, thus providing very little for the player to get ahold of with the chin. Second, without a chinrest, the top of the instrument was subjected to extreme wear from the constant rubbing of the male player's whiskers. Some fine old instruments were worn through in the chinrest area as a result of excessive use without the protection of a chinrest.

Types of Chinrests

The cheaper chinrests are made of plastic. Better ones are made of wood. Some go across the tailpiece. Others are positioned in the middle of the instrument. But the majority of chinrests are positioned to the left of the tailpiece. An assortment of chinrests is pictured in Figure 3.1.

Selection of a Chinrest

The comfort and security of the player are the first things to consider when selecting a chinrest. A person with a long neck may find one of the higher chinrests desirable and vice versa. A square-jawed person may find the flatter type chinrest more comfortable than the deep-cupped type. Color of wood used in the chinrest can be another factor in selection. The best way to find a satisfactory chinrest is to go to a dealer or repairman who has a variety of chinrests to choose from. By trying one after another one will find the one best suited to his physical makeup and way of holding the instrument.

Figure 3.1. A variety of chinrests. (Courtesy Scherl & Roth, Elkhart, Indiana)

The Problems of Skin Irritation

There is constant friction between the chinrest, the base of the violin or viola, and the player's neck and chin. Many players, particularly men, have extreme difficulty with irritation of the skin in this area. The degree of the problem depends upon the nature of the individual's skin, the amount of pressure used to hold the instrument, temperature, and climate. To counteract this skin problem, some players have experimented with sponge-rubber pads glued to the chinrest. Others have experimented with chamois covers. Both of these latter devices are intended to protect the skin on the neck. A clean cloth, such as a handkerchief, placed between the neck and the instrument, can also do much to reduce the cause of skin irritation.

Clamping the Chinrest on the Instrument

The chinrest is clamped onto the instrument by two threaded sleeves, which fit over two oppositely threaded projections, one from the chinrest itself, and one from the foot, or clamp. This portion of the chinrest is shown in Figure 3.2. To secure the chinrest to the instrument, a small nail or a chinrest key is inserted into the hole in one of the chinrest sleeves. By tightening one and then the other of these sleeves, the chinrest can be secured firmly to the instrument. To avoid damaging the wood of the instrument, caution should be used when inserting the chinrest key or any other metal tightening device. Also, the sleeves should not be screwed too tight. Overtightening will crush the wood of the instrument.

Care

The chinrest requires little care. It should be cleaned occasionally with soap and water, and the screw sleeves should be checked occasionally to see that they are tight.

SHOULDER PADS

Purpose

The purpose of the shoulder pad is to fill the space between the top of the left shoulder and the back of the violin or viola. Its effect is to reduce or eliminate the need to elevate the left shoulder. It provides a nonslippery surface against which the shoulder can press in the holding process. (It is the upward pressure of the shoulder and the downward pressure of the chin that hold the instrument, with the help of the left hand.)

Types of Shoulder Pads

Shoulder pads range from the simplicity of the turned back lapel, as used by the late Fritz Kreisler, to the relatively more complex "Resonans" and "Menuhin" types. There are probably a dozen different shoulder pads available. Eight are shown in Figure 3.3.

MENUHIN AND LARK

These two shoulder pads are virtually identical. A velvet covered piece of plastic is affixed to spring steel legs, which have rubber covered feet. The feet clamp over the edges of the instrument.

FORTE PRIMO AND FORTE SECONDO

These shoulder pads bear the imprint Willy Wolf (Holland). The Forte Primo is straight with concave sides. The Forte Secondo is kidney shaped. The pad is sponge rubber and may be raised or lowered by adjusting the height of the feet. The feet clamp over the edges of the instrument.

RESONANS

This pad has a metal crossbar covered with velvet. Rubber covered feet clamp onto the edges of the instrument. These feet fold flat for easier storage of the pad in the case. The

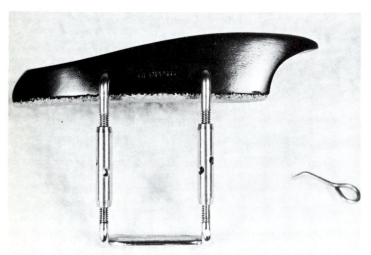

Figure 3.2. Back view of chinrest with tightening key.

Figure 3.3. Shoulder pads: left, from top to bottom, Menuhin, Lark, Forte Primo, Forte Secondo; right, from top to bottom, Resonans, Newsky, J-P-Egenter-Ajust, Poehland. (Courtesy Albert C. Muller & Sons, Inc., Sacramento, California)

feet may be bent inward or outward to fit instruments of different widths. Position of the pad on the instrument can be adjusted. The pad is made in three sizes—low, medium, and high. The viola model can be adjusted for width.

NEWSKY

Made in Finland, this pad comes in low, medium, and high for violin and viola. It is also available for 1/4, 1/2, and 3/4 sized violins.

J-P-EGENTER-AJUST

This is a velvet covered pad with a triangular mounting.

POEHLAND MODEL C

This pad is crescent shaped and concave. It is made of sponge rubber covered with velveteen or corduroy. It attaches to the end pin and the rubber band loops over the corner of the bout. The position of the pad can be adjusted by sliding it along the strap.

PLAY-ON-AIR (Not shown)

This is an inflatable, pillowlike pad.

Care

About the only care required by shoulder pads is that the rubber, which covers the feet, be replaced occasionally. This rubber deteriorates and rots off leaving the metal feet bare. In this condition they can mar the varnish on the ribs and back of the instrument. Also the rubber band will have to be replaced occasionally on the Poehland.

ROSIN

Rosin is hardened pitch from which the turpentine has been distilled. It is available in several qualities and at least two shapes—round and oblong.

Figure 3.4. Rosin in oblong and round cakes and powdered rosin. (Courtesy Scherl & Roth, Elkhart, Indiana)

Purpose

Rosin is rubbed onto the bow hair to make the hair sticky enough to grip the string and set it into vibration. (See Figure 2.6.) The hair does not have sufficient gripping power to do this by itself, a fact that is immediately evident if one draws a newly rehaired bow, which has not been rosined, over the string. Little or no sound will be produced, and until the bow has been well rosined, it will not produce a steady tone. After rehairing a bow, repairmen usually apply a liberal amount of powdered rosin to the hair. If powdered rosin is not used, extensive use of cake rosin will be needed to make the bow grip the string consistently. Rosin has been brought out recently in liquid form. It is used in this form by some repairmen in place of powdered rosin. No evaluation of this product is available.

Shapes of Rosin Cakes

Rosin is generally made in either round or oblong cakes. The round cake usually has a protective cloth cover which keeps the fingers out of contact with the rosin and protects the cake. The oblong cake usually has a wood or cork outer cover which keeps the fingers off the rosin and also helps to prevent the cake from being completely demolished if it is dropped on the floor. This type is recommended for beginners.

Qualities of Rosin

The variation in rosins lies in the coarseness of the grit that they dispense to the bow hair. A good rosin gives the bow the ability to "grab" the string without being rough or coarse.

Cello rosin is softer and more coarse than violin rosin. Bass rosin is gummy in consistency. It is made in several degrees of hardness.

Rosin will melt or become soft if subjected to too much heat. And since rosins come in varying degrees of hardness, it follows that a soft rosin may be used in cool climates but may not be satisfactory in warm climates.

The choice of rosin finally rests with the player. He must experiment until he finds a type that suits him, his bow, and his instrument. (Refer again to *Rosining the Bow,* Chapter 2, p. 19.)

TUNING PEGS

The tuning pegs are the four wooden pegs that are located in the peg box at the top of the instrument.

Purpose

Tuning pegs, as the name implies, are used by the performer to tune the strings. Except for the bass, which uses a machine head (see Figure 1.15), standard tuning pegs for the string instruments are made of hardwood such as ebony, rosewood, or boxwood. The string is inserted through a hole in the peg, and then by turning the peg one way or the other, the pitch of the string is raised or lowered.

Figure 3.5. A set of matched pegs, tailpiece, and end pin. (Courtesy Albert C. Muller & Sons, Inc., Sacramento, California)

Figure 3.6. Pegs and peg box. (Courtesy Scherl & Roth, Elkhart, Indiana)

The primary requirements of the peg are that it turn easily and smoothly, that it may be "set" at any of the infinitesimal number of points in its circle, and that it will stay, or hold, wherever it is set.

For a peg to meet the demands listed, it must be perfectly matched to the holes in the peg box, a condition not always found in instruments after a period of use. Pegs are tapered and peg holes are bored conically to match the taper of the peg. The taper is what makes it possible to set the peg so that it will not slip. By forcing the peg inward as it is turned, it is possible to set the peg very tightly.

Care

If pegs are in good condition, there is no need to do anything to them between string changes. By applying a small amount of peg compound to a peg when a string is changed, it should continue to function well indefinitely.

Poor quality pegs, or pegs that are not properly fitted to the instrument, will cause trouble until the basic problem is corrected by a competent repairman. No amount of peg compound, chalk, or rosin will make them work smoothly and hold.

The practice of using chalk on pegs to make them hold is acceptable only on an emergency basis, and then not on a good quality instrument. Chalk is a coarse, gritty, abrasive substance. It extracts the natural oil from the wood and will cause wear to both the peg and the peg hole.

Peg Compound, Peg Soap, Peg Dope

Peg compound is also called peg soap or peg dope. The individual products may appear to be different, but they are all basically the same. They consist of an abrasive substance mixed with jewelers rouge. A light coating on the peg lubricates the peg at the same time that it provides a gritty, holding quality.

Pegs can become worn or peg holes enlarged to the point that the peg no longer fits the peg hole. The result is that the peg no longer turns smoothly and it becomes difficult to set the peg so that it will not slip. In many cases an application of peg compound will solve the problem. More severe problems of slipping or sticking require the attention of the repairman, who may find it necessary to ream the holes and reshape or replace the pegs. This is not a job for the layman.

PATENT PEGS OR TENSION PEGS

Any peg that incorporates a screw or other mechanical device is classified under the heading "Patent Peg" or tension pegs. There are a number of such pegs on the market, some of which are described below.

Purpose

All of the patent pegs have a common aim and purpose—to make it easier to tune the instrument. The two main reasons patent pegs have been developed are (1) young players have difficulty setting pegs so that they will not slip; (2) good peg action is a quality that is not invariably present in school-grade instruments.

The beauty of the patent peg is that it can function perfectly despite the condition of the peg box; patent pegs are designed to act independently of the peg hole into which they are inserted. They supply their own bushings and their own holding tension. They should be installed by a skilled repairman. Breakage and mechanical defects can occur, but they are infrequent.

Types

ROTH-CASPARI PEGS[1]

The Roth-Caspari pegs look from a distance like ordinary pegs. They are distinguished by a screw that is located in the center of the knob. The ease with which the peg turns is regulated by this screw. The action of the peg is tightened by turning the screw to the right and eased by turning the screw to the left.

These pegs are available for 1/2, 3/4, and 4/4 sized violins, for viola, and for 1/2 and 3/4 sized cellos. They can be purchased from music dealers or repairmen. They should be fitted to the instrument by a repairman.

SCHALLER PEGS

"S" (Schaller) pegs are available for violin, viola, and cello. This peg is made of plastic and has a tension regulating device similar to the Roth-Caspari. They are available for 1/2, 3/4, and 4/4 sized violins, for viola, and 3/4 and 4/4 sized cellos.

Recommendations

Patent pegs are strongly recommended for the intermediate grade instrument, which is equipped with gut and gut-core strings. At this stage of development the student's fingers are usually not yet strong enough or well enough coordinated to turn and firmly set an ordinary peg. The slipping that results is a cause of great frustration to both student and teacher. Patent pegs can remove this source of frustration.

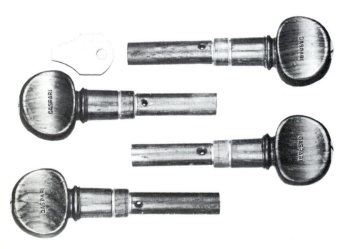

Figure 3.7. Roth-Caspari pegs. (Courtesy Scherl & Roth, Elkhart, Indiana)

TUNERS OR ADJUSTERS

A tuner is a small metal device consisting of a thumbscrew and a hook over which the end of the string is looped. Tuners are fastened to the tailpiece by inserting the threaded sleeve through the appropriate hole at the wide end of the tailpiece and securing it with the round nut, which is part of the tuner. Tuners are used on violins, violas, and cellos. By turning the thumbscrew to the right the pitch of the string is raised. By turning it to the left the pitch is lowered.

Purpose

Tuners are used with metal strings to enable the player to tune these strings more easily and accurately than can be done with the tuning peg. For this reason the device is sometimes referred to as a "fine tuner."

When to Use Tuners

As stated in the section, *Strings,* tuners should always be used with metal-core strings, since the pitch of these strings is altered considerably with the slightest change of tension, and the tuner makes possible the most minute adjustment in tension. Tuners should not be used with gut or gut-core strings, since these strings must be moved one way or the other across the nut in order to effect a change in pitch. This movement across the nut cannot be accomplished readily by increasing or decreasing tension on the tailpiece side of the bridge through the use of the tuner. Hence, the tuner is of no practical value in the case of gut strings.

It is recommended that string instruments for young beginners be equipped with steel strings and tuners. Steel strings stretch very little and are affected by temperature changes far less than gut strings; and if the pegs are in good condition, the child will probably be able to make all necessary tuning adjustments with the tuners. This removes the danger of the peg slipping and releasing the tension of the string or strings. The latter is an annoying experience. One string slipping usually leads to another. On cellos this can be a test of strength. You may win eventually, but you will very likely lose your patience in the process.

Types of Tuners

Tuners are made in a variety of types. In principle a threaded sleeve fits through the hole in the tailpiece that corresponds to the string with which the tuner is to be used. A round nut is screwed down over this sleeve, holding the tuner firmly on the tailpiece. A prong, or hook, projects up through the slot ahead of the hole, or out beyond the front of the tailpiece. The loop-end of the string is placed over this prong.

A rather special tailpiece with fixed tuners is made by "Thomastik." This consists of a molded plastic tailpiece of which the tuners are a permanent, integrated part. On this tailpiece the conventional gut tailpiece loop is replaced with wire or by the Sacconi tailpiece adjuster. The "Thomastik" is made for violin, viola, and cello.

Tuners are not made for bass since the bass is already equipped with a mechanical screw-type tuning device. With the exception of the "Thomastik," tuners may be installed and removed from the tailpiece at will. Not every tuner works satisfactorily with the small sized violins. Because of the small amount of clearance between the top of the violin and the

---

1. (The name Roth-Caspari is registered at the U.S. patent office, all rights reserved.)

bottom of the tailpiece, some tuners, when turned too far, will press down into the top and cause ugly scars. A string-mounted tuner designed to prevent this problem is now available for 1/4–1/16 sized violins. (See Figure 3.8A.)

Care

It is possible for the threaded screw of the tuner to become gritty with rosin dust. As a result it may become hard to turn. If this should happen, the tuner should be removed and washed in warm soapy water. A small drop of light oil should be placed on the screw. If the threads become stripped, the tuner should be replaced.

Figure 3.8A. An assortment of tuners. The tuner that is second from the left in the middle row is an example of a string-mounted tuner. (Courtesy Shar Products Company)

Figure 3.8B. View of a full set of tuners on a violin. (Courtesy Scherl & Roth, Elkhart, Indiana)

THE BRIDGE

Purpose

The bridge is an extremely important part of the string instrument, for it is through the bridge that the vibrations of the strings are carried to the instrument itself where the tone generation and resonance takes place.

Bridges are made of seasoned maple. Violin and viola bridges are designed somewhat differently from cello and bass bridges, and, of course, the size of the bridge is in proportion to the instrument. The design of the bridge is both practical and aesthetic.

Fitting the Bridge

Essential to the optimum function of the bridge is the exactitude with which it is fitted to the top of the instrument. "Fitting" a bridge is a job for a professional repairman. It involves thinning the feet of the bridge and carving them to match the contour of the top of the instrument. Next the top of the bridge is curved to match the contour of the fingerboard and to bring the strings to the correct height above the fingerboard. Notches are made carefully in the top of the bridge to space the strings at the correct distance from each other.

Most repairmen have personal idiosyncrasies about cutting wood away from one part of the bridge or another. This process amounts to a ritual in most shops and is predicated upon the repairman's intuitive sense of what is right for a given instrument. The placement of the bridge in relation to the *f* holes is also very important.

Figure 3.9. Violin bridges. (Courtesy Scherl & Roth, Elkhart, Indiana)

To recapitulate, the four most obviously important factors in fitting a bridge are:

1. Shaping the feet to the contour of the top of the instrument.
2. Achieving the correct distance between the strings and the fingerboard.
3. Spacing the strings correctly.
4. Finding the most desirable position for the bridge in relation to the *f* holes. Generally, this is in line with the inner notches in the *f* holes.

Bridge Height

The bridge should be high enough to allow the following clearances between strings and the top of the fingerboard at the bridge end. These distances are for standard or full-sized instruments; smaller instruments are slightly less.[2]

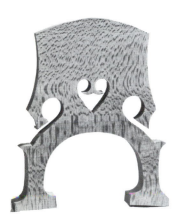

Figure 3.10. Cello bridge. (Courtesy Scherl & Roth, Elkhart, Indiana)

Figure 3.11. Bass bridge. (Courtesy Scherl & Roth, Elkhart, Indiana)

Gut Strings				
Violin	E	1/8″	G	3/16″
Viola	A	3/16″	C	4/16″
Cello	A	1/4″	C	5/16″
Bass	G	7/16″	E	5/8″

All Steel Strings				
Violin	E	3/32″	G	5/32″
Viola	A	9/64″	C	3/16″
Cello	A	11/64″	C	1/4″
Bass	G	21/64″	E	7/16″

Author's Note: Authorities differ on these measurements. Climate and personal preference must also be considered.

Bridge Curvatures

Obviously, the bridge curvature must conform to the curvature of the fingerboard. However, in the last few years two distinctive curvatures have been developed.[3]

Viennese Curvature

Possesses less curve—(not as round)—and is slightly lower at the A and D (violin) strings. It enables the player to perform more rapidly and to develop better and faster technique. Another advantage is the reducing of fatigue since the actual distance between two strings is shorter and less motion of the arm is required. The Viennese curvature of the bridge requires perfect alignment of the fingerboard; otherwise, the player is apt to touch two strings simultaneously.

Figure 3.12. Repairman fitting bridge. (Courtesy Scherl & Roth, Elkhart, Indiana)

---

2. "You Fix Them" (Second Edition), Scherl and Roth, Inc. Reprinted with permission.

3. *Ibid.*

BRIDGE DIAGRAMS

These illustrations are drawn to exact measurements for all string instruments. In addition to proper curvature for each model, the small indentations in the curve indicate the correct string spacings.

In the center of each diagram the vertical lines crossing the horizontal bar indicate the correct string spacings at the fingerboard nut of the various instruments.

The measurement on the lower left corner of each diagram is the correct height between the end of the fingerboard and the fourth gut wound string on each instrument.

The measurement on the lower right corner of each diagram is the correct height between the end of the fingerboard and the first string of each instrument.

(Note: refer to previous section, "Bridge Height" for proper measurement when using steel strings in place of gut.)

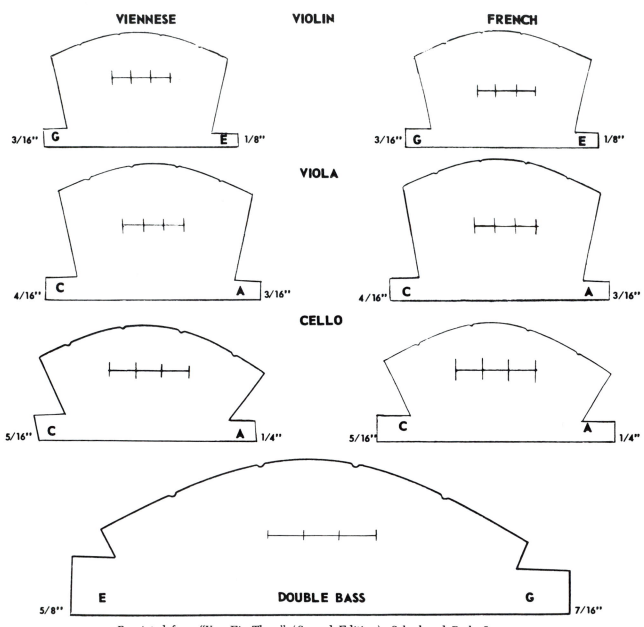

Reprinted from "You Fix Them" (Second Edition), Scherl and Roth, Inc.

French Curvature

Slightly rounder and a trifle higher at the A and D (violin) strings. It is usually necessitated because the fingerboard has not been "dressed" perfectly. The advantage is the elimination of the problem of playing two strings simultaneously. The disadvantages are the wider travel of the bow and greater fatigue of the bow arm.

SPECIAL BRIDGES

The coming of metal strings brought with it some problems. The metal string, especially the violin E, acts as a blade or a sawtooth as it moves back and forth across the bridge in the tuning process, causing it to cut more deeply into the top of the bridge. This brings the string closer and closer to the fingerboard, which eventually causes buzzes and rattles.

Bridges with Ebony Inserts

One solution to this problem was the construction of a bridge with an ebony insert, or inserts (see Figure 3.13), which withstands the wearing affect of the string better than maple. Another solution has been to place a small piece of chamois or skin under the string, or a thread winding around the string, or a small piece of paper folded several times, to act as a buffer. This second technique also serves to reduce some of the metallic sound of the wire string. Some metal strings are supplied with a small rubber "tone filter," which is intended for this purpose. (See Figure 4.1.)

Roth-de Jacques Bridge

The Roth-de Jacques bridge has adjustable feet, which are joined to the bridge by an interlocking swivel joint. Under tension the feet adjust automatically to the curvature of the top. (Figure 3.14)

Starker Bridge

Janos Starker, the famous cellist, has taken an ordinary bridge and bored a conical hole in the bottom of each foot. This process is supposed to increase the power and resonance of the instrument.

Figure 3.13. Bridges with ebony inserts.

Figure 3.14. Roth-de Jacques bridges. (Courtesy Scherl & Roth, Elkhart, Indiana)

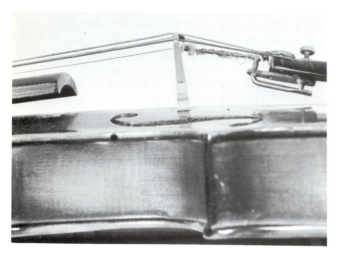

Figure 3.15. A neglected bridge which has become warped.

Figure 3.16. Correct way to return the bridge to an upright position.

EXACT BACK TIP ANGLE

Figure 3.17. Correct position of the bridge. (Courtesy Scherl & Roth, Elkhart, Indiana)

CARE OF THE BRIDGE

The bridge is a relatively delicate part of the instrument. Its narrow width and small feet support the combined tension of the four strings. Each time the strings are tuned, the tendency is for the bridge to move minutely toward the fingerboard. In time this will cause the bridge to tilt forward until it falls or cracks; or the bottom part of the bridge may remain in position and the top portion above the weak midsection will tilt forward, causing the bridge to warp. (See Figure 3.15.)

These problems can be avoided if the position of the bridge is observed periodically and corrected if needed. Exerting pressure at the top of the bridge in the direction of the tailpiece will return it to its upright position. But this must be done carefully to avoid pushing the bridge backward so far that it falls over. To avoid this, the fingers of one hand should grasp the string directly behind the bridge while the fingers of the other hand gently push the bridge to an upright position. This technique, as well as the correct position of the bridge, is shown in Figures 3.16 and 3.17.

MUTES

Purpose

The mute is a device, which, when placed upon the bridge, deadens, dampens, or reduces the amount of tone produced by the instrument. It also changes the quality of the sound. Muted passages are used by composers to achieve contrast and special effects.

Physically the mute acts as a clamp on the bridge and reduces the free passage of vibrations through the bridge to the top of the instrument. For many years the design of mutes was limited to two types. One was three pronged; the other five pronged. They were made of hardwood (ebony), metal, or leather with wire reinforcing. They clamped onto the top of the bridge. Each affected the tone of the instrument in its own special way.

Beginning with the music of Debussy and Ravel, composers have made increasing demands upon orchestra players in regard to speed and frequency in the use of the mute. Split-second application and removal is not uncommon, and a composer may ask for the mute to be used a dozen or more times in a movement or section of music. As a result, "attached" mutes were developed.

Figure 3.18. An ebony mute. (Courtesy Scherl & Roth, Elkhart, Indiana)

Foreign Terms for Mute

As a musician, teacher, or director of an orchestra, one needs to be acquainted with some of the foreign terms for the mute, its application, and its removal. Italian, German, and French are the most important, and Italian is used most frequently.

	Word for Mute	*To Apply*	*To Remove*
Italian	Sordino (i), Sord.	Con sordino	Senza sordino
German	Dämpfer	Mit Dämpfer	Ohne Dämpfer or Dämpfer weg. or ab.
French	Sourdine(s)	Avec les sourdines	Otez les sourdines

Mute Problems

The mute has always presented a series of problems to the orchestra musician. First, it was an easy piece of equipment to forget. It could be left in the instrument case backstage, or at home in the suit worn at the last concert. Second, if the player was well disciplined and remembered to take the mute onto the stage, finding the best place to keep it was a problem. If it was put on the music stand, it was usually knocked off when a page was turned. If it was put in a coat pocket, the player might have difficulty retrieving it in a hurry when it was needed. In full dress the player usually put the mute in the vest pocket. But what to do with it in rehearsal when vests and coats were not worn? And last, but by no means least, in the process of frantically fumbling for a mute—in the coat or vest or on the stand or chair—it was not unheard of to drop it onto the floor. Mutes are most often called for in quiet moments, and the clatter of a mute as it strikes the floor is not conducive to a harmonious relationship between the conductor and the offender. Orchestra players long ago learned the technique of maintaining a steely and eyes-averted detachment during this kind of episode, giving the conductor and the audience no help in identifying the culprit.

Attached Mutes

The kind of trauma described above and the simple need to find a better way, led practical and inventive minds to discover a mute that could be attached to the instrument. This solution meant that the mute would always be with the instrument; it simplified the process of application and removal; and it eliminated the chance of the mute falling to the floor.

The new mutes fit securely over the strings just behind the bridge. To mute the instrument, the device is pushed toward the bridge. The off position is achieved by returning the mute toward the tailpiece.

The Roth-Sihon mutes, shown in Figure 3.20, are available for violin, viola, cello, and bass. It is recommended that all school instruments used on the secondary level be equipped with a mute of this or some other style, which can be attached to the instrument.

Other Special Mutes

TOURTE MUTE

The Tourte is another attached mute. It is made of rubber and sits on the strings behind the bridge when not in use. For muting it is moved forward and fastened over the bridge (Figure 3.23).

HALL MUTE

The Hall mute is a two-pronged mute made of aluminum. It also produces a pleasant and resonant tone.

PRACTICE MUTE OR TON WOLF

Practice mutes are heavy metal devices, which, when placed upon the bridge, reduce the volume of the instrument to nearly zero. Using a practice mute, it is possible to practice in an apartment or rooming house without disturbing occupants of adjacent quarters (Figure 3.24).

Figure 3.20. Sherl-Roth mutes. (Courtesy Scherl & Roth, Elkhart, Indiana)

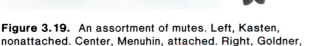

Figure 3.19. An assortment of mutes. Left, Kasten, nonattached. Center, Menuhin, attached. Right, Goldner, attached. (Courtesy Shar Products Company)

Figure 3.21A. Roth-Sihon mute in "off" or nonmuting position.

Figure 3.23A. Tourte mute in "off" or nonmuting position.

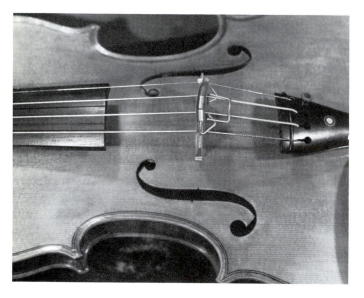

Figure 3.21B. Roth-Sihon mute in "on" or muting position.

Figure 3.23B. Tourte mute in "on" or muting position.

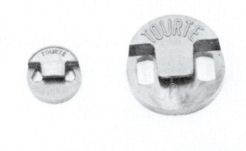

Figure 3.22. Tourte mute. (Courtesy Albert C. Muller & Sons, Inc., Sacramento, California)

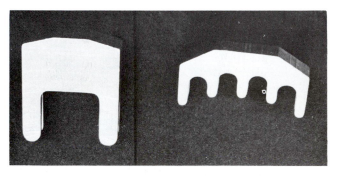

Figure 3.24. Practice mute. (Courtesy Albert C. Muller & Sons, Inc., Sacramento, California)

Figure 3.25. Wolf suppressor.

WOLF SUPPRESSOR OR ELIMINATOR

The term "wolf," when used in regard to a string instrument, denotes a note or notes that produce an undesirable resonance pattern, causing that note(s) to have a different tone quality than the other notes on the instrument. The wolf tone can be described by such words as super-resonant, boomy, or hollow. Wolfs are undesirable, not only because they produce unevenness in the scale of the instrument, but because the note on which the wolf occurs does not respond to the bow as the other notes do. The wolf is balky and undependable, and requires special treatment; it must be favored.

A wolf frequently occurs on C or C♯ on the violin, and on F or F♯ on the viola and cello. It is most evident on the bottom string; however, it will usually be present in the upper octaves of the same note. Wolfs are to be found in very fine instruments and are attributed to some idiosyncrasy in the design of the instrument. Most repairmen are reluctant to attempt structural changes to cure the wolf.

Pressure just behind the bridge or under the tailpiece will suppress the wolf. A device has been contrived to accomplish this. It consists of a piece of cork and a screw mechanism, which makes it possible to press the cork onto the top behind the bridge. Another device, which suppresses the wolf, consists of a metal sleeve that is screwed onto the bottom string just behind the bridge.

TAILPIECE GUT, TAILPIECE ADJUSTER, TAILHANGER

The term "tailpiece gut" is becoming less and less literally descriptive with the passing of time. The term refers to the material (gut, nylon, or wire) that is attached to the tailpiece and then looped over the end button, thus anchoring the tailpiece to the instrument. The term "tailhanger" is used in *The Complete String Guide* (ASTA, MENC, NSOA) in a generic sense, regardless of the material used. But "tailpiece adjuster" is still in common use.

The tailhanger must be strong enough to resist the combined pull of the four strings without stretching. Traditionally a short piece of gut was used, for the violin a piece about

the diameter of a cello A string, and proportionately larger sizes for the larger instruments. The two ends of the piece of gut are inserted into holes on the underneath side of the tailpiece. These two ends are heated and flared and thread is wrapped tightly up against the flaired end to prevent the ends from slipping back through the holes in the tailpiece. The loop, thus formed, is placed over the end button. If the tailpiece gut is cut to the correct length, the end of the tailpiece will be directly over the saddle. Gut has been used for this purpose because it is extremely strong and durable. But it does become weak with age, and damp weather softens it, increasing its tendency to break. Greater durability and ease of installation account for the current prevailing use of devices such as the Sacconi tailpiece adjuster. (See Figure 3.26.)

Importance of Tailpiece Adjuster (Tailhanger)

The tailpiece adjuster is a true lifeline. Without it, all is lost. Four strings hanging from the scroll, limp and useless, is a sad but ludicrous sight. Truthfully, the breaking of a tailpiece gut is calamitous. In addition to totally immobilizing the instrument, the sudden and complete release of tension can cause the bridge to snap, the sound post to fall; and the flailing tailpiece can seriously scratch or gouge the top of the instrument. The only sure way to prevent this kind of occurrence is to check the condition of this part as you would strings, bow hair, etc. If it begins to fray, have it replaced. If gut is used, this usually means a trip to the repair shop, for the majority of players do not have the skill to make this kind of repair.

Because the breaking of the tailpiece gut is an unpleasant thing to have happen, substitutes for gut have been sought. Wire has been substituted for gut on the bass. And another recent development is described below.

Sacconi Tailpiece Adjuster

Inventive genius applied itself to the solution of the tailpiece gut problem for the violin, viola, and cello. The Sacconi tailpiece adjuster is the result. This ingenious device is made of an extremely strong synthetic, which is claimed to be ten times stronger than gut. The ends, which are threaded, are inserted into the tailpiece in the conventional manner. Nuts are screwed down until the tailpiece is in the correct position. The loop is placed over the end button and the job is done. It is clean, simple, quick, and easy. No tools are required. In addition to being many times stronger than gut, the material is said to be weather and waterproof.

BOW GRIPS

Most of the information regarding bow grips is covered in the chapter on the bow; however, there are two items in this category, which, because of their "do it yourself" aspect, may logically be dealt with here. The first of these is the Rolland bow grip; the second is the thermal grip.

Rolland Bow Grip

This is a small, soft rubber device, which is slid over the existing bow grip. It is shaped with a depression into which the right thumb fits while playing. Its purpose is to provide

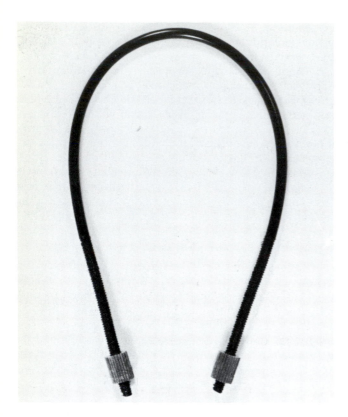

Figure 3.26. Sacconi tailpiece adjuster.

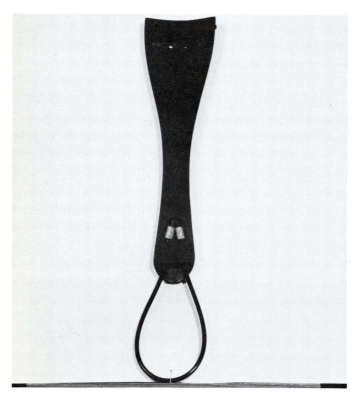

Figure 3.27. Sacconi tailpiece adjuster inserted into tailpiece.

Figure 3.28. Rolland bow grip. (Courtesy Scherl & Roth, Elkhart, Indiana)

a positive place for the thumb and thus prevent the thumb from wandering toward the middle of the bow or into the hollow of the frog. It can prevent the "roving thumb" problem and lend security to the student who is so afflicted. The Rolland bow grip is shown above. The Alshin Bowmaster, a similar device, is a longer, contoured sleeve of plastic rubber, which slips onto the "grip" area of the bow. It comes in three sizes: small for kindergarten through third grade students, middle for fourth through sixth grade students, and large for older students and adults. To obtain the Alshin Bowmaster, write to 5300 Ocean Blvd., Sarasota, Florida 33581.

Thermal Grip

This is a general term used to describe a bow grip which consists of two pieces of thin plastic tubing that are shrunk onto the stick by heat. The longer of the two pieces is placed on the stick in position and heated. It shrinks tightly onto the stick. The short one is placed over the long one at the end near the frog. This is shrunk onto the stick and a grip is formed. The plastic is very tough and durable. Anyone can make this installation with the help of a match, candle, or lighter.

BOW GUIDES

Bow guides fall into the same controversial category as finger placement aids. Some teachers will not use one or the other because of their strong belief that students should be able to overcome their problems with their own resources and help from the teacher. Other teachers, feeling that if a child is not able to overcome a problem within a reasonable time, find there is nothing inherently wrong with using an aid designed to help remedy a particular problem.

Pictured in Figures 3.29 A and B are two devices designed to help a student bow at the correct angle. Both clamp onto the top of the violin so that the guide is halfway between the bridge and the fingerboard. The bow is positioned in the channel created by the design of the guide which, in turn, guides the bow in a straight line. The "Tone Shaper" from Shar Products fastens with a velcro strap. The Canapini "Violin Bow Control" fastens onto the bridge.

CELLO END PINS

Purpose

The cello end pin is as much an integral part of the cello as is the bridge or the tailpiece. And although it is not proven to be directly related to the playing properties of the instrument, it has a great deal to do with the player's comfort and security. The end pin is to the cellist what the shoulder pad is to the violinist and violist. It puts the instrument at the correct height and makes it possible for the player to hold it firmly. An indication of the importance of this part of the

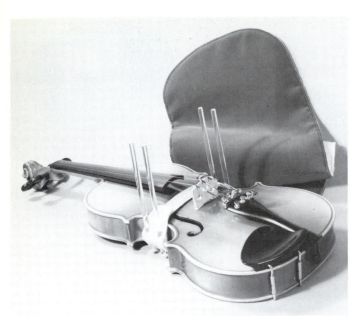

Figure 3.29A. Tone shaper. (Courtesy Shar Products Company)

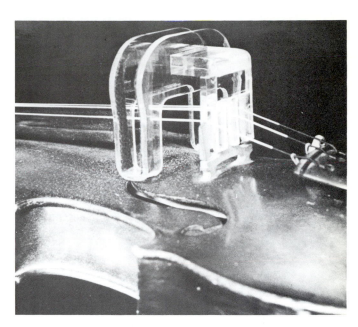

Figure 3.29B. Canapini violin bow control.

instrument is the fact that the first thing a cellist does after sitting down to play is to look for a hole for the end pin.[4]

Parts of the End Pin

The end pin consists of the following parts:

1. A wooden (usually ebony) sleeve or socket, which fits into a hole at the base of the cello.
2. A metal rod, which is inserted into the hole in the sleeve. This rod has either a sharp point or a rubber tip and a restraining band, which prevents the rod from slipping into the sleeve. The rod sometimes has grooves or notches to receive the point of the thumbscrew.
3. A metal sleeve, which fits around the socket and contains a thumbscrew. The thumbscrew is used to set the rod at the desired position.

Function and Problems of the End Pin

The rod, or peg, is adjusted by the player as needed and is secured by the thumbscrew. It is important that the thumbscrew hold the rod firmly. And it is important that one of the following conditions be met:

1. The tip of the end pin rod be sharp.
2. The tip be of soft rubber, which will not slip.
3. An end pin holder be provided.

Unless one of these conditions is complied with, the cellist is confronted with a difficult, frustrating, and nearly impossible situation. In order to meet the first requirement, the point of

the end pin will need to be sharpened periodically with a steel file.

The restraining sleeve, which was mentioned above, deserves a special bit of discussion. It seems inconceivable that an end pin could be made without some means to prevent it from slipping completely inside the instrument. Probably no end pin is made without such a device, but with repeated use, and sometimes mistreatment, it is broken or dislodged. Sometimes this restrainer is a pin through the rod; sometimes it is a sleeve around the rod; sometimes the end of the rod is flaired. It appears that time and use can destroy the effectiveness of any of these methods, and the result is that there is nothing to prevent the pin from slipping completely inside the cello, or becoming stuck in the socket with the point recessed in the socket so that it cannot be grasped by fingers or pliers. The latter is worse than the former. When the rod slips into the instrument, it can usually be retrieved by turning the instrument belly-down and rolling it back and forth until the rod can be grasped through one of the *f* holes. When the rod becomes stuck in the socket, it usually means that the entire end pin assembly must be removed in order that the pin can be driven out. This means releasing the tension on all the strings and freeing the tailpiece gut from the end pin.

An additional common problem with the less expensive end pins is that the sleeve into which the thumbscrew is threaded is not thick enough to provide a firm purchase for the thumbscrew. Unless it is given careful use, the sleeve threads become worn and the sleeve must be replaced.

BASS END PINS

Bass end pin assemblies are heavier and larger than the cello's; the rod is larger in diameter and shorter. The purpose of the end pin is to raise the instrument to the correct height for the player and to anchor the instrument in the desired spot.

Everything that is said about cello end pins applies to bass end pins.

---

4. There is a good deal of experimentation going on at the present time with cello end pins of various designs. The Tortellier is one that has gained some acceptance. The objective of these new end pins is to elevate the bottom of the cello so that it comes closer to being horizontal. This reduces the cello's contact with the body, and, according to proponents of these devices, elevates the finger board and thus places the hand in a more advantageous position to function. Another device called "Cellimate" fastens on the end of the end pin. It has a point which can be swiveled to adapt to the angle at which the cello is held. It is available from M & M Distributing, P.O. Box 1411, Ann Arbor, Michigan, 48106.

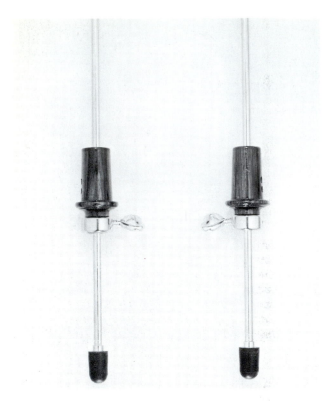

Figure 3.30. Cello end pins. (Courtesy Scherl & Roth, Elkhart, Indiana)

Figure 3.31. A cello end pin rest. (Courtesy Shar Products Company)

Figure 3.32. Cello end pin rests. (Courtesy Shar Products Company)

CELLO AND BASS END PIN RESTS

Purpose

The purpose of all of the gadgets in this category is to give the player the security of knowing that the instrument is going to stay where it is put. Since a player may encounter hardwood, tile, concrete, or carpet as floor material, he or she should be ready to cope with any situation. A sharp steel point may embed itself satisfactorily in wood, but it will be less successful on concrete, and some people are sensitive about their carpet or rugs.

Several different methods of coping with this problem have been developed. They are listed and described below.

Rubber End Pin Holders

In this category there are several styles on the market. The Waller end pin rest consists of a piece of sponge rubber with a metal cover plate. The cover is made with a depression in the center into which the end pin is placed. The sponge rubber is supposed to prevent the rest from sliding about, but it is not completely satisfactory on all surfaces.

Another type is made of rubber. A hollow throat receives the end pin and a flat base makes contact with the floor. The throat forms a flexible joint with the base.

Cello Boards

Cello boards are used in schools as much as any other device. They are inexpensive to produce, foolproof, and virtually indestructible if made of relatively hard wood.

A piece of wood 1/2 inch to 3/4 inches thick is cut 3 inches wide and about 28 inches long. A hole large enough for a chair leg (about 2 inches in diameter) is drilled at one end and a series of 3/8 inch diameter holes are drilled at an angle halfway through the board at varying distances from the large hole (Figure 3.34).

The left leg of the cellist's chair is inserted into the large hole, and the end pin is placed in the hole that puts the cello at the most comfortable angle for the player.

Cello boards are not the most convenient device if they must be moved about frequently. But they serve admirably in the orchestra rehearsal room where they can be left in place.

Figure 3.33. Combination cello end pin. (Courtesy Albert C. Muller & Sons, Inc., Sacramento, California)

There are also contrivances made of leather or web belting, which function on the same principle as the cello board. Loops are secured to the legs of the chair and a cuplike device receives the end pin.

DAMPIT

Dampit is a humidifier for violin, viola, cello, and bass. Dampit is a perforated plastic tube with a sponge inserted into the tube. The sponge is moistened by dipping the Dampit in water. The Dampit is inserted into the instrument through one of the *f* holes. A rubber disc, which is larger than the *f* hole opening, prevents the Dampit from falling into the instrument. Each Dampit is packaged with a humidity gauge, which may be used to determine when the Dampit should be placed in the instrument (Figure 3.35).

BASS STOOLS

The bass player has the option of standing or sitting while playing. If the rehearsal or performance is extended, or if there are long waiting periods, he or she will probably choose to sit. Most professionals sit. They use a stool that has been adjusted to their height.

Teenage bass players tire quickly. They should have a suitable stool. Too often this is not provided, and the results are not conducive to a good rehearsal situation. Since these students feel that they must sit, and they should not be denied this comfort, they place chairs behind them into which they noisily collapse each time the director stops the orchestra, or they have a thirty-two bar rest. This kind of activity is disruptive and interferes with the concentration level of the entire orchestra.

Figure 3.34. Cello board.

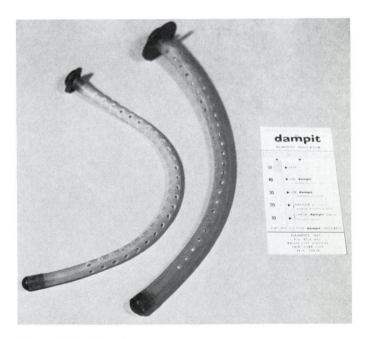

Figure 3.35. Dampit.

Figure 3.36. Wenger bass chair. (Courtesy Wenger Corporation, Owatonna, Minn.)

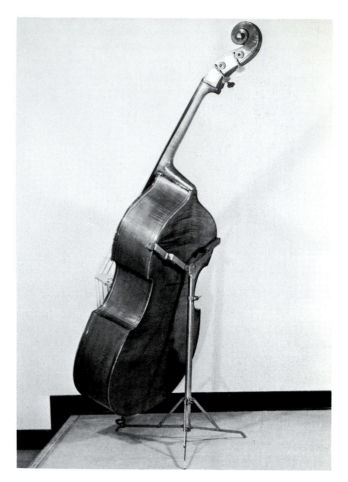

Figure 3.37. String bass stand.

Figure 3.38. Two views of the bass string winder. (Courtesy Albert C. Muller & Sons, Inc., Sacramento, California)

Any stool that is suited to the height of the player is satisfactory. The player sits on the edge of the stool with the right leg on the floor, and the left leg supported on a rung of the stool.

The Wenger bass chair is designed strictly for the bass player. It is made of metal. The height of the seat is adjustable. It has a back support.

BASS STANDS

Bass stands are used in dance bands when the bass player is required to move quickly from the bass to another instrument and vice versa. In such a situation there is often no time to pick up the bass from a position on the floor; it must be ready to play. A stand such as the one shown in Figure 3.37 is used for this purpose.

BASS STRING WINDER

This device is alleged to "take the work out of string winding." And it surely does reduce by a great deal both the time and the physical effort involved in winding a new string onto a bass. The bass string winder fastens easily onto any of the bass wing nuts and makes it possible to "crank" the new bass string to its approximate pitch in a matter of seconds and with a much easier physical action than is required without this device.

CELLO CHAIRS

The desirability of a straight-backed, unslanted chair for cellists is important enough to warrant mention here. Chairs with seats that slope down toward the back are extremely uncomfortable for cellists. The cellist needs to sit forward on the chair, with his or her back away from the back of the chair, and a sloping seat makes this difficult. With a flat seat the cellist can assume a comfortable position and retain it without effort.

Most metal folding chairs have a sloped, contoured seat, which is designed to throw some of the person's weight against the back of the chair. For this reason they are unsuitable for cellists and most other seated players, for that matter. A flat seated, wooden desk chair is much better suited to the cellist's special needs.

Figure 3.39. A cello chair. (Courtesy Wenger Corporation, Owatonna, Minn.)

The Wenger Corporation, maker of a variety of music-related furniture and equipment, makes a special cello chair in several sizes. (See Figure 3.39.)

CASES

Violin and Viola Cases

Violin and viola cases are generally of the shaped type, that is the outline of the case conforms roughly to the shape of the instrument.

Oblong cases are also available. They have the advantage of providing more inside room for storage of shoulder pads, strings, and rosin.

Cases today are either of plywood construction covered with plastic or leather, or of a new molded plastic process. The main requirement of a case is that it be functional. It should be sturdy so that it can stand abuse. The hardware should be made of sufficiently heavy metal so that hinges and clasps do not wear out. When looking at a plastic case, the hinges should be carefully examined to determine whether they are suitably attached. If in doubt, choose a better quality case. The metal should be rust and corrosion proof. The exterior should be of tough, durable material.

The interior of the case should be lined with soft material and provide a snug fit for the instrument for maximum protection against shock. Pockets, or compartments, should be big enough to accommodate rosin, strings, and perhaps a shoulder pad. They should be glued and hinged strongly

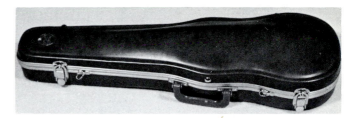

Figure 3.40. Shaped case. (Courtesy Scherl & Roth, Elkhart, Indiana)

Figure 3.41. Oblong case. (Courtesy Scherl & Roth, Elkhart, Indiana)

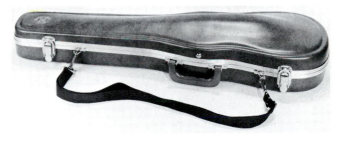

Figure 3.42. Violin case with strap. (Courtesy Scherl & Roth, Elkhart, Indiana)

enough to prevent them from coming apart. The bow holder at the narrow end of the case should be nailed and glued so it will not come loose, and the bow clamps should be of a good quality spring steel so that they do not lose their shape and their usefulness.

Many student cases are made with two rings affixed to the handle side of the case. A carrying strap may be snapped into these rings (Figure 3.42). By slinging the strap over the shoulder, a child can have free hands for carrying books or riding a bicycle.

A canvas cover is highly recommended for the protection of good quality cases. A cover will double the life of a case. It is generally not practical to equip school cases with covers because of the cost of covers.

Figure 3.43. Cello bag.   **Figure 3.44.** Hard cello case.
(Courtesy Scherl & Roth, Elkhart, Indiana)

Cello and Bass Bags

Cello and bass bags are made of canvas or duck. The better bags have a fleece lining or inner coating. A recently introduced cello bag of excellent quality is lined with foam rubber and is reinforced in the neck area (Figure 3.43).

The bag keeps the instrument dry and prevents nicks and scratches, but it does not protect against hard blows by heavy objects. A sleeve for the bow is located in the front of the bag and a music pouch in the rear. The quality of the bag depends upon the weight of the canvas, the thread used, the kind of material used to bind the seams, and the quality of the zippers or snaps.

Hard Cello Cases

Every artist-quality cello should be furnished with a hard case to protect it against damage. The same criteria that apply to violin and viola cases applies to the hard cello cases. In the cello case the end pin is held in a slotted retainer at the base of the case, and a strap holds the neck at the top. The combined weight of the instrument and this type case can come to eighteen pounds and more. The size and weight make it prohibitive for a young child.

Trunks for Cellos and Basses

Professional cello and bass players who must travel and send their instrument as baggage often make use of trunk type cases. These are heavily reinforced pieces of luggage and require several men or a mechanical lift to handle them. They are fitted inside so that the instrument is held tightly in padding with the use of straps.

PITCH PIPES

Pitch pipes with four pipes (one pipe for each string) are available for violin, viola, and cello. The pitch pipe can be helpful in teaching students to tune their instruments and to make them conscious of the importance of checking their strings each time they practice. It is particularly important that students without a piano in their home be supplied with a pitch pipe.

STUDY QUESTIONS

1. What are the reasons for using a chinrest?
2. What are the reasons for using a shoulder pad?
3. Name two or three brands of shoulder pads.
4. Describe two advantages of the attached mute.
5. Under what circumstances is it advisable to use patent pegs?
6. Under what circumstances is it advisable to use tuners?
7. List three steps involved in fitting a bridge.
8. List the Italian, German, and French terms for mute.
9. What is the effect of a mute upon an instrument?
10. Describe the function of the Sacconi tailpiece adjuster.
11. What is the purpose of the cello and bass end pin?
12. Describe one cello end pin holder that is practical for school use.

4 Chapter

Strings

Strings
Corda (Italian)   *Corde* (French)
Saite (German)

Strings are to the violin, viola, cello, and bass what the reed is to the oboe. They must be well made of good material, properly matched, and suited to the instrument if the instrument is to function at its best. Strings are made of several different kinds of material—gut, synthetics, and metal.

Players develop preferences for certain types of strings. Some prefer metal; others prefer gut and gut wound with silver or aluminum. Still others prefer to intermix these types. Some recommendations and options regarding types of strings and their use are made following the descriptions of the various types of strings.

QUALIFICATIONS OF A GOOD STRING

The first requirement of a string is that it produce a pure fundamental tone, undistorted by pitch fluctuations or faulty overtones. The second is that it is responsive throughout its playing range to the great variety of demands placed upon it—a broad range of dynamics, quick spiccato notes, heavy chords and accents, etc. The third is that it stretch completely in no more than three days. The fourth requirement is that it give a reasonable length of service. Under most circumstances this should be at least one year. Of course, a heavy schedule of playing can reduce this span to six months or even less.

HISTORICAL DEVELOPMENT OF STRINGS

Strings, like most products, have gone through a process of change. And, like the early resistance to the automobile, changes in the materials used and the design of strings has met with occasional resistance. For instance, fifty years ago the wire E string for the violin was relatively new. Violinists were reluctant to accept this metal substitute for the thin-gauge gut they had been using, even though the gut string was extremely undependable. Players were sure that the wire string would not have the "sweet" quality of the gut string, and there was widespread doubt about the advisability of subjecting a fine old instrument to the added tension created by a wire string.

But the wire E had more power and brilliance than the gut string, and it did reduce the probability of the E string breaking in the middle of a recital or concerto, which was a common experience with the gut E. So, of course, the wire E was finally accepted, and today the gut E is rarely used. Later, in addition to the E, other strings were made of metal and various alloys. These strings, too, were accepted slowly. Today there is little real antipathy toward the metal strings.

SELECTION OF STRINGS

Many very fine players use metal strings. Others are convinced that gut-core strings are superior. Still others continue to use those gut strings that are available. Most personal preferences for particular strings or string combinations are developed through a trial and error method. The player tries various strings until he finds what works best for him and is best suited to his instrument.

The instrument itself can dictate the types of strings that should be used. For instance, the stronger new instruments are better able to withstand the added tension produced by the metal strings than are the old instruments. But it must be restated that in the case of advanced players, personal preference, rather than scientific evidence, is most frequently the determining factor in selecting string types.

For optimum results in the areas of intonation and equalization of tone from string to string, strings should be matched according to gauge, a matter that the player should take up with a competent string dealer or repairman. Problems of a thin tone or lack of responsiveness can sometimes be cured by changing the gauge of the string.

Advantages of Metal Strings for Students

Where students are concerned, some practical considerations are more important than aesthetic considerations when selecting the types of strings to be used. Metal strings are preferred for young players because they hold their pitch better than gut-core strings. Furthermore, an instrument equipped with metal strings and tuners is far easier to tune than one with gut-core strings.

By the time students reach junior high school, have graduated to a full-size instrument, and are tuning their instrument with a minimum of assistance, they are ready for a change from metal to gut-core strings. This type of string frequently improves the tone quality of student instruments.

TYPES OF STRINGS

Strings are made of a variety of materials—gut (not of the cat), aluminum, silver, chromesteel wire, metal alloys, combinations of synthetics and plastics. The violin E, formerly made of gut, has been replaced by a single strand chromesteel wire. All other strings for all the instruments are made with a solid or multistrand core and are wound or wrapped with aluminum, silver, an alloy, or synthetic. The core of the string can be made of gut, steel, single strand or multistrand wire, or synthetic. Names such as "Flexocore," "Chromcor," "Perlon" core, "Spirocore," "Sensicore," etc., are applied to various brands.

Specific Recommendations

FOR BEGINNERS

Matched sets of metal strings are recommended for beginners, and the instrument (except for the bass) should be equipped with tuners. Because of the increased demand for small sized instruments for small beginners, string makers have made available strings in sizes ranging from 4/4 down to 1/16 for violin, three sizes for viola, 4/4 to 1/8 for cello, and three sizes for bass. Among brands that are made in these sizes are Chromcor, Dominant, and Super-Sensitive. A list follows of some of the brands of metal strings ("metal" is used generically to identify strings with something other than a gut or nylon core.)

Aricore (Perlon Core)
Chromcor
Dominant
Flexocor
Jargar
Prim
Super-Sensitive

FOR ADVANCED PLAYERS

As stated above, by the time students are in junior high school and have graduated to a full-sized instrument, the more advanced players, at least, may find that their instrument sounds better with some aluminum and silver-wrapped strings with a gut or synthetic core. This is not stated as a fact but as a possibility; for even among advanced players and professionals there are strong personal feelings and prejudices in regard to strings. About the only thing that can be agreed upon is that there is a difference in the "feel" of playing on metal ("Perlon," etc.) strings and gut-core strings.

The following combinations are recommended:

For Beginners
Violin, Viola, Cello—All metal with tuners
Bass—G . . . Gut or metal
      D . . . Gut or metal
      A . . . Silver wound or metal
      E . . . Silver wound or metal

For Advanced Players (unless all metal strings are used)
Violin—E . . . Metal
      A . . . Aluminum wound or gut
      D . . . Aluminum wound
      G . . . Silver wound
Viola—A . . . Metal, aluminum wound, or gut
      D . . . Aluminum wound
      G . . . Silver wound
      C . . . Silver wound
Cello—A . . . Aluminum wound, metal, or gut
      D . . . Aluminum wound
      G . . . Silver wound
      C . . . Silver wound
Bass—G . . . Metal or gut
      D . . . Metal or gut
      A . . . Metal or silver wound
      E . . . Metal or silver wound

Note: If metal strings are used, it is recommended that they be used in complete sets. The exception is when one of these strings is used as the top string in combination with gut-core strings.

USE OF TUNERS

Tuners should always be used with metal-core strings since metal-core strings are under considerable tension, and the pitch is altered by the most minute change in tension. The tuning peg should be used to bring the string to the approximate pitch when the string is first installed. The tuner is used for fine-tuning thereafter. With tuners these strings can be brought to the desired pitch easily. Without tuners, getting them in tune is a frustrating and time-consuming task.

There is no advantage in using tuners with gut-core strings. This type of string requires more change in tension to effect a pitch change than can be practically accomplished with a tuner. In brief, with gut strings the tuner is more bother than it is worth and is best avoided.

TONE FILTERS

A "tone filter" is a piece of rubber or plastic shaped like a miniature doughnut. Small pieces of leather or thread windings serve the same purpose. This device is placed between the string and the bridge to cushion the contact of the string on the bridge. It helps prevent rattles and buzzes, which can occur from the contact of the string and the bridge, and helps prevent the metal string from cutting too deeply into the bridge.

BRIDGE AND NUT ADJUSTMENT FOR METAL STRINGS

When metal strings are used on any of the stringed instruments, the bridge should be cut down and the notches in the nut cut somewhat more deeply than is normal so that the height of the string above the fingerboard will be reduced. Without this adjustment, the player must use an excessive amount of force to press the string to the fingerboard.

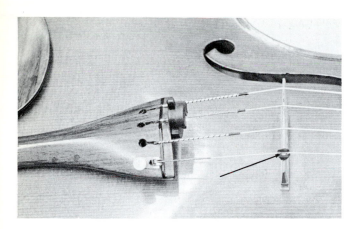

Figure 4.1. Tone filter.

PUTTING STRINGS ON THE INSTRUMENT

The order in which the strings are placed on the pegs is the same for all four of the instruments, with the single exception that the G and C are sometimes interchanged on the viola in order to reduce the acuteness of the angle of the C string between the nut and the peg. The standard and accepted order of matching strings to pegs is shown in Figure 4.2.

"Stringing up" is a string player's colloquialism. It refers to the function of putting a string or strings on a string instrument. There are two basic steps involved in this process. (1) The loop end of the string is secured in the correct hole in the tailpiece, or on the correct tuner. (2) The other end of the string is fed through the hole in the correct peg, secured on the peg, and tightened to the desired pitch. This two-step process is not difficult, but it is extremely important that it be executed carefully. Neglect of any of the details can result in a false string or in slippage of the string on the peg, causing the string to either go flat or slip off the peg entirely.

Because strings break, and because the teacher will find it necessary to replace broken strings for most elementary pupils, it is of primary importance that the student learn well the steps involved in changing a string. This process is now described in detail:

1. Remove any pieces of the broken string from the tailpiece and the peg.
2. Check to see if the peg concerned is working smoothly. If it is not, apply a small amount of peg dope.
3. A light application of graphite (lead pencil) in the notch of the bridge and the nut will help the string to move smoothly over these points.
4. Select a good quality string of the correct gauge and size.[1] Be sure strings are matched for type.
5. Remove the string from the envelope or string tube carefully. Do not twist, bend, or kink the string. Note: It is desirable to keep wound strings straight, either in a tube or string case.
6. If the string is metal, place the string on the tuner, as shown in Figure 4.3.

---

1. It should be kept in mind that ½ and ¾ size strings are available for violin and viola in Type 5.

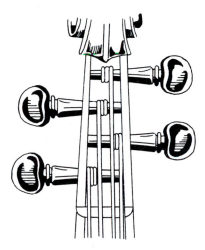

Figure 4.2. Strings and pegs.

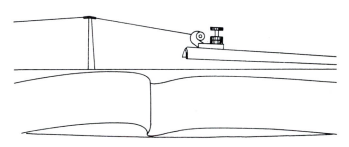

Figure 4.3. Metal string looped over tuner.

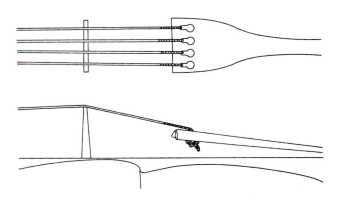

Figure 4.4. Gut string inserted into tailpiece.

If it is a gut-core string, insert the knotted end of the string through the hole in the tailpiece and pull the string toward the bridge. See Figure 4.4.

Make sure that the knot is well forward in the slot by tugging firmly on the string.

7. If the peg end of the string has a twisted or rough winding designed to prevent slippage, it is enough to insert the end of the string through the hole in the peg. The length of string allowed to protrude through the peg increases proportionally with the size of the instrument. About 5/8 inch is sufficient for the violin with only slightly more for the viola. For the cello 3/4 to 1 inch should be allowed, and for the bass 1 1/2 to 2 inches.

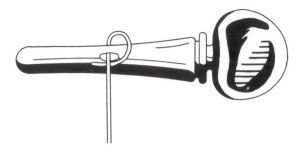

Figure 4.5. String inserted through peg.

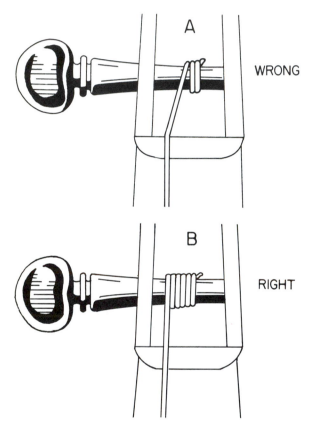

Figure 4.6. A. Wrong way to wind string. B. Right way to wind string.

Figure 4.7. Pegs in right position to turn.

If the peg end of the string has no coating or winding, more of the string must be inserted through the peg in order that the end of the string can be looped back under the main body of the string. When tightened, the end of the string will be cinched against the peg. See Figure 4.5.

Difficulty is sometimes incurred in feeding the string through the peg—the top, right peg in particular. A pair of tweezers, or small pliers, should be carried in the case for these occasions. With tweezers the string can be pulled through the peg even if only a quarter of an inch of the end is all that can be fed through with the fingers.

8. Wind the string onto the peg carefully in order that it will have a straight or an inward pull on the peg. The importance of winding the string properly cannot be overstated since it has a significant bearing upon the ease with which the peg may be set in tuning. It can be seen in Figure 4.6, example A, that the pull of the string is outward, tending to loosen the peg.

Winding the string as shown in Figure 4.6, example B, on the other hand, results in assistance from the natural pull of the string in keeping the peg tight.

9. Bring the string up to pitch slowly. Do not tune it higher than the desired pitch; this may damage the string. Also do not pull or stretch the string excessively. The strings should now appear as shown in Figure 4.2.

10. To be grasped and turned easily, the pegs must be in the positions shown in Figure 4.7. If, after a string is fully stretched, the peg is in an awkward position, it is possible to alter the position by pulling more or less of the string through the peg. By pulling more of the string through the peg, the peg will not have to be turned so far to produce the desired pitch, and vice versa.

11. After the string is completely stretched, it should not be allowed to slip to a loose condition. When retightened, it will again do some stretching, and this can be an annoyance.

CARE OF STRINGS

If the rosin dust is wiped from the strings after each extended playing, nothing else will need to be done to keep the strings in good playing order. If the string is in good condition when put on the instrument, and if it is kept clean, it will not present problems until age and wear begin to affect it.

It has already been stated that the life of a string normally depends upon the way it is used and how much it is played. The age-at-purchase of the strings that contain gut is an important predictor of their life span. String envelopes are not dated, and gut-core strings frequently are stored in plastic tubes with no more than a brand label. The only way to be assured of buying fresh strings is to buy from a dealer whose rate of stock turnover is known to you.

SOME STRINGS PROBLEMS AND THEIR SOLUTIONS

Strings can and do cause problems, and some strings may have inherent problems. A number of these problems are discussed below. Causes and solutions are given when known.

Problem: Strings break at bridge when first tightened.
Cause: Bridge notch is too narrow, or bridge has been planed so thin it cuts the string instead of providing a bearing surface.
Solution: Have bridge re-cut if possible; if not, replace.

Problem: Strings break at nut when first tightened.
Cause: Notch is too narrow and string is pinched, or a rough or sharp surface has developed.
Solution: Have repairman widen or smooth the notch.

Problem: Gut and wound strings are difficult to tune. They can be tuned just above or just below the correct pitch, but not to it, precisely.
Cause: The string may not be sliding along the notch in the nut.
Solution: Loosen the string and remove it from the notch. Run a lead pencil (graphite) in the notch several times. If this does not correct the problem, see your repairman.

WHEN TO REPLACE A STRING

Some strings let you know clearly when they are ready to be replaced. But in some cases the time for replacement comes and goes before the need is obvious, unless the player is aware of the subtle signs that develop. The consequence is that the player uses a false or faulty string without knowing it. Described below are a few of the obvious signs of impending trouble and suggested action.

Gut Strings

Problem: Fraying, particularly where the fingers contact the string most frequently. Dark discoloration in the same area.
Cause: String absorbs oil and moisture from the fingers, darkens, and unravels.
Solution: Snip off loose ends as close to the string as possible, as long as the string still performs satisfactorily. Learn to judge the point of no return, and replace the string when that point occurs.

Wound Strings

Problem: Winding separates. Winding breaks and unravels.
Cause: Flaw in string. Sharp edge on nut. Finger nails too long. Wear.
Solution: Correct possible causes and replace string.

Problem: String wears flat on side next to fingerboard. String becomes false.
Cause: Age and use.
Solution: Replace it before it breaks.

Single Strand Wire Strings

Problem: String wears flat on side next to fingerboard.
Cause: Age and use.
Solution: Replace it before it breaks.

Nearly any of the problems listed above can cause the string to buzz, rattle, produce poor tone quality, or become "false."

REPAIRING A BROKEN STRING

If a string breaks close to the peg or the tailpiece, it may be temporarily repaired in an emergency by tying the broken ends together. A knot that will not slip, such as a square knot, should be used. This kind of repair should be considered temporary and the repaired string should be replaced with a new one as soon as possible.

FALSENESS

A string is false when it fails to produce a pure representation of the desired pitch. That is to say, the open string sounds impure, does not ring true, and other notes on the string produce a distorted pitch. This condition makes itself most evident in the case of open strings, harmonics, and double stops.

When a string is false, it sets up an irregular vibration pattern, which gives off overtones other than those normal to the fundamental pitch. The result is a pitch that sounds sharp or flat regardless of where the finger is placed to stop the string. *Immediate replacement of the string is the only solution to this problem.* Do not delay in replacing a false string. The fingers will adjust to compensate for the "out-of-tuneness" of the string. In compensating, they are learning incorrect placement, which, if prolonged, will take valuable time to correct.

Testing for False Strings

One way to check strings for "falseness" is to play the interval of a minor sixth in a high register, using the three pairs of strings, and keeping the hand in the same relative position as you cross from one pair of strings to the next. The example shown below is for the violin. Corresponding intervals and positions can be applied to the viola and cello.

The hand remains in the same position as the fingers move across to the next pair of strings. If the distance between the fingers remains the same on the three pairs of strings, and a true minor sixth is produced, the strings are not false. If an adjustment is necessary in the spacing of the fingers, the string upon which the adjustment must be made is false.

Another method of checking for false strings is by playing 5ths. Begin in first position, using the questionable string as one of the pair. Move the hand upward, using the same finger to play the 5th. If a noticeable adjustment becomes necessary to keep the 5th true, one of the strings is false. By doing the same thing with the next pair of strings, the false string can be identified.

Still another way to check a string for falseness is to play the open string in question using a fast bow. Release the bow from the string while in motion allowing the string to ring. If the pitch changes noticeably when the bow is removed, the string is false.

A FEW FINAL REMARKS ABOUT STRINGS

1. Always keep a complete set of extra strings on hand.
2. Buy only good quality strings. Do not mix types other than as recommended. Correct gauge is important.
3. Wipe the rosin from the strings after each playing.

4. Through experience try to determine the useful life of a string and change it before it goes false, unravels, or breaks.

STUDY QUESTIONS

1. What are the Italian, French, and German terms for string?
2. Describe the material or materials used in several types of strings.
3. What kind of strings are preferred for young beginners? Why?
4. What is a tone filter?
5. Why is it important to wind the string onto the peg in a specific way?
6. What is meant when a string is said to be false?
7. Discuss several string problems and their solutions.

Care and Maintenance of the String Instruments

It has been said that the great artist will play beautifully in spite of any odds. It could also be said that the beginning student would sound no better on a fine Stradivari than on his $100.00 production-line instrument. Both of these statements may be true; but fine performers are generally very meticulous about the care and condition of their instrument, and the least defect is corrected by a master repairman at the earliest possible moment. This would seem to indicate the high regard the artist-performer has for the condition of the instrument. In order that the ultimate sound be as aesthetically and musically pleasing and correct as possible, it is equally important to provide the beginning string player with a good quality instrument in good condition so that he or she can listen, relate to, and reproduce a good quality string sound.

Initial responsibility for the condition of the beginner's instrument is the teacher's. (Minimum standards and details of shop adjustment are detailed in Chapter 14, Selecting Instruments, Bows, and Cases.) Then, in addition to teaching the student to play the instrument, care for it must also be taught.

Care of the string instruments can be separated into two categories. The first is the kind of thing that the player is responsible for. The second is the kind of repair that should be left to the expert craftsman.

THE PLAYER'S RESPONSIBILITIES

1. Do not expose a string instrument to extremes of temperature.
2. Provide a humidifying device in a dry climate. Keep the instrument as dry as possible in a damp climate.
3. Protect the instrument against hard knocks or jolts. Check for openings or cracks.
4. Wipe rosin dust from the strings, instrument, and bow before returning the instrument to its case. Polish the instrument and bow occasionally with a recommended polish such as Hill, Roth, or Lewis.
5. Check the tilt of the bridge periodically. The tuning process tends to pull the top of the bridge forward (toward the fingerboard). It should be vertical or lean backward minutely. Also check the position of the bridge feet. They should be opposite the inside notches of the *f* holes and square across the strings. Release the string tension slightly before moving the bridge.

6. Check strings to see if they are false, frayed, or unravelling.
7. See that the tuning pegs work smoothly. Apply peg dope if needed.
8. Check tailpiece gut or tail hanger. If it is badly frayed it should be replaced.
9. Periodically tighten the nut that secures the tuner(s).
10. Always loosen the bow before returning it to the case. If bow hair is smooth or sparse because of breakage, have bow rehaired. If stick is warped, have it straightened.

REPAIRS TO BE LEFT TO THE EXPERT

1. Adjusting the sound post. (See Figure 5.1.)
   The sound post must be of good wood, correct diameter and length, cut to conform to top and back, and properly positioned.
2. Cutting and fitting the bridge.
   The bridge must be of good wood (maple). The feet must be of the proper thickness and conform to the top. The curvature of the top must place the strings at the proper height above the fingerboard. The notches must not be too deep.

Figure 5.1. Workman setting sound post. (Courtesy Scherl & Roth, Elkhart, Indiana)

Figure 5.2. Sound post setting tool. (Courtesy Scherl & Roth, Elkhart, Indiana)

Figure 5.3. Workman reaming peg holes. (Courtesy Scherl & Roth, Elkhart, Indiana)

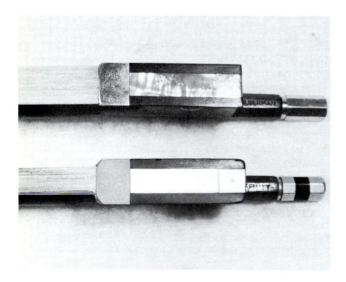

Figure 5.4. Top, rehaired bow. Below, bow that needs to be rehaired.

3. Dressing the fingerboard.
The fingerboard becomes pitted and grooved from the pressure of the fingers and the vibration of the strings. It then becomes necessary to plane the fingerboard until it is smooth. A properly dressed fingerboard has a concave dip lengthwise to provide clearance for the strings to vibrate, and the contour of the fingerboard and the curve of the bridge should conform in order to ensure the proper height of the strings above the fingerboard.

4. Repairing cracks and openings.
Simple openings between the back or top and the ribs are repaired by gluing and clamping. Cracks in the top or back may require that the instrument be opened.

5. Cleaning.
Cleaning of heavy rosin and dirt accumulations is a job for an expert. The varnish on a string instrument is delicate and may be damaged permanently by mistreatment.

6. Reaming peg holes and fitting new pegs. (See Figure 5.3.)
The need for this is rare. If an instrument is originally fitted with good pegs that fit well, it will take years of use to wear them to the point that they need to be replaced. Should it become necessary, it is a job for an expert.

7. Replacing a bass bar.
This is another major job that is rarely necessary. It is sometimes resorted to in an effort to improve the tone or response of an instrument.

8. Rehairing the bow. (See Figure 5.4.)
The hair wears smooth with playing until it no longer grips the string. How soon this happens depends upon the quality of the hair to begin with, and the amount of use the bow receives. Some players find it necessary to have their bow rehaired every month, others every two months, or six, or twelve. An annual rehairing is usually adequate for school bows.

The practice of washing the bow hair has strong proponents and opponents. Those who defend the practice contend that washing gets rid of the accumulated oil and grease and improves the condition of the hair. Opponents of the practice claim that washing the bow hair softens or removes the barbs on the hair, thus reducing its ability to "grab" the string. Those who argue this line also point out the possible danger of swelling and cracking the frog by allowing water to work into it. This danger alone should be enough to divert one from a practice that has doubtful results. Furthermore, by the time a bow is dirty enough to be considered in need of washing, it should be rehaired.

BUZZES AND RATTLES

Buzzes and rattles originating with the instrument can be a source of great annoyance to the player. Sometimes they are extremely hard to locate and correct. Some of the commonest causes of buzzes or rattles follow.

A button or piece of jewelry on the wearing apparel, which touches the instrument
A loose tuner
Loose chin rest
Tailpiece contacting the chin rest

Loose purfling
Open seam
Crack
String too close to fingerboard

Obviously, some of these causes are remedied very easily by the player. Others require the assistance of a repairman. The first four in the list can be prevented by simple precautionary measures, which have been mentioned already. If a crack or open seam is suspected, it can usually be located by tapping with the knuckle around the edges of the top and the back. If the seams are tight, the tapping produces a solid and resonant knock. If a seam is open, the slight flap of wood against wood can be heard.

Whether a crack in the top is tight or open is determined by pressing lightly on either side of the crack. If the wood on either side of the crack can be depressed, the crack is open. All cases of open seams or cracks, nut height, bridge, or fingerboard adjustments should be handled by a qualified repairman.

BOW PROBLEMS

Most bow problems and damage should be referred to a repairman. Some of the problems that can occur are discussed below.

Problem: Hair is so short the bow cannot be loosened or so long the bow cannot be tightened.
Cause: Hair cut too short or too long when placed in the bow.
Solution: Return to dealer or take to repairman for rehairing with correct length hair.

Problem: Entire hank of hair pulls out at tip.
Cause: Loose plug.
Solution: Return bow to repairman.

Problem: A number of individual hairs pull out of tip.
Cause: Poor knot or insufficient bonding of ends of hair.
Solution: Return bow to repairman.

Problem: Bow becomes warped.
Cause: Failure to loosen bow; uneven distribution of hair.
Solution: Repairman will straighten bow over flame. If hair is uneven, bow must be rehaired.

Problem: Tip breaks when bow is first tightened or after some use.
Cause: Faulty grain in wood or tip damaged by blow.
Solution: May or may not be repaired depending upon nature of break.

Problem: Screw turns but hair does not tighten.
Cause: Threads on screw or eyelet are stripped.
Solution: Replace eyelet or screw. Care must be taken to match eyelet and screw since sizes are not standardized.

The preceding lists of problems that can occur to string instruments and bows are purposely detailed in order to make the future teacher aware of the many kinds of things that

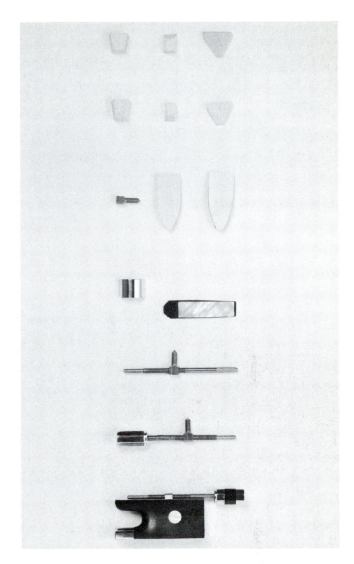

Figure 5.5. Wedges and parts of the frog. (Courtesy Scherl & Roth, Elkhart, Indiana)

can happen to this equipment. These lists are not intended to imply that these many kinds of problems will face the teacher frequently and consistently. Most of them need never occur. And chances are that if an instrument is in good condition to start with, and is given normal attention and care, its most serious needs will be new strings periodically. The bow, if kept in good working order, should never require anything more than rehairing.

The string instruments must be handled with care. They cannot be knocked or banged around without being damaged. With consideration for their frailty and the use of common sense, they will remain trouble free for years. A String Instrument Inspection Record will be found in Appendix II. Use of such a form on a regular basis can be an invaluable aid to keeping instruments in good condition.

You Fix Them, a practical repair manual published by Scherl & Roth, Inc., should be in every instrumental music teacher's library. It tells what you can fix and how to go about it.

If there is no repairman in your area, and you are forced into making repairs that ordinarily would be done by a professional, or if you simply want to learn to do more repairs yourself, you will need to acquire special knowledge, skills, and tools. The American String Teachers Association's *ASTA Stringed Instrument Repair and Maintenance Manual* was designed for just such a situation. It is an exhaustive treatise on string instrument repair, replete with helpful photographs. Edited by John D. Zurfluh, Sr., the manual contains articles on instrument and bow maintenance and repairs by thirteen repairmen from the United States and Canada. The manual is published looseleaf, three-hole punched, to be placed in a binder of your choice. According to the editor, this format was chosen to facilitate an individual's adding his own materials or any that might be produced by ASTA at a later date.

STUDY QUESTIONS

1. List seven or eight aspects of instrument maintenance for which the player should be responsible.
2. List five or six aspects of maintenance that should be handled only by a repairman.
3. What are some causes of rattles and buzzes?
4. Describe some of the problems that can beset a bow.

Part II

There are many aspects of string playing that are common to the four-string instruments. For example, shifting is a process of moving the hand from one place to another on the fingerboard, and even though it may be accomplished in a slightly different manner on each instrument, the basic movement is the same. Spiccato means to bounce the bow against the string, whether it is on the violin or the cello. Intonation is a problem of finger placement on the string, which is common to players of all string instruments, and a trill is a trill regardless of the instrument involved. Some techniques, such as vibrato, are treated generally here and are given more specialized consideration in the chapters dealing with the individual instruments.

These functions and the terms that denote them form a common core of technique and language for the strings. Therefore, for ease of reference, as well as to avoid needless repetition, these techniques are dealt with in the single chapter that follows.

Techniques which Apply to All of the String Instruments

The four string instruments have much in common. Each is made of wood; each has four strings; each is played with a bow. Tone is produced by drawing the bow on the strings or by plucking them. Pitch changes are produced by placing the fingers of the left hand at various points along the string.

The violin and viola may be played in either a standing or seated position. The cello is always played in a seated position (unless the cellist is strolling). The bass player may stand or use a stool.

Because of the many basic similarities in the way these four instruments are played, techniques, as they apply to all of the instruments, will be discussed in general terms in this chapter. In the chapters devoted to the individual instruments, these same techniques may be discussed in more specific terms with application to the instrument in question.

HOLDING THE INSTRUMENT

Many students have great difficulty attaining an acceptable playing position. Holding the violin and the viola is difficult and awkward. The cello and bass are somewhat easier to hold since the floor helps support them. A quick perusal of some of the miserable positions that can be found among intermediate and some advanced players is ample evidence of the need to maintain constant vigilance during the early stages of the learning process. Constant attention and prodding by the teacher will be needed during the first year of instruction if acceptable results are to be achieved in this all-important area of instrument and bow position.

The way in which the instruments should be held is covered in considerable detail in the chapters on the respective instruments. This has been considered to be necessary because of the brief, and sometimes incomplete, manner in which the matter is handled in some method books. Some books have very good pictures or drawings that show how to hold the instruments. Others contain poor illustrations or none at all. At least one method takes care of the matter with the statement: "Your teacher will show you how to hold the instrument." The difficulty some students have in learning to hold the instrument, and the shortage of help in some of the instruction books, is pointed out here simply to bring the problem into perspective.

TUNING

Sources of Pitch

In an experienced orchestra the oboe provides the A. All instruments in the orchestra tune to this source of pitch. In school groups an electronic A, or a tuning bar, is frequently used as the pitch source. At home the student may use a piano, organ, tuning fork, or pitch pipe. The latter comes in two types. One type is the A alone; another is a group of four tubes, which correspond to the four strings. Pitch pipes or tuners, as they are sometimes called, are not always reliable. Even those that are accurately in tune must be blown gently to avoid distortion of the pitch. Even so, they are better than having nothing to tune to.

Steps in Tuning

In tuning it is important that the tuning tone be established clearly and steadily. Only then will it be possible to match it.

On the violin, viola, and cello the A is invariably tuned first; then the other strings are tuned to the A. The top two strings are usually tuned first, then the two middle strings, followed by the two lower strings. This order is not sacred and can be varied if desirable.

One approach in a heterogeneous string class or ensemble is to tune all the A's and D's first, then the G's followed by the E's of the violin and bass, and finally the C's of the viola and cello. This procedure can produce greater accuracy in tuning and, at the same time, make the students aware of the intervallic relationships from one instrument to another.

Because the pitch of the bass strings is so low, and because the bass is tuned in fourths instead of fifths, it is not practical to tune the bass by sounding two open strings simultaneously. Instead, students may tune one string at a time to the piano or along with the other instruments. More advanced players may tune using natural harmonics, which puts the pitch in a more easily discernible register.

Following is a list of points to be kept in mind in learning to tune the violin, viola, and cello:

1. Listen carefully for at least five seconds to the tuning note.
2. Tune the A string carefully and quietly.

3. Use a steady, light bow. This will avoid pitch fluctuations and distortions.
4. Tune the two top strings together until the interval of the fifth is perfect. (When "perfect," no beats will be apparent.)
5. With metal strings use tuners or adjusters. Avoid turning pegs unless absolutely necessary.
6. When turning peg, always grasp the scroll between the fingers and squeeze the peg in toward the pegbox as it is turned. This keeps the peg seated and prevents slippage.
7. Minute pitch adjustments of gut-core strings can be made by pushing on the string just above the nut to raise the pitch, and by rubbing the finger along the length of the string or pulling it slightly to lower the pitch.
8. Avoid any exaggerated or rapid increase or decrease in tension through extreme tightening or loosening of the string. To bring a string to the desired pitch, it should first be lowered slightly and then raised to the correct pitch.

Tuning a string instrument is not easy. It calls for a well-developed sense of pitch and a good deal of strength in the fingers that turn the pegs. More often than not the young beginner does not have either of these requirements in sufficient degree to do the job. The teacher must accept the fact that he or she is going to have to tune the beginner's instrument for a considerable time. When the teacher feels that the student has developed to the point when he or she can begin to tune the instrument, the teacher should then begin to provide the motivation and instruction that will lead to the student's ability to tune independently at the earliest moment, first tuning by plucking the strings, then by using the bow.

TECHNIQUES OF THE LEFT HAND

Intonation

Intonation is the word used to describe the degree of in-tune-ness or out-of-tune-ness of a player's or a group's performance. Acceptable intonation is a prime objective of every instrumentalist and vocalist. It surpasses every other musical goal in importance; for without acceptable intonation, all other aspects of performance—rhythm, tone, expression—are wasted.

Without going into a long and involved discussion of intonation expectations, it should be stated here that a first-year student is not expected to perform with the same intonation standards as a third-year student. During the early months of instruction you will be pleased if the student puts the finger on the right string for the right note. If, at first, the notes produced are recognizable as what they are supposed to be, intonation is regarded as satisfactory. As the student progresses, the accuracy of intonation should also progress to the point that high school students' intonation should be judged quite strictly.

Achieving acceptable intonation on a string instrument is at once easier and more difficult than on the woodwinds and brasses. These latter instruments have natural limitations in

the form of the keys, which are pressed down to produce various pitches. No woodwind or brass instrument is acoustically perfect; so just pressing down the correct key does not automatically produce the exact pitch desired. It is necessary, therefore, for players to "favor" certain notes on their instrument in order to play in tune. Needless to say, this matter is not given serious consideration in the early stages. But it becomes a matter of real importance and concern as the woodwind and brass players move into the advanced stages of instruction. This "favoring" of a note is done on a string instrument by moving the finger forward or backward on the string; it may amount to nothing more than an infinitesimal rolling of the finger when the finer shades of intonation are at stake. The string instruments do not have the advantage the woodwinds and brasses have of a specific key or combination of keys to produce a specific note; but neither do the strings have any limit on their ability to produce *perfect* intonation. The trumpet and clarinet players may find beginning intonation less of a problem than the violinist, but later the clarinetist will be fighting certain notes on the instrument in the middle and upper registers, and the trumpeter may find problems with notes that utilize the third valve. At this stage the string player can blame no one and nothing but himself.

In the early stages of string instruction it is imperative that the instrument be properly adjusted, the strings in good condition, and the instrument carefully tuned by the instructor for each lesson. Neglect of any one of these matters can impair the young student's attempts to play in tune. (The value of tuners and metal strings from the standpoint of easy tuning and staying in tune has already been discussed.)

When the fingers of the left hand are first placed on the string, the problem is to get the child to place them at the point on the string that produces the correct pitch. There are approximations that can be used, such as: the first finger should be placed on the string "so far from the nut" in terms of inches.

Finger Placement Aids

Various devices have been tried in an attempt to assist young students to orient their fingers correctly to the strings. A few of these devices, or techniques, are listed below:

1. Pieces of adhesive tape are placed under and perpendicular to the strings to mark the places where the fingers are placed.
2. A piece of string or thread is stretched across the fingerboard and fastened with cellophane tape. This provides an elevated strip, which is easy for the finger to feel.
3. Finger positions are marked on the fingerboard with chalk, crayon, or pencil.

There is a continuing pedagogical argument about the use of aids, or crutches, such as those described above. One side of the argument abhors the use of anything but the ear in the note-finding process and claims that the child will remain dependent upon the aid long after its period of usefulness. The other side is willing to accept anything that can assist the young student over some of the early hurdles on the premise that success is thus more easily achieved, and suc-

Figure 6.1. Tape marking the place for the first and second finger on the violin.

cess breeds success. As far as the author knows, no research has been done with a control group to prove or disprove either of these arguments. If, in the teacher's judgment, the student will be helped by a finger placement aid, the teacher must also determine at what point the student can proceed satisfactorily without a crutch.

Vibrato

Among the functions of the left hand, vibrato is second only to intonation in importance; for when the vibrato begins to develop, the player begins to move out of the beginning student category onto the path that leads to artistry. It is the vibrato that imbues the tone with warmth, vitality, and luster.

The vibrato is produced by a back and forth rolling motion of the finger on the string. This motion alternately raises and lowers the pitch, but it does it in such a way that the listener is not aware of pitch fluctuation but rather of the beauty vibrato adds to the tone.

It is the flexibility in the width and speed of the vibrato that is largely responsible for the tremendous range of expression of which the string instruments are capable. It is the variety and expressiveness of the vibrato that has led to the contention that the strings have the closest kinship to the human voice of all of the instruments.

The vibrato should never be purely mechanical. To be truly effective it must respond to the emotional stimulus of the music. It depicts calmness and serenity through its own lack of agitation. It heightens the drama and intensity of the music by becoming more rapid, more violent, more agitated. Those vibratos that are too slow or too fast, too wide or too narrow, function at a constant speed, or impair intonation, are detrimental to the ultimate in performance in the same way that a wobble or a quiver can make a voice unpleasant.

The actual movement of fingers, hand, and arm in producing vibrato will be discussed in relationship to each instrument. The preparation of these movements can be assisted through various kinds of exercises and practice. Joints can be flexed and the hand and arm can be put through motions that will condition them to produce a vibrato. But a degree of physical coordination and emotional compulsion that verges upon a mystique seem to be needed before the vibrato will function freely. For some it comes as naturally as eating. For others it remains elusive, defying long and arduous effort to acquire it. To repeat, exercises may condition the mechanism but they will not "cause" a vibrato to function.

Students should not be encouraged to use vibrato too early in their development. It should wait until intonation is reliable, since the movement of the fingers and the fluctuation of pitch in the vibrato can cover up poor intonation. If poor intonation persists, the vibrato should be avoided and the student should practice with a "dead" hand.[1] As stated earlier, the vibrato should not be mechanical. With some players a constant vibrato becomes a habit, and curbing the vibrato when desirable or requested is hard for them.

Shifting and Positions

Shifting positions on a string instrument is the process of moving the hand closer to or farther from the nut. The positions available to the string player begin with half position and progress up the string to seventh, eighth, or even ninth position.

The availability of numerous positions expands the capability of the string instruments in the following ways:

It extends the overall range of the instruments by extending the high range.
It extends the playing range on each string.
It facilitates the playing of certain note combinations or sequences that otherwise would be awkward.
It makes the portamento possible.

If the string instruments could play only in first position, two limitations would be imposed upon them. First, the number of notes that could be played on each string would be those that can be reached in first position. Second, the high range would be limited to the notes that can be reached with the little finger while playing in first position on the top string.

By utilizing the higher positions it is possible to play many more notes on each string and the overall range of each instrument is expanded by more than two octaves. In the examples on page 56 the range of notes played on each string, using first position, is compared with the expanded range using the higher positions. Overall ranges using first and fifth positions are also shown.

---

1. This term describes a manner of playing that is devoid of any left hand expression. In performance the string player uses an almost continuous vibrato. If the composer wants a passage played without vibrato, he writes *non vibrato* at the beginning of the section. On the other hand, if he wants to assure that a passage will be played with full vibrato, he writes *molto vibrato*. Actually, neither term is used very frequently. The excitement of the music—if it is convincingly written—is usually enough to stimulate the players to use *molto vibrato;* so they do not need to be told. *Non vibrato* is a special effect, and no special effect should be overworked.

CHART SHOWING EXTENDED RANGE USING 5TH POSITION

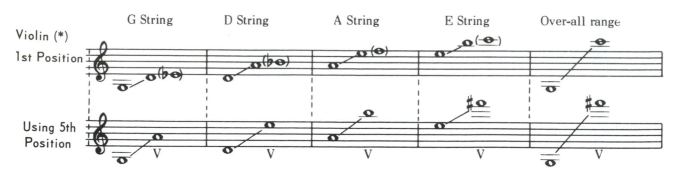

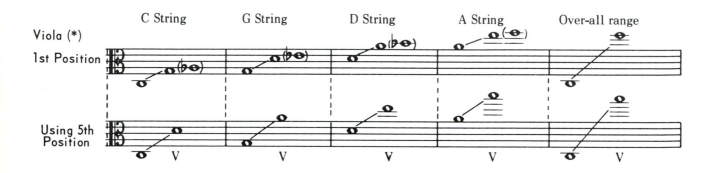

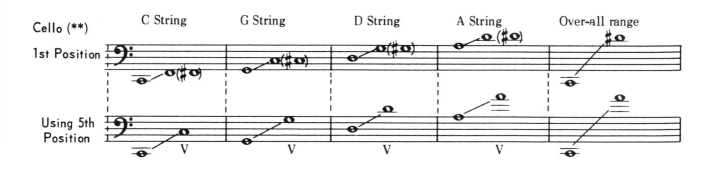

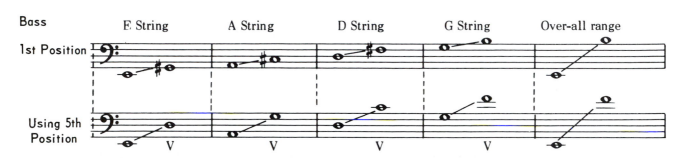

(*) The notes in parentheses are reached by extending the 4th finger.

(**) The notes in parentheses are reached by using the forward hand extension.

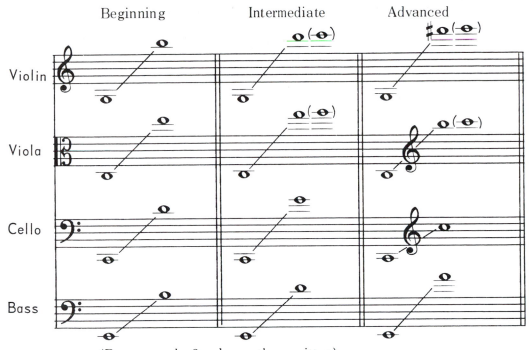

(Bass sounds *8va* lower than written)

In the chart above, beginning, intermediate, and advanced ranges are shown for each instrument. The beginning range does not exceed first position. At the intermediate stage the violin and viola are in third position, the cello in fourth position, and the bass in third position. The advanced stage makes use of fifth through seventh positions. It should be understood that standard solo and orchestral literature require the player to exceed the top limit shown in this chart.

Moving from one position to another is called shifting. Every string method includes an explanation of the positions and how to shift. Many exercises are devoted to acquainting the students with correct shifting techniques, to the orientation of the hand and fingers to the various positions, and to developing facility in getting from one position to another easily and accurately. It is important for the students to realize that as they move into the higher positions, the fingers will be placed progressively closer together.

A thorough knowledge of the positions and shifting techniques, which are both fluid and accurate, are essential equipment for the advanced player. Bass and cello players will begin shifting early of necessity. Violinists will find that they must know at least third and fifth positions if they are to conquer even a small part of the standard repertoire. Violists can get by for a longer period of time without going above third position.

A shift can be made purely for the purpose of getting to the next desired position. When this is the objective, the shift is made as unnoticeably as possible. To accomplish this the fingers move lightly and quickly to the next position. A shift may be made from one position to another using the same finger or a different finger. What precedes and follows the shift determines this, and there are too many possibilities to cover here.

SULLA CORDA

The aim of the shift may be to play a particular group of notes on one string rather than move to the next higher string, thus avoiding a change in tone quality. When a composer wants to give a player this kind of direction, the term *Sulla* (sul, sull', sulle) *Corda,* or *Sul* followed by the letter name of the string is used. In the example below the cellist knows that the composer wants the first four measures played on the D string.

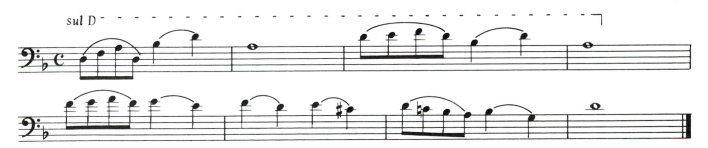

A famous example of playing for an extended period on one string is the *Air* by J. S. Bach as arranged for the violin by the great 19th century German violinist, August Wilhelmj. Wilhelmj transposed the *Air* from the D Major Suite to the key of C, which meant that the lowest note in the piece would be G. The highest note is B♭, a minor tenth above. He then indicated Sul G at the beginning of the piece. Over the years the piece became a favorite encore known as the "Air for the G String."

The higher positions on one of the three lower strings may be used to achieve a more intense quality of tone than can be realized by playing the notes in a lower position on a higher string. For example, notes played in fifth position on the violin G string can be far more intense and dramatic than the same tones played on the D string. An excellent example of this is found in the opening section of the Ravel *Tzigane* for violin and piano. Ravel has designed this unaccompanied recitative so that it mounts higher and higher on the G string in both pitch and intensity until it seems that the instrument shrieks with passion.

The Portamento

Many times the shift has an ulterior purpose. This purpose it to produce a slide or *portamento* from the note that is being left or to the note being approached. This effect gives a poignant stress to the note or sequence of notes and enhances the emotional impact of the interval.

An experienced and competent performer will know when a portamento is appropriate and when it is not, without any indication from the composer. If, however, the composer wants to make certain that a portamento is executed in a particular spot, he may write the word portamento over the interval or use the musical shorthand, which is a slanted line between the two notes in question. This symbol is another example of the exactness of musical notation; the length of the line is indicative of the scope of the portamento. A short line tells the player to make only a slight slide. A longer line extends the length of the slide.

Example 1 leaves the amount of portamento up to the player's discretion. Example 2 indicates that there should be a little portamento, but not too much, to the high B. This portamento is executed by placing the second finger on the string below the B with nearly normal pressure and sliding into the B.

Example 1

Example 2

Example 3 calls for a heavier, more continuous slide between the two notes than do either of the previous examples. And example 4 could be called either a portamento or an unarticulated *glissando*. Example 5 is a true chromatic glissando. It is played with one finger, which slides down the string, articulating each note.

Example 3

Example 4

Example 5

The portamento must be used with discretion. It is inappropriate in music preceding the Romantic period. Mechanically, the slide must be executed with taste. It must not be too long, too slow, or too heavy, and it must not be overused. Experience, maturity, good taste, and good examples after which to pattern will create the restraint needed in the use of this device.

Indicating Fingerings and Positions

Composers who are not string players usually leave the matter of fingering and positions up to an editor or the player; or they collaborate with a performer during the writing process and bring out a fully edited score upon publication. Standard editions of orchestral literature contain a minimum number of fingerings. This is a detail that the composer is often incompetent to execute or one he chooses not to spend time on. On the other hand, some solo literature is extensively edited with fingerings. There are advantages as well as disadvantages to this. A carefully edited piece of music can convey nearly everything that the composer had in mind. This is helpful, especially to those who feel that they need this kind of assistance. But the artist-performers, and I refer to the majority of highly skilled players, have their own way of doing many things. Ranking foremost among these is fingering. So any piece of music that has been edited is a reflection of the kinds of fingerings preferred by the editor, based, of course, upon what he or she felt the composer intended. If the edition is cluttered with fingerings, the better

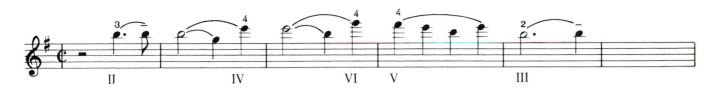

players will look for another edition; for they prefer a relatively clean copy into which they can insert those notations they feel they need. This is not to say that specific wishes of the composer should not be put down; they should. So should fingerings where they are helpful and where they will expedite the player's understanding of the music or speed his ability to execute a difficult passage.

Fingerings and positions can be indicated in two ways. The fingering can be written above or below the notes with Arabic numerals; or the position may be written above or below the notes with Roman numerals. Most editors simply use fingerings. If a misunderstanding is possible, they use Roman numerals to indicate the string they intend the notes to be played on. I means the top string; II is the second; III the third; IV the fourth. Because the Roman numeral sometimes stands for a string and sometimes a position, confusion is possible. Occasionally, the composer's or editor's intention can be deduced only by drawing conclusions from the use of similar markings elsewhere in the music where the intent is clear.

In the above example, Arabic numerals indicate the fingers that are to play the notes. (Mendelssohn Violin Concerto). The positions utilized in these five measures are written here below the staff only to indicate the shifting that takes place. It is not customary to mark positions in this way except in student literature.

Positions are often indicated by Roman numerals in study materials such as etudes and scales. One reason for using Roman numerals to indicate positions in this type of material is to acquaint the student with the positions he is using. Another is that extended passages or an entire etude may be in one position; that is, it was written to be played in one position as an aid to learning that position. In such cases there may be a statement at the head of the etude indicating that it is to be played in a particular position; or the Roman numeral symbolizing that position may be used at the start of the etude; or the etude may be labeled "Etude in 3rd Position." In the following examples it is to be assumed that the player will stay in the indicated position until another position is indicated.

Double Stops

The term double stop denotes the technique of playing on two strings simultaneously. The three upper instruments are capable of playing double stops with many combinations of fingering. The bass is less disposed toward double stops because of the difficulty of keeping more than one of its large strings vibrating and because of the limited number of intervals that the hand can encompass. For these reasons double stops on the bass are generally limited to combinations that utilize an open string. Even this demand is restricted to advanced solos and is virtually never encountered in orchestral works.

The violin and viola are capable of playing double stops ranging from unison to tenths. Larger intervals are possible if an open string is the bottom tone. Advanced instruction on these instruments includes scales in thirds, sixths, octaves, and tenths. The reach is greater on the cello, so fewer combinations are possible, although thirds, sixths, and octaves are not uncommon in solo writing.

Double stops are most effective in the low and middle section of the instrument's register, in the positions that make use of maximum string length.

Double stop writing is limited almost exclusively to solos although a composer may occasionally write double stops for one or more of the sections of the strings. Combinations of open strings are not unusual, as well as combinations using one open string while the fingers function on an adjoining string.

Thirds and sixths are the most frequently used double stops because they are the most pleasant and sonorous to hear, and because they are the easiest to manage on the instrument. Fifths are difficult to play in tune. The finger must be pressed flat across the two strings and must be straight across in order to get a perfect fifth.[2] Tenths are difficult but possible on the violin and viola, since they stretch the hand to capacity. Octaves can be played throughout the violin and viola range.

---

2. This applies only to perfect fifths. A diminished or augmented fifth is played with two fingers as will be seen in the examples on pages 60 and 61.

Normally, the first and fourth fingers are used except when an open string is involved in which case the third finger plays the upper member of the octave. Fingered octaves use a 1–3, 2–4 finger pattern. They are very difficult and are limited to the most advanced players in solo work. In playing octaves and tenths the cellist uses the thumb to play the lower note and the third finger to play the upper note.

Examples of some double stops and their fingerings follow. Needless to say, either note in the following examples may be altered chromatically.

SOME DOUBLE STOPS AND THEIR FINGERINGS
VIOLIN

SOME DOUBLE STOPS AND THEIR FINGERINGS
VIOLA

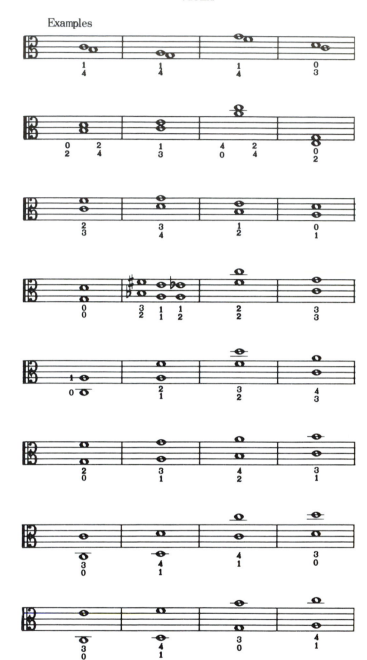

The examples given above and on page 61 are selective only. Each of the string instruments, except the bass, is capable of playing most major and minor 2nds, 3rds, 6ths, 7ths, perfect, diminished, and augmented 4ths, 5ths, and 8vas throughout the range of the instrument, limited only by the bottom string capabilities and the practicality of the high positions.

SOME DOUBLE STOPS AND THEIR FINGERINGS
CELLO

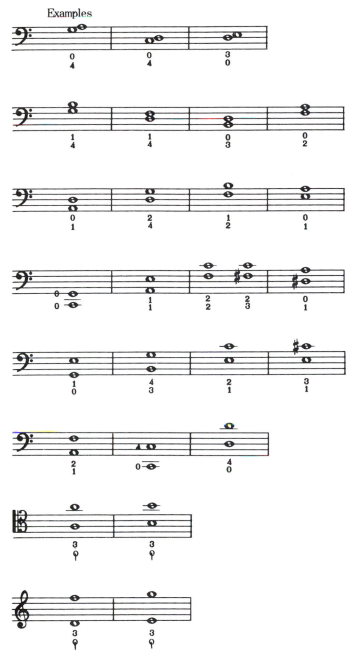

ϙ is the sign for thumb position.

DIVISI

In orchestral writing, if a composer or arranger writes two notes and expects both notes to be played by each player, the intent is often indicated with the term *non divisi*. In German the term *nicht geteilt* is used. *Divisi* or *geteilt,* on the other hand, tells the players that they are to play only one note of a two-part divisi. Some conductors have players divide on each stand, the outside player playing the top note while the inside player plays the lower note. Other conductors have the first stand play the top, the second stand the lower notes, etc. When more than three notes are written, special arrangements must be specified by the conductor, the concert master, or the section leader in order to cover all parts. Examples of typical *divisi* and *non-divisi* writing follow.

Starting with Berlioz, Wagner, and Richard Strauss and continuing through Debussy, Ravel, Sibelius, and into the present, multipart writing for the strings is commonplace. The opulence created by this kind of scoring seems to answer the need for rich, lush textures of sound. It is not unusual to have each section of the strings divided into two, three, or four parts. This is done by writing the parts on separate staves. (See page 62.)

In Ravel's *Daphnis and Chloe Suite* three separate lines are utilized for the viola part. In Sibelius' *The Swan of Tuonela* the first and second violins are each divided into four parts, the violas and cellos into two separate parts, which, in turn, have frequent two-part *divisi.*

Pizzicato

WITH THE RIGHT HAND

Pizzicato is the process of producing tone by plucking the string. Normally, pizzicato (abbreviated pizz.) is performed by the right hand. On the violin, viola, and cello the pad of the first finger is used, with the thumb placed against the side of the fingerboard to support the hand and arm. On the bass the first, and sometimes the first and second fingers are used, with the thumb again braced against the side of the fingerboard.[3]

For the playing of extended pizzicato passages the bow is held in the remaining fingers of the right hand or is laid down. If an isolated pizzicato note or chord occurs, with little time for preparation, the bow may be held in its normal manner and the finger (thumb for the cellist) is simply straightened to pluck the string or strings. For an extended passage, the composer will do well to allow time for the player to prepare for the pizzicato, as well as to regrasp the bow following the pizzicato passage. Without adequate time to get set for the pizzicato, the player must make a mad scramble, hoping to get his finger on the right string in time, a maneuver that does not always meet with total success.

Following a pizzicato note or passage the word *arco,* which is the Italian word for the bow, is placed before the next group of notes to tell the player to again use the bow. This term is used as universally as the term pizzicato. Once in a great while a French edition directs the player to *reprenez l'arche.*

---

3. In dance music the bass is part of the rhythm section and plays pizzicato exclusively. Because of this, many dance bassists move the right hand and arm rather freely rather than keeping the thumb against the fingerboard. In slow tempi the arm is partially dropped or pulled away from the fingerboard between beats. This serves to keep the arm loose and relaxed, and the motion, which is a rhythmical one occurring on the beats between the notes (beats 2 and 4), can actually help the player to keep a steady beat. When playing a "four beat" figure (a note on each count of a four beat bar), or a fast tempo that put the notes closer together, the hand is kept closer to the strings.

TILL EULENSPIEGELS LUSTIGE STREICHE

In the proper execution of pizzicato the string is pulled sideways. If pulled vertically, the string slaps against the fingerboard, making an unmusical sound, which is only acceptable as a special effect when asked for by the composer. The quality of sound is regulated by the point at which the string is plucked. Toward the bridge the tone will be hard and brittle; well up the fingerboard the tone will be soft and limp.

One, two, three, or four strings may be played pizzicato in one stroke. In playing chords, cellists, and sometimes violinists and violists, use the thumb; the first finger is most often used on violin and viola, in which case it is flattened across the strings involved. In chord playing, more hand and arm action is required than in the playing of single notes, so the thumb is taken away from the fingerboard.

Composers use pizzicato for punctuation, percussive effects, and for relief or change. The music of the early composers made only infrequent use of pizzicato. A charming example is the slow movement from the Haydn F Major Quartet Opus 3, No. 5. In this movement the first violin plays a lovely muted melody to the harplike pizzicato accompaniment of the other three instruments.

Tchaikovsky was enamored of the sound of pizzicato in the orchestra and made frequent use of the technique. The third movement of his Symphony No. 4 in F minor uses the strings exclusively in pizzicato fashion. In a case such as this, where the bow is not used for an extended period, and there is time to pick it up again, it is generally laid on the music stand. Another famous pizzicato passage is found just after the opening woodwind chords in Tchaikovsky's Overture to Romeo and Juliet.

The full string section playing pizzicato has a certain special appeal to most audiences. The reason probably lies in the novelty of seeing and hearing these normally smooth, singing instruments produce percussive sounds, which are uncharacteristic of their otherwise sweet and gentle nature, plus the spectacle of these bowed instruments producing sounds without the bow. Leroy Anderson has capitalized upon this special appeal of the pizzicato in his piece for strings called *Jazz Pizzicato*. Composers who write for school groups have

Figure 6.3. Pizzicato on the cello.

Figure 6.4. Pizzicato on the bass (with a French bow).

Figure 6.2. Pizzicato on the violin and viola.

Figure 6.5. Pizzicato on the bass (with a German bow).

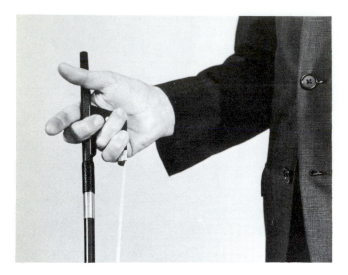

Figure 6.6. Holding the German bow for pizzicato.

also recognized the merits of pizzicato selections and have produced numerous compositions in various grades of difficulty. They are popular with both young and mature audiences.

LEFT-HAND PIZZICATO

In advanced solo literature for the violin and to a lesser extent the viola and cello, pizzicato is also performed by the left hand. The fingers of the left hand pluck the string in the direction of the palm of the hand. Single notes or groups of notes can be played in this fashion. Considerable strength and control are needed to play left-hand pizzicato, and, at best, not a great amount of tone can be produced. A small plus sign (+) is placed over notes that are to be played pizzicato with the left hand.

Descending scale passages can be played in this manner. The fourth finger plucks the string to produce the note that is stopped by the third finger. The third and second fingers follow suit, and the first finger plucks the open string. The following passage would be played in this way.

Because the little finger is relatively weak and ineffectual in this manner of playing, the notes that it would play in the above passage are often played by striking the string with the bow, as follows:

Patterns in which bowed notes and pizzicato notes alternate are found in the violin solos of Paganini, Sarasate, and other composers of virtuoso violin pieces. Such passages are usually brief and are performed at a fairly rapid tempo.

Trill

"A trill consists of the regular and rapid alternation of a given note with the note above."[4] The trill may be a half or a whole step above the lower, or principal, note depending upon the underlying harmonic structure. On the string instruments the finger playing the lower note remains static while the trilling finger moves rapidly onto and off the string.

Trills can be of short or long duration, lasting for as short a time as a 16th note or as long as several measures. Two important qualities in a trill are evenness and clarity. Both are dependent upon strength and control in the fingers of the left hand. Most books of studies have lessons for the development of the trill, all of which have the same purpose, building strength and elasticity in the fingers. To produce a clear trill the finger must strike the string firmly and leave it instantaneously.

The second finger is generally the strongest; consequently most performers produce their best trill with this finger. The third finger is next in efficiency; the little finger generally ranks from poor to fair. Trills that might involve an open string on the lower note are usually taken in a position, although it is possible to trill with the first finger. The bass is rarely asked to trill because of the slow response of its strings.

In early music the trill is usually started from the higher note. (This is referred to as starting the trill from above.) This produces an *appoggiatura* to the principal note. In most cases the trill lasts for the full duration of the note and is ended with a turn utilizing the note below the principal note. When the trill is in a cadential position it frequently ends with an anticipation of the note of resolution.

Since the Romantic period, practice is to start the trill on the principal note. It may or may not be ended with a turn. Circumstances dictate this matter. Cadential trills are frequently begun slowly; they may be ended in a rhythmical manner with the principal note and the trill note receiving equal amounts of time in a measured fashion.

---

4. Grove's *Dictionary of Music and Musicians.*

A series of trills is usually played with no ornamentation.

This is by no means meant to be a treatise on the trill. *Grove's Dictionary of Music and Musicians* gives three pages to the discussion of the shake or trill, and there is widespread disagreement among the musicologists about the interpretation of the entire field of ornamentation, including trills and their beginning and ending. The important thing to remember here is that a trill that functions well may be adapted to any situation.

Tremolo (Finger)

The word "finger" is added here to differentiate between this tremolo and the more common tremolo that is played with the bow. The finger tremolo is patterned after the piano tremolo wherein two or more notes are played alternatively in rapid fashion.

The string instruments are also capable of playing tremolo in double stop combinations.

In this example the lower notes are slurred while the upper note is sustained, or less commonly, alternating double stops.

In orchestra music the types of tremolo illustrated above would usually be played *divisi*. The single tremolo is encountered quite frequently in orchestra music.

In the slow movement of his violin concerto, Mendelssohn makes very effective use of this device in combination with double stops.

Harmonics

Natural Harmonics

A natural harmonic is a tone produced by placing a finger lightly on a string at one of the string's natural division, or nodal, points. This causes the string to vibrate in segments instead of as a whole. The result is called a harmonic. The harmonic is soft in volume and flutelike in timbre.

The sign commonly used for a natural harmonic is a small circle placed over the fundamental note. Diamond shaped notes are also used. By touching the string lightly at that point, the desired harmonic is produced. In example 1, the finger touches the string at its mid-point. This produces the harmonic one octave above the fundamental open D. By placing the finger lightly at the 1/4 division point, as in example 2, the harmonic produced sounds two octaves above the fundamental open string.

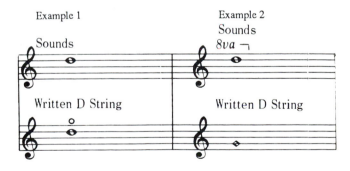

Harmonics, which can be produced on the G string of the violin, are illustrated in example 3. By simple transposition the harmonics available on the other strings and other instruments can be found.

Example 3

NATURAL HARMONICS ON THE VIOLIN G STRING

Example 4

ARTIFICIAL HARMONICS

ARTIFICIAL HARMONICS

So-called "artificial" harmonics are produced by stopping the string with a finger and then touching the string lightly at the interval of a 3rd, 4th, or 5th above the stopped point. In this way harmonics of the shortened string are produced. Harmonics that are two 8vas, two 8vas and a 3rd, and two 8vas and a 5th above the fundamental can be played. The first of these (two 8vas) is the most common. It is used in playing scale-wise passages and other melodic passages with the flutelike harmonic quality. Some artificial harmonics and the method of writing them are shown in example 4.

TECHNIQUES OF THE BOW

Holding the Bow

The bow is held in the right hand. With the exception of the Butler bass bow, the bows are held in basically the same way. The thumb is placed on the underneath side of the stick, near the frog. The four fingers are placed on top of the stick, curving over the stick to form a grip.

This grip must be relaxed but firm. It must be capable of manipulating the bow with the utmost delicacy at one moment and with fierce roughness the next, with snail-like slowness and tremendous speed. It must be able to make short, staccato notes and then connect notes imperceptibly, to stay on the string or bounce off, to be at the frog or at the point, or on the top string or the lowest string all in fractions of seconds.

The precise manner of holding the bow is as controversial as the question of how the left thumb is placed on the neck, but the bow grip has been regarded as of greater importance. The reason so much importance has been placed upon this matter is due to the difficulty so many players have in achieving a bow grip with which they are satisfied and comfortable in all circumstances. Many diverse demands are made of the bow; it is expected to do many things. If it balks or fails in any of its duties, the performer comes to one of

two conclusions—either the bow itself is inadequate to the task, or the grip needs to be adjusted. Once the first question is resolved satisfactorily, the second becomes the center of attention. The search is always for a panacea.

Over the years this search for the perfect way to hold the bow, a grip that would make it possible for any player to execute the most difficult and intricate bowings with ease, has led to the formation of several so-called "schools" of holding the bow. The Russian, the German, and Franco-Belgian schools of violin bowing are the most prominent. Without going into a lengthy account of each of these schools, it is safe to say that they evolved as did schools of painting. That is, a great artist (who was usually a teacher also) did what was instinctive to him and produced the results he desired. Others observed, copied, or were taught his techniques, and a "school" was born. Each school has recognizable characteristics which distinguish it. In the case of the schools of bowing, the distinguishing characteristics are the placement of the first finger on the stick and the consequent attitude of the wrist and elbow.

The most convincing argument against the position that there is only one correct way to hold the bow is the fact that these several schools of bowing have emerged through the years. If one way of holding the bow were so much better than another, why did not one method become universal? The reason is, of course, that each individual's bone and muscle structure is unique. Being unique, it is therefore impossible for one individual to do something in precisely the same way as another. Modifications to suit individual differences are necessary. No teacher should insist that every pupil adopt his or her system, approach, or mannerisms any more than everyone should have to wear size nine shoes and live in a brown house.

Since the onset of the twentieth century and the internationalization of the world through improved transportation and communications systems, the nationalistic aspects of the various schools of bowing have disappeared. In fact, today the terms "German school" or "Russian school" are viewed more with historic interest than as terms having meaningful current applicability. It is not important that the characteristics of these schools be known, but it is a matter of interest; therefore they are described briefly below.

RUSSIAN SCHOOL

The Russian school put the stick at the top of the third joint of the first finger, nearly into the palm, with the hand tilted toward the point. This puts the wrist into a high arch and makes it possible to apply the full weight of the arm with ease. (Figure 6.7.)

GERMAN SCHOOL

The German school went in the opposite direction, putting the first joint of the first finger in contact with the wood and maintaining flat fingers and a rather flat wrist. This grip produces a very low wrist position at the point of the bow. (Figure 6.8.)

FRANCO-BELGIAN SCHOOL

This was a compromise between the Russian and German positions. The second joint of the first finger was the point of contact, the hand tilted slightly toward the tip, and the wrist in a moderate arch. (Figure 6.9.)

Function of the Bow

The bow's purpose is to draw tone from the instrument. To accomplish this the hair of the bow is placed on the string at right angles and is then moved horizontally across the strings. The friction produced by the hair and the string cause the string to vibrate. Presto, tone is created. Nothing could be simpler.

There are five basic factors that bear on this very simple principle. They are:

Bow direction (up or down)
Amount and speed of bow
Point of contact on the string
Amount of pressure or weight
Amount of hair in contact with the string

All of the infinite number of strokes and subtleties of which the bow is capable are produced by the variables inherent in these five factors. Bow direction stands in a special category because there are only two directions for the bow to travel—up or down. (On the bass and cello this really amounts to left or right, but common practice over the years has been to use the term "up" and "down" in reference to all the strings.) But the remaining factors are capable of a nearly endless number of variations. True, the full bow is the most that can be used. However, skillful manipulation can deceive the listener into believing that the bow has no stopping point. On the other end of the spectrum, as little as 1/16th inch of bow may be used to play a note. So the amount of bow can range from a fraction of an inch to the full bow; and added to this is the factor of speed, which can range from unbelievably slow to incredibly fast.

As to point of contact, the bridge and the fingerboard are considered the reasonable limits. However, it is not uncommon in the music of the Impressionists to be directed to play "over the fingerboard," a technique called *flautato* or *flautando*, which produces a breathy, flutelike quality. The

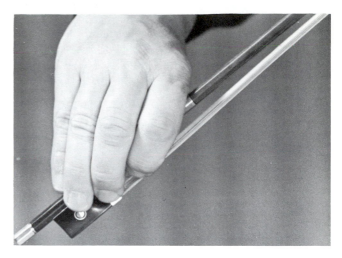

Figure 6.7. Holding the violin bow (Russian school).

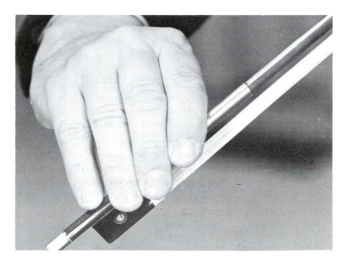

Figure 6.8. Holding the violin bow (German school).

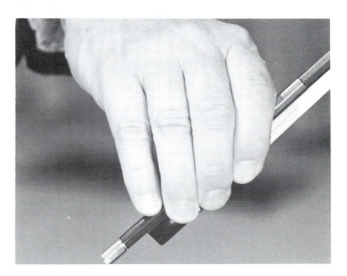

Figure 6.9. Holding th violin bow (Franco-Belgian school).

other extreme is behind the bridge, a manner of playing which is required very infrequently and yields a sound that is more like a squeak or whistle than a musical tone. Between these extremes lie the infinite number of points of contact from which the player may choose in order to attain the particular volume and quality of tone he wants at a given moment.

Pressure, or weight, is directly related to speed and point of contact. Each influences and is influenced by the other. Pressure of the bow on the string is not increased without moving the point of contact closer to the bridge, and vice versa.

The tilt of the bow governs the amount of hair that is in contact with the string. Tilt changes from frog to point because of the movements of the hand and arm, and because of the need to use more hair and pressure from the middle to the point. It is in this way that the tone and volume throughout the length of the bow is equalized, the heavy lower half using less hair and the upper half using additional hair and pressure as needed.

Tone Production

Learning to "dig in" with the bow and draw a full tone is a long process in most cases. Many students are well into, and some well beyond, the intermediate stage of progress before they acquire this concept. The big string tone is a product of the following factors:

1. Controlled strength in the right arm, hand, and fingers.
2. Proper balance between bow-speed and pressure.
3. Correct distance of the bow from the bridge in relation to speed and pressure.

There is a great deal of force and counterforce at work in the bowing process. The first place this happens is between the thumb, which presses up, and the fingers, which press down. The second instance is the pressing down of the bow on the string and the resistance of the string. The thumb and the first finger form a lever action, which, if applied to excess, could break the bow. The string and the little finger balance this action. This function of the little finger accounts for the importance of having it on top of the stick for the violin and viola.

The arm also plays an important role. From the middle to the point, pressure on the string is exerted through the thumb-first finger lever with its counterbalances. From the middle to the frog the natural weight of the arm comes into play. This weight must be controlled by the shoulder muscles in order to keep the lower-half volume in balance with the volume capability of the upper half. Tone production is dependent upon all of these factors being in proper balance.

In general the player should have the sensation of pulling on the down bow and drawing on the up bow.

Dynamics

There are several overall guiding principles in regard to dynamics. They are: (1) the softest tone is produced by the least amount of bow pressure, (2) the loudest tone is produced by the greatest amount of bow pressure, and (3) as pressure is increased, the point of contact moves closer to the bridge.

Correlated with this principle is one having to do with the amount, or length, of bow used in regard to dynamics. This principle can be stated as (1) the softest tone is produced by using the least amount of bow, and (2) the loudest tone is produced by using the greatest amount of bow.

Of fundamental importance are

1. Point of contact between bow and string.
2. Speed of the bow.
3. Amount of hair contacting the string.

The question of the amount of hair to use is relatively simple. If more tone is desired, the bow is brought to a more upright position, and more hair is brought in contact with the string. For less tone, reverse the procedure.

Point of contact is a somewhat more complex matter because it is directly related to bow speed. And bow speed is dictated by duration of note, point of contact, pressure, and desired tone quality. If two given notes are of the same duration, and require the use of the full bow, then pressure and point of contact are the factors that will govern the dynamic produced. If something less than a full bow is required to produce the note, then bow speed also enters into the matter, in which case the principle stated above applies.

Bowing directions cannot be given in absolute terms. But it is possible to reduce a few matters to simple terms, which will apply in most situations. They are

Forte
Exert pressure on the bow.
Use as much bow as possible.
Keep the point of contact close to the bridge.

Piano
Exert little or no pressure. Use a light bow.
Limit the amount of bow used.
Keep the point of contact away from the bridge.

Bowings

The term "bowings" refers to how the bow functions in relation to the music. It involves whether the bow will go up or down, stay on the string or bounce, start and stop abruptly or smoothly, slur notes or play them separately. The basic orchestral bowings and their symbols will be discussed below, but in order to understand them it is first necessary to become acquainted with the vocabulary of the bow. Some of these terms have already been presented and should be reviewed. (See Figure 2.3.) Others will be new.

BOW DIRECTION

Down Bow
The bow travels in a frog-to-point direction. A down bow may begin at the frog or at any point above the frog. See A in Figure 6.10.
The sign for down bow is almost universally ⊓.
Some old editions use ∧, which is an inverted up-bow sign.

Up Bow
The opposite of down bow. The bow is drawn in point-to-frog direction. See B Figure 6.10. The sign for up bow is ∨.

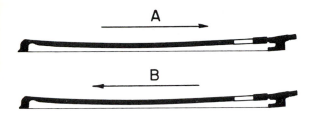

Figure 6.10. Line drawing showing bow direction. A. Down bow; B. Up bow.

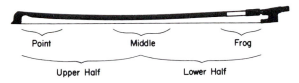

Figure 6.11. Divisions of the bow.

DIVISIONS OF THE BOW

For convenient reference the bow is divided into six playing areas:

Whole Bow	(W.B.)	Upper Half	(U.H.)
Point	(Pt.)	Middle	(M.)
Frog	(Fr.)	Lower Half	(L.H.)

These are terms with which conductors and string players must be familiar. They consitute the common language of the orchestra. It should be understood that no area of the bow is used exclusive of another. The upper half includes the point, which is simply the top two to six inches of the upper half. The middle includes portions of both the upper and lower half; and the frog, like the point, is the lowermost part of the lower half.

The area near the frog is the heaviest part of the bow and consequently is used for the heavy bowings. The point is the lightest part. It is in this area that soft tremolo is played. If a conductor's admonition is, "Play at the point" or simply "Point!!" be assured he wants very little volume.

If a conductor orders "on the string," it will be in regard to a passage that could very possibly be interpreted to be played off the string (spiccato) as well. In quiet passages, which need special control, such as a staccato passage at a moderate tempo, many conductors prefer to have the bows left on the string. They believe that the string section can achieve increased uniformity and precision in this way.

"In the string" means that the hair is to maintain firm and continuous contact with the string. Increased pressure is usually part of this concept. The sound resulting from this approach is the opposite of the flautato, which is a light, airy sound.

USE OF THE BOW

It is possible to digest some basic principles of bow use, which are based upon the laws of physics, and are influenced by tradition and the need of the player for comfort and security. Immediately following are the various divisions of the bow and the kinds of bowings that are most frequently performed in those divisions.

Down Bow
 When the music begins on a strong beat.
 For heavy accents and chords.
 For diminuendo on one note or a slur.
Up Bow
 When the music begins on a weak beat.
 For pick-up note(s).
 For crescendo on one note or a slur.
Lower Half
 Heavy accents and chords.
 Heavy repeated staccato notes, on or off the string.
 Heavy marcato.
Middle
 Spiccato
 Détaché
 Staccato
 Ricochet
Upper Half
 Détaché
 Spiccato
 Staccato
 Marcato
 Tremolo
 Ricochet
Point
 Tremolo
 Light détaché and staccato
 Ricochet
Full Bow
 Long sustained tones
 Long slurs
 Long, heavy staccato or marcato

BOW USE AND DISTRIBUTION

One of the most common faults among young string players is failure to distribute the bow intelligently and practically. "Running out of bow" is frequently experienced by the young player. It is caused by the failure to plan ahead. The solution to "running out of bow" is simply to "save the bow." "Saving the bow" is a relatively simple concept to demonstrate and is not difficult to put into practice. All that is needed is a little self-discipline.

"Running out of bow" is a problem that shows up in long notes, usually whole notes or longer, in moderate to slow tempi. (The factor involved is not actually the note value but the duration of the note in actual time—seconds.) Any note that must be held for more than three to five seconds is a long note for a young player. The natural, youthful instinct is to keep moving, get it over with and onto the next thing. So the youth hurries through the first part of the note with the bow, realizing too late that there is not enough bow for the balance of the note.

In addition, most young players do not avail themselves of the full bow. They avoid the frog area like the plague, automatically cheating themselves out of usable bow. The most plausible reason for this is that the arm must put out extra lifting effort in this part of the bow; so following the line of least resistance, that area of the bow is avoided. A contributing factor is that it is more difficult to make a smooth change of bow at the frog than three to four inches ahead of

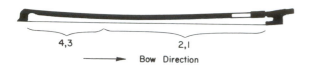

Figure 6.12. Poor distribution of the bow. (The numbers 1, 2, 3, 4 represent four counts.)

the frog. The number of bows on which the hair is black from disuse in this area is adequate substantiation of this statement.

To summarize this point, the student who is unschooled in the art of bowing resists using the portion of the bow just ahead of the frog. If the bow is placed on the string at the frog at the start of a piece, or if something compels the bow to arrive at the frog, the student seems to want to get it away from that area as fast as possible. If the note is to be held for four counts, the young player will more often than not expend three-fourths of the bow on the first two counts, leaving too little bow for the remaining two counts (Figure 6.12).

This use of a disproportionate amount of bow on the first two counts causes the first two counts to be louder than the last two. In addition, there will be no sense of *sostenuto,* and the last two counts will necessarily be "squeezed out." A full string section playing in this manner produces a most unsatisfactory and unschooled sound.

Two things must happen if this very undesirable practice is to be corrected.

First: The student must learn to use the precious inches of bow at the frog. Any kind of inducement or coercion is fair to achieve this end. Mostly it is a question of breaking down resistance.

Second: In playing any long note, the student must begin the note at the extreme point or frog, however it occurs in context. Then, a conscious effort must be made to allocate a given amount of bow to each count. The simplest rule for the child is to get to the middle of the bow at the middle of the note. This, at least, assures the student of an equal division of the bow.

A more advanced approach is to use the bow faster in the upper half where there is less bow and arm weight and more slowly in the lower half where the bow may be moved very slowly without the tone breaking.

Another aspect of bow distribution involves the problems inherent in figures made up of notes or slurs of unequal duration. For example:

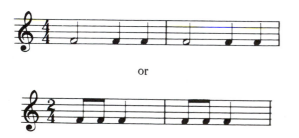

These examples are extremely elementary, but they clearly demonstrate the point. If the short notes are played with the same amount of bow as the long notes, without compensating for weight and pressure, the short notes will be considerably louder than the long notes. Again, in this case the solution is simple—use less bow on the short notes than on the long notes. To illustrate:

W.B. U.H. U.H. W.B. L.H. L.H.

Playing the short notes alternatingly at the U.H. and L.H. is good as long as the pattern continues. This technique applies regardless of tempo. Of course, as the speed of the figure increases, less bow is used. At fast tempi very little bow is used, as little as three to five inches on the long note and one inch on each of the short notes. But each long note permits the bow to regain its position.

This principle becomes more difficult to apply when the figure does not allow for natural compensation. For example:

In this case the accent on the first beat is helped by the fast movement of the bow, which is necessary if the bow is to reach approximately the same point for each up bow.

Somewhat more difficult to manipulate is a figure such as that shown at the top of page 71, which is to be played softly and without accent.

To achieve the desired results the down bow must be light and quick in the first four bars and the up bow held back. In the next bars this is reversed.

Intelligent use of the various areas of the bow, learning to maneuver the bow to the desired spot for a figure, moving the bow quickly and lightly and having it compensate for a preceding or succeeding slower bow, are skills that must be developed to reach an artistic level of performance. However, these skills are of a highly sophisticated nature and would be dealt with more appropriately in a treatise on advanced techniques.

There are some well-established practices in bowing orchestra music that are based upon the natural laws of bow direction as they apply to and are governed by the music that motivates them. In her book, *Orchestral Bowings and Routines,* Elizabeth A. H. Green outlines some of the basic principles of orchestral bowings and gives musical examples to illustrate the application of these principles. She enumerates thirteen rules that apply to basic bowings and nine that apply to what she labels "artistic bowings." Toward the end of her book, she recapitulates the thirteen basic rules in simple form.

No. 1.   The note on the first beat of the measure is down-bow.
No. 2.   The note before the bar-line is up-bow.
No. 3.   If the note before the bar-line is slurred across the bar-line, play it down-bow.

Moderato

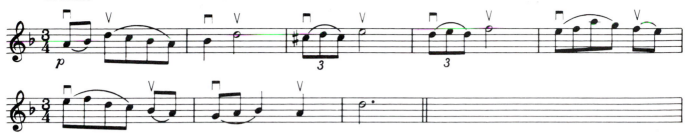

No. 4. An odd number of notes before a bar-line (without slurs) starts up-bow.

No. 5. An even number of notes before a bar-line (without slurs) starts down-bow.

No. 6. Alternate bowing, down and up, on after-beats. If rhythmic figures between rests have an even number of notes, chance a down-bow on the first note: if an odd number of notes, try an up-bow on the first note.

Note: Teachers must guide herein with their fuller knowledge. These short rules will cover most rhythm found in the easier music.

No. 7. In groups of four notes, starting on the beat, play the first one down-bow.

No. 8. Chords are played down-bow.

No. 9. Link the dotted eighth and sixteenth.

No. 10. Link the quarter and eighth in six-eighth time.

No. 11. The dotted eighth and sixteenth is not linked when the execution of the figure is too fast to perform the link feasibly, and the linked bowing is often omitted in soft passages where extreme neatness and clarity are desired. In this case, the dotted eighth is up-bow at the point and the sixteenth is down-bow.

No. 12. If your closing chord has a little, short note before it, play the little note up-bow starting near the frog.

No. 13. In four-four time a half-note on the second beat of the measure is down-bow.[5]

TYPES OF BOWINGS (See Appendix 1 for a more extensive list of bowing terms.)

Détaché

Separte bows. One note per bow alternating up and down bow. Played in the middle or upper half generally. Hair flat on the string. From one-third to one-half the bow is used.

Slur

Two or more notes played in one bow. Any part of the bow may be used.

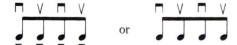

5. Reprinted from *Orchestral Bowings and Routines* by permission of the author and copyright (1949, 1957) owner, Elizabeth A. H. Green. Edwards Letter Shop, Ann Arbor, Michigan. It is forbidden to mimeograph or further reproduce this material.

Portamento Slur (Portato)

This is a type of slur in which each note gets a slight articulation. It is a cross between a slur and a slurred staccato.

Staccato

A short, quick stroke played with the bow on the string. The stroke begins and ends abruptly and requires the following procedure: pressure is applied to the bow so the bow bites into the string; this is immediately followed by a partial release together with a quick movement of the bow, ending with a clean stop.

Amount of bow and area used depends upon length of note and volume. This can range from one or two inches of bow in the upper half for "pp" to the full bow for "ff."

There is a limit to the speed of the staccato. When the speed of the notes exceeds this limit, they are played spiccato.

Marcato (Martelé)

A heavy staccato stroke, usually played in the middle or upper half. Limited speed. Medium to loud volume.

Spiccato

A stroke in which the bow bounces onto and off of the string. The fingers, wrist, and arm make the stroke. The mid-area of the bow is used, above the middle for a lighter stroke, below the middle for a heavier stroke. The bow bounces onto the string to produce the note, bounces away, and repeats this procedure. Up and down strokes are used. The stroke can be played from medium to fast tempi. The length of the notes depends upon how long the hair is allowed to remain in contact with the string.

Sautillé

This is the first cousin to the spiccato. In the sautillé the natural spring of the bow is depended upon. It is played very near the middle of the bow and at a rather fast speed. At slower speeds the spiccato is used.

Slurred Staccato

A series of staccato notes played while the bow is moving in one direction. This calls for an abrupt start and end of each note. Slurred staccato is usually played up bow although down bow staccato is occasionally asked for in virtuoso solos. Up and down bow staccato involving two or three notes at a moderate tempo is not unusual in orchestra playing. If circumstances suggest it, the skilled performer will play the up-bow staccato groups by lifting the bow between notes. When played rapidly, this is referred to as flying staccato.

Sul ponticello

This term indicates that the bow is to be drawn deliberately close to the bridge. The effect produced is a shrill, piercing quality. It is employed most frequently with tremolo but occasionally with sustained tones.

Sul tasto, sulla tastiera

The bow is drawn close to or over the fingerboard. The result is a soft, flutelike quality of tone.

Col legno

With the wood. This means literally to hit the string with the back, or stick of the bow. The sound is percussive and the pitch only faintly apparent. Only notes of very short duration can be performed since no sostenuto is possible. This is an effect and is never used for an extended period.

Linked or Hooked Bowing

Series of dotted eighth-sixteenth, dotted quarter-eighth or quarter-eighth notes in 6/8 time may be played either with separate bows or in the same direction of the bow with a stop between the notes, depending upon tempo and style. When these figures are played with the bow moving in the same direction, it is called linked or hooked bowing. When the tempo in which the figure occurs exceeds the practical limits in which the hooked bowing can be executed, the figure is often played with separate bows, using an up bow on the long note.

Chords

Three- and four-note chords are effective on violin, viola, and cello and are not difficult if the notes of the chord are properly arranged. Short three-note chords can be played as a unit, that is the three notes can be played simultaneously. This is accomplished by exerting sufficient pressure with the bow upon the middle string of the chord.

If the chord has a duration in excess of a quarter note, it is played as though the lower two notes were grace notes to the top two.

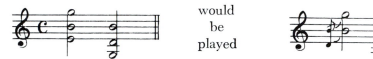

In this way the effect of the chord is produced and the top notes can be held as long as the bow can reasonably sustain them. This same principle of "breaking" chords pertains to four-note chords.

The length of time the bow remains on the lower notes of the chord before moving to the upper notes is dependent upon the style and period of the music, the tempo, and the context in which the chord is placed.

Chords are played more easily down bow than up bow because of the weight of the bow and arm at the frog, but they can be played either way. If consecutive chords are spaced or separated, they should be played with a series of down bows.

If they should be connected, or played as part of a legato line, they should be played up or down bow as the bowing comes.

When chords appear in the orchestra music of Haydn, Mozart, Beethoven, and other composers of that period, they are usually played *divisi*. That is, the notes of the chord are divided between the two players on a stand. In a three-note chord, the outside player takes the two upper notes, the inside player the two lower notes. These notes are played as double stops. The reason for doing this is to keep the music rhythmically clear and precise, an impossibility if twenty or thirty players are "breaking" a chord. This practice, obviously, does not apply to solo playing.

The following are some excerpts from the first violin part of the Symphony No. 35 ("Haffner") by Mozart. Chords are shown as they are written by Mozart and as they are played according to common orchestral practice.

Note that the chords, which are played *divisi,* are played with the bowing as it comes. In cadential situations such as the two which follow, some conductors ask that the chords be divided and played with consecutive up and down bows, as they come. Others prefer the increased punctuation and finality that comes from playing all of the chords down bow. This is purely a matter of personal taste.

The chords at the end of the finale should be played *divisi* and with up and down bows, with the exception of the last three, which are spaced by rests. The fact that Mozart wrote the consecutive chords in the third and fourth bars from the end without staccato dots makes it important that they be played without unnatural spaces between them.

In the later symphonic works of the Russian and German composers and in Italian opera orchestrations, full chords for the strings are common. The full, rich, dramatic character of this music is enhanced by the strings playing their heavy, sweeping chords.

Anyone wanting to pursue the matter of orchestral bowing to the level of professional orchestra expertise is referred to *Manual of Orchestral Bowing* by Charles Gigante. Gigante has had many years of professional orchestra experience as a violinist and presents in this *Manual* a carefully thought out approach to mastering the many kinds of bowings professional orchestra violinists must execute. The book is published by ASTA and is available from Theodore Presser, Publishers. Another excellent resource is the video, *Guide to Orchestral Bowings through Musical Styles* by Marvin Rabin and Priscilla Smith. It is available through the University of Wisconsin Extension Division.

STUDY QUESTIONS

1. List several sources for the tuning note A.
2. What is the most important goal of every string player?
3. Describe three "finger placement aids" for young beginners.
4. Why is the vibrato so important?
5. List three capabilities made possible by shifting positions.
6. Explain *sulla corda*.
7. Explain *portamento*.
8. Explain *double stop*.
9. Explain *divisi*.
10. Explain *pizzicato*.
11. What are the two methods of producing harmonics?
12. Where is the term "arco" used?
13. Explain *finger tremolo*.
14. List five factors pertaining to bow use which govern tone production.
15. Explain *flautando*.
16. Draw the symbols for down bow and up bow.
17. Discuss several types of bowing styles.
18. When is the term *divisi* used in reference to playing chords?
19. Explain the following: ⊓, ∨, W.B., M., Pt., L.H.
20. Define: col legno, détaché, marcato, tremolo, ponticello.

Part III

Chapters 7, 8, 9, and 10 deal with teaching each of the string instruments. These chapters do not pretend to take the place of a step-by-step method. A good method presents one concept at a time in a logically progressive order and provides well-conceived drills to assist in the mastery of each concept. There is no substitute for this complete and sequential approach.

There are many successful approaches to teaching strings. Each teacher develops techniques that seem to work well in achieving the goals set for the students. Suggestions made on the following pages are to be considered as one possible approach to teaching the string instruments but by no means the only one.

The aim of the following chapters is to present objectives for each of three developmental stages—beginning, intermediate, and advanced—and suggestions that will help to achieve these objectives. These objectives are not often spelled out in method books. By familiarizing themselves thoroughly with the contents of these chapters, plus the chapter, "Techniques Which Apply to All of the String Instruments," the teachers will be in a position to direct the students to maximum achievement as they make their way through a suitable method.

Teaching the Violin

The violin is the soprano of the string family. It is the melody instrument. In the orchestra there are more violins than any other instrument. In a symphony orchestra there may be as many as twelve to sixteen first violins and ten to fourteen second violins.

In school string programs the large majority of students begin on the violin. Out of a class of thirty beginners in an elementary spring program, there may be two violas, two or three cellos, and one or two basses, the balance violins. This imbalance is not desirable, but it is a fact in most cases. It is no wonder, then, that when we think of school string programs we think first of the violin. It is important, therefore, that the teacher-candidate become well acquainted with the violin.

SELECTING THE CORRECT SIZE VIOLIN

The teacher's first responsibility is to see that each student is equipped with an instrument of the correct size. Violins are made in sizes ranging from full (4/4) down to 1/16. There is a size for every size child, and it is important that the right one be selected. Some age-range suggestions are found in Table 13.1, page 142. These are admittedly rough; since children grow at varying rates.

The objective is to find an instrument that is neither too long nor too short. If it is too long, the arm will have to stretch out too far to reach the first position; the elbow cannot form an easy angle; the arm will tire quickly; the fingers will be unable to assume the proper attitude on the strings; and the distance between notes will be too great for the child to manage easily. If it is too short, the arm will be constricted; the elbow will be at too acute an angle; the spacing between notes will be too narrow for the width of the child's fingers.

The most common sizes are 1/2, 3/4, and 4/4. Most school-age children can be adequately fitted with one of these sizes. If a child is between 1/2 and 3/4, it is best to choose the 1/2 size. The child will be comfortable with it until growth indicates a 3/4 is needed.[1]

One way to determine if an instrument is the correct size is shown below. The instrument is held in playing position. The arm is extended so that the fingers touch the scroll. If the fingers easily encircle the scroll with the elbow bent slightly, the violin is the correct size. This is demonstrated in Figure 7.1. Figure 7.2 shows the same procedure being followed with an instrument that is too large.

---

1. See more about selecting the correct sized instrument in Chapter 13, p. 142.

Figure 7.1. Young student with correct size violin.

Figure 7.2. Young student with too large a violin.

If school instruments are not available, and the parent must purchase an instrument, the matter of economics enters the picture. Some parents will resist buying a small violin knowing that they will have to arrange for a larger one when the child has grown—in perhaps one or two years. Fortunately, many dealers have rental or trade-in plans, giving the purchaser a full, or very liberal, allowance when a small instrument is traded for a larger one. Under such an arrangement, the parent is not jeopardized financially.

A Complete Outfit

Every violin outfit should be complete and in good working order. It should include the following:

A well-made violin with proper strings, tuners and pegs that work properly, strings at proper height and properly spaced, and a satisfactory chinrest.
A bow full of good hair, properly rosined, a frog that fits properly and slides smoothly, and a screw that works easily.
A shoulder pad that is fitted to the child.
A cake of rosin.
A case that fits the violin, has a good bow holder, pockets for rosin, and a place for the shoulder pad, closes securely, and has fasteners which work and keep the case closed securely, has a good handle and a carrying strap (also see Figures 3.40–3.42).

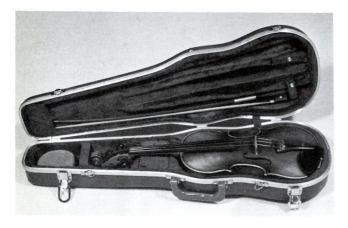

Figure 7.3. A complete violin outfit.

FIRST STEPS FOR THE BEGINNER

The first lessons are extremely important—and the most difficult. The child must begin to learn some of the following:

To take the violin from the case carefully and put the shoulder pad on it.
To take the bow from the case, tighten it to the proper tension and rosin it.
Hold the violin correctly.
Hold the bow correctly.
Know the names of the strings.
Place the bow on a given string and draw the bow correctly to produce a tone.
Recognize the printed notes that correspond to the open strings.

Learn the rhythmical value of notes and rests.
Learn to keep a pulse and play given notes and rests within that pulse.

The above tasks must be approached in a manner and at a pace that suits the age and maturity of the child. While with one child this may be a slow and uncertain process, with another it may be accomplished with speed and surety.

Because the holding of the violin and the bow are two separate, distinct, and exacting tasks, some methods postpone these matters so that the child can begin almost immediately to play music. This is, of course, the primary objective, one the child feels should be accomplished the minute the violin is taken from the case.

One method has the violin played in guitar-fashion. It is held under the right arm and the strings are plucked with the thumb. The left hand is held in relatively normal position, fingering notes, which are taught by rote or by numbers.

Several methods modify this approach to the degree that the instrument is held under the chin in normal fashion, with the left hand holding the violin by the neck or the upper right bout, but the right hand plucks the strings rather than playing them with the bow. After following this pizzicato approach for a few lessons, the bow is introduced and normal procedure is followed.

Most traditional methods advocate a bow-on-the-strings approach from the beginning. Among these methods there are fundamental differences. These differences can be described as follows:

The whole-note or whole-bow approach
versus
The quarter-note or partial-bow approach

The note-reading approach
versus
The rote approach

The whole-note approach is typical of the early methods. The theory was that the use of the full bow should be inculcated in the pupil from the outset. It was reasoned further that if the pupil could draw a full bow properly and with ease, all other bowings would be easier.

The quarter-note approach and the pizzicato approach are examples of much recent educational psychology, which contends that children will learn more quickly and more cheerfully if they can realize success in terms they can measure, in this case playing music on the violin. There is no question about the greater difficulty in drawing a full bow in contrast to a short bow, using the middle of the bow. So the pupil learns to control the bow in small amounts, gradually increasing the use to the full bow.

Advocates of the rote approach maintain that note-reading interferes with the important and difficult process of learning to hold the violin and the bow. These two functions are so complex that full attention should be given to them, without the distraction of learning notes and counting. Shinicki Suzuki, the now-famous Japanese violin teacher, has had phenomenal success with this approach in Japan. He has had thousands of Japanese children under his instruction and has proved that he can get results. His system includes close parental involvement, private and group instruction.[2]

2. See Chapter 11 for a fuller discussion of the Suzuki method.

In the school instruction program there are several drawbacks to the use of the rote method. The first is that time for individual attention is limited. Second, parental involvement is virtually impossible to achieve to the degree it is needed in this kind of an approach. Third, the objective of the school program is to develop orchestra players; therefore reading music is a prime requisite and needs to begin early.

Some teachers have had success using a rote approach for the first few lessons before introducing note-reading. This makes it possible to concentrate fully on the violin and the bow, give the pupils an early sense of achievement, and then present notes as a new and interesting aspect of their progress.

Holding the Violin

The violin is placed on the left shoulder, about 45° to the left of a straight forward position. The end pin button touches the neck. The shoulder should remain in a normal position; it should not be raised to meet the shoulder pad. The shoulder pad rests on the collar bone and the inner part of the shoulder. The fingerboard should be about parallel with the floor.

To achieve the proper setting of the violin, have the pupil stand facing you. The stance should be straight but relaxed, the arms hanging normally at the sides, weight balanced on the feet. Place the violin in position on the pupil's shoulder, pushing it lightly but firmly under the chin and against the neck.

At this point, still holding the instrument, ask the pupil to press the chin and jaw down upon the chinrest until the student has the feeling of holding the instrument alone. The head should be turned so that the sight-line is toward the scroll and tilted so that the side of the jaw touches the chinrest. This process should be repeated several times before having the pupil perform it alone.

When ready to do this without help, have the pupil hold the violin by the right side of the lower bout, as shown in Figure 7.5 and place it in position. When it is in position, tug it gently to make sure the grip is firm.

Figure 7.5. The violin held by the lower right bout prior to placing it in position on the shoulder.

Left Arm and Hand Position

With the violin securely in position, the left hand should be raised to the neck of the instrument. The neck is held between the thumb and the base of the first finger as shown in Figure 7.6. *The wrist should be straight.*

The pad of the thumb is held lightly against the side of the neck with the end of the thumb extending slightly above the fingerboard. The amount of thumb that projects above the fingerboard depends upon the length of the fingers and hand. The longer the fingers, the lower the neck will be on the thumb. The shorter the fingers, the lower the thumb will be on the neck, even to the point of being under the neck.

The arm should be swung to the right until it is well under the violin. Its exact position varies depending upon which string is being played on. It moves to the left when the fingers are on the E string and to the right when on the G string.

The hand should be turned in so that the palm is close to and nearly parallel to the neck. This position is necessary so that the fingers can be poised over the strings at all times.

Figure 7.4. Correct position of the violin.

Figure 7.6. Correct position of the thumb and hand on the neck.

Sitting Position and Rest Position

The violin is held the same whether the player is standing or sitting. A comfortable seated position is attained by sitting straight with the left foot slightly forward. The feet should be on the floor, not wrapped around the chair legs or over the chair rung. Small chairs should be provided for small children. Sitting position is illustrated in Figure 7.7.

During long periods of rest in orchestral music, the violin is put in a position of complete rest by being placed under the arm or across the lap. This position is shown in Figure 7.8.

Figure 7.9. The violin in partial rest position.

Figure 7.7. Correct playing position while seated.

Figure 7.8. The violin in complete rest position.

If the rest is of long enough duration to warrant taking the instrument down from the shoulder but not long enough to warrant putting it on the lap, it is held vertically on the knee as shown in Figure 7.9. This might also be described as "at the ready"; the instrument can be very quickly raised to playing position from there.

Common Faults in Holding the Violin

The violin is held too far to the left or right. Either extreme causes problems for the bow and the left arm.

The angle of the violin is too flat. This makes the bow arm raise excessively to reach the G string and puts the head and neck in a strained position.

The violin is tilted at too much of an angle. This puts the E string at a difficult angle for the bow and repudiates the assistance that gravity lends to the bow.

The violin is held too high or too low. Both positions are detrimental to good bowing, shifting, and to appearance.

The arm is held too far to the left. This puts the fingers in an unsatisfactory position and causes problems in shifting.

The violin is held in the crotch of the hand. This impedes good fingering and makes for excessive motion in the shifting process.

The wrist is bent inward so that the palm of the hand is in contact with the neck. This is a common and extremely bad position since it precludes correct finger action and later on makes shifting nearly impossible.

The wrist is bent outward. This position strains the wrist and arm muscles and is in no way helpful.

TIGHTENING THE BOW

At this point the violin should be returned to the case, and the bow removed from the case. Before turning the bow over to the pupil, the teacher should demonstrate how to tighten it and how to loosen it.[3] Determining the approximate number of turns to the right to tighten the bow and using the same number to the left to loosen it again eliminates the guesswork from this procedure and is generally a satisfactory technique at this stage. The student should be warned about overtightening the bow and impressed with the need to loosen it before returning it to the case. Reasons for the foregoing are discussed in the section on the bow.

The teacher should also show the student how to rosin the bow and explain how often and how much the bow should be rosined. This is also covered in the section on the bow. The student should also be impressed with the need to keep the fingers off the hair.

HOLDING THE BOW

Before having the pupil hold the bow, some teachers establish the position of the thumb and fingers by having the pupil hold a pencil or similar object. The advantage is that the pencil is familiar to the pupil while the bow is unfamiliar. In addition, the pencil is light in weight, and being short, presents no balance problems. The length and weight of the bow are the first factors that stand in the way of a good bow grip.

Another technique to establish the shape of the hand is to have the pupil hold a ball that fits comfortably into the hand, and attempt to transfer that hand position to the bow.

Teaching the Bow Grip

Next the teacher hands the bow to the pupil who takes it in the left hand, holding it by the screw button with the thumb and first finger. The hair is facing up. The right hand is held with the palm facing upward, and the fingers slightly curved. The pupil places the bow into the right hand, which takes it as follows (see Figure 7.10):

The point of the thumb is placed on the underneath side of the stick with the right part of the thumb touching the grip and the left side touching the lower, inside edge of the frog. The first joint of the thumb is bent outward.

The first three fingers curve over the top of the bow with the knuckles slanted toward the tip. A point just above the second joint of the first finger rests on the grip. The second finger curves over the stick and touches the thumb. The third finger curves over the stick and touches the frog. The tip of the little finger rests on top of the bow just ahead of the screw. The second and third fingers should touch each other. There are small spaces between the first and second and third and fourth fingers. The fingers should neither be spread nor squeezed together, but assume as easy and natural a position as possible.[4]

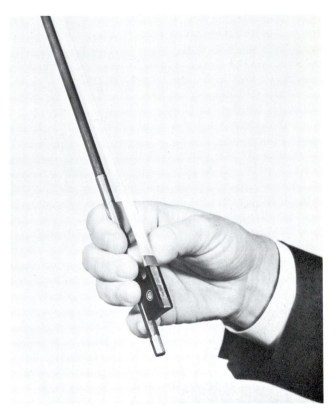

Figure 7.10. Correct position of thumb and fingers on the bow from below.

All of the fingers should be curved. The greatest problem in this regard is with the little finger. In too many cases it is held straight and stiff, a condition that causes problems in acquiring a smooth change of bow at the frog. Also, with many children, the thumb bends *in* instead of *out*. This makes the thumb inflexible and stiffens the hand and wrist, conditions that impair satisfactory bowing.

With the hand still palm-up, check the position of the fingers and thumb. Adjust if needed. Now have the pupil "squeeze" the muscles in these fingers, maintaining the same position on the bow. This should be repeated several times. It firms up the grip and helps to give each finger a sense of where it belongs on the bow.

The arm should now make a half turn to the left so that the hair is pointing down. This is the pupil's first exposure to the playing attitude of the bow. The student now senses the need for balance and sees the need for a firm, relaxed grip. Rotating the arm to the right and back again is a good exercise in itself. It also exposes the position of the fingers for easy examination (see Figure 7.11).

The following aids to teaching correct bow use are credited to Suzuki and Rolland.

1. *Thumb under the frog.* The right thumb is placed on the outside of the frog (on the flat surface) instead of between the hair and the stick.
2. *Early bow hold.* The right hand is placed on the stick three to four inches ahead of the frog. This method has two advantages: (1) a short-armed child can more readily reach the tip of the bow, and (2) placing the hand nearer

---

3. In groups the teacher can demonstrate this procedure to the entire class and have them tighten and loosen the bow under supervision.
4. Suzuki advocates having small children initially place the thumb below the frog, on the ferrule.

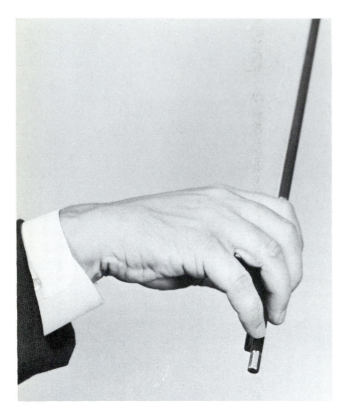

Figure 7.11. Correct position of fingers from above.

the balance point results in easier handling of the bow by the young player. As the student progresses, he or she should be encouraged to move the bow hand nearer to the frog.

Common Faults in Holding the Bow

The thumb is inserted too far through the bow.
The thumb bends *in* instead of *out*.
The thumb is positioned too far from the frog.
The fingers are spread too far apart.
The little finger is flat instead of curved.
The entire hand is too far up the bow.

THE BEGINNING OR OPEN STRING STAGE

The various "stages" used in this book may be related to school levels as follows:

Beginning—Elementary
Intermediate—Junior High
Advanced—High School and beyond

It must be understood that these "stages" do not connote neat, pat compartments into which students can be conveniently placed for the simple prescribing of appropriate materials and procedures. Each student progresses at a different rate; and while one student may excel in reading ability and have poor intonation, another may not read well but have excellent intonation, etc. Students of the same age group may be located in any of the three stages of development, and a given student may be a cross between beginning and intermediate or intermediate and advanced.

Objectives

To hold the instrument and bow correctly.[5]
To draw the bow parallel to the bridge.
To draw the bow on the proper string.
To draw the bow for the specified duration.
To make satisfactory bow changes from up to down and down to up.
To identify the strings by their letter names.
To know the signs for down bow and up bow and follow these directions.
To be able to identify the following parts: bridge, fingerboard, neck, chinrest, shoulder pad, bow, frog, point, hair, screw, upper half, middle, lower half.
To associate a printed note with the corresponding open string.
To know the names of the notes corresponding to the open strings.
To know how to count quarter notes, half notes, whole notes, and their corresponding rests in 2/4 and 4/4 time.
To keep one's place while playing a line of music.

Most method books spend several lessons on the open strings, so the pupils must learn their identity on both the instrument and the printed page. To review, they are:

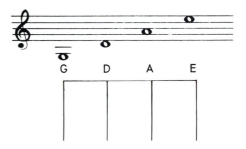

Using only open strings allows the pupils to concentrate on how they are holding the instrument and the bow, which is of paramount importance during this formulative period. The students may place their left hand on the upper right bout during the open string stage of instruction.

At the outset the pupils should not be expected to hold the instrument in position for more than a few minutes. However, the arms will soon become accustomed to the position, and within two to three weeks, it is not unreasonable to expect ten to fifteen minutes of steady practice.

The first lessons will consist of open string notes and rests. The rests allow the pupils to check their position and look ahead to see what is coming. Drawing the bow parallel to the bridge and producing a smooth, even tone are the aims of these first lessons, plus learning to follow the written music and keep a steady beat.

When first using the bow, many children have difficulty staying on one string. They may start the bow on the right string but touch one of the adjoining strings during the progress of the bow. This is not unusual, for it takes some time for the arm and wrist to make the adjustments needed to keep the bow in alignment.

---

5. During the open string stage it is permissible for the left hand to support the violin by holding it by the upper right bout. This rests the left arm and hand.

Exercises to Aid Bow Alignment

The following two exercises can help the alignment problem. They help the arm to sense the planes of the various strings as well as the distance the bow moves to get from one string to another.

EXERCISE NO. 1 TO ORIENT THE BOW TO THE STRING PLANES

1. Put the point of the bow on the A string. Press. Hold for four counts.
2. Lift the bow one inch above the string. Move to the middle. Press. Hold for four counts.
3. Repeat.

This should be done on each string that is being used in the lessons. Gradually move closer to the frog in step 2. The exercise is done silently.

EXERCISE NO. 2 TO ORIENT THE BOW TO THE STRING PLANES

1. Put the bow on the A string two inches from the point. Press. Hold for four counts.
2. Keeping pressure on the string, elevate the arm until the bow is fully on the D string. Hold for four counts.
3. Move back to the A string for four counts.
4. Lower the arm until the bow is fully on the E string and hold for four counts.
5. Move back to the A string.
6. Repeat.

Do the same exercise with the bow at various locations, i.e., middle, frog, and points between. Also use the D as the fulcrum.

Another problem beginners have is keeping the bow parallel to the bridge and at a more or less constant distance from the bridge. To cure a wandering bow, students should draw slow bows, watching the point of contact. To cultivate a straight bow, students should practice Exercise No. 1, observing the angle of the bow in a mirror. Also notes on the open strings should be played while observing the bow in a mirror.[6]

It is difficult, at first, for young violinists to know when their bow is not straight, and watching the bow in a mirror is not a foolproof method of checking its alignment. Another device that is often helpful is to point out that when the middle of the bow is placed on the string, the bow, the forearm, and the upper arm form three sides of a square, and that they should be in the same plane. Using this perspective, it is also relatively easy to tell if the wrist or upper arm is too high or too low.

If some children's arms are too short to draw the bow to the point without pulling the bow out of line, the best solution is to get a shorter bow. If this is not practical, they can be told *not* to draw the bow beyond a given point. This point can be marked with a piece of adhesive tape.

Tilt of the Bow

If the method being used employs quarter notes in the upper half of the bow, the angle or tilt of the bow is no concern, since, in the upper half, the hair is kept flat on the string.

6. For devices designed to help students bow straight see Figures 3.29 A and 3.29 B

A

B

Figure 7.12. A. Correct position of the bow at the point. B. Correct position of the bow at the frog.

However, when the lower half is used, the pupils must become aware of the need to tilt the bow as it approaches the frog.

At the frog the bow should tilt in the direction of the fingerboard at an angle of 15°–25°. The cause of this tilting is the curve of the wrist. The effect is to use less hair, thus balancing the tone with the remainder of the bow and facilitating a smooth bow change at the frog.

Common Faults of the Open String Stage

The instrument is allowed to sag.

The thumb and fingers slide out of place on the bow.

The bow is drawn at an angle to instead of parallel to the bridge.

The distance of the bow from the bridge varies excessively.

The bow touches two strings at the same time.

The pupils lose their place in the course of a line of music.

The pupils fail to count steadily and are unsure in the reading process.

The bow is tightened too tight or is not loosened when returned to the case.

LOCATING THE NOTES

After a few weeks of playing only open strings the pupil will be chomping at the bit to begin playing "real music." The first step is to use the first finger on the A or D string. Sound the pitch of the desired note and help the pupil locate the correct place for the first finger. On a 4/4 violin the first finger will be located about 1 1/8 to 1 1/4 inches from the nut to produce a B on the A string. The distance will be about one inch on a 3/4 violin. Measurements are all relative and are not completely trustworthy. The pupils must now begin to use their sense of pitch. If they have real trouble finding the notes, use one of the devices described on pages 54–55.

The same procedure is followed for the second finger. At this point the relationship of one finger to another enters. The distance of the second finger from the first should be discerned visually while the interval is listened to. The first finger should be kept on the string when the second is being used, and the first and second when the third is being used.

Half Steps and Whole Steps

The element of half steps and whole steps enters now. When the second finger is close to the first a half step is produced. In first position this is about one-half inch distance from finger contact point to finger contact point. The fingers will be about one inch apart for a whole step. If the fingers are broad enough, they may touch each other when forming half steps. There will be a space between the fingers when forming whole steps. The following are some of the symbols used to indicate half steps and whole steps.

Symbols for Half Steps	*Symbols for Whole Steps*
1/2 step	Whole Step
	W. S.

When the second finger is a whole step above the first, it is sometimes referred to as the "high" second. When it is close to the first, it is called "low" second.

During this stage it is important that the hand maintain its location and that the fingers are placed on the strings with the ends of the fingers depressing the strings and the first

joint nearly vertical. It is also important that the fingers develop strength in order to stop the strings firmly; it is the efficacy of this action that determines, to a degree, the clarity of intonation and tone.

Some methods endeavor to simplify matters during this stage by keeping the same fingering pattern on each string. This is accomplished by changing key as needed. The pattern is:

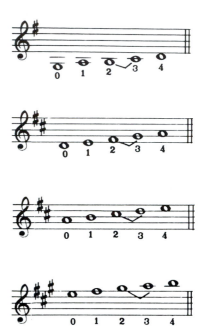

Other methods vary the interval and finger pattern on the premise that the student should acquire flexibility early.

The fourth finger is introduced somewhat later. It should be delayed until the other fingers are fairly well established. When the fourth finger is brought into play, all fingers should be placed on the string and strength applied. This will build the muscles. Since the fourth finger is the weakest, it should, at this point, be given full use and extra exercise. The following exercise will do wonders for the fourth finger if done for a couple of minutes each day. The fourth finger should be raised as high as possible and brought down onto the string with a snap. The exercise is to be done on each string.

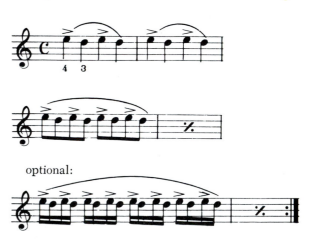

optional:

Common Faults During This Stage

The pupil is inconsistent in the placement of the fingers. In other words, the pupil is playing "out of tune."
The half steps are too wide and/or the whole steps are too narrow.
The first joint of the finger collapses so that it is flat on the string instead of vertical.

THE INTERMEDIATE STAGE

Objectives (All Appropriate Previous Objectives Continue)

To play in tune.
To learn to tune the instrument.
To play with a pleasant tone.
To play with a range of dynamics from pp to ff.
To attain a velocity measured by slurred 16th notes at ♩ = 66–76 and bowed 16th notes at ♩ = 56–66.
To use the bow skillfully in a variety of bowings, i.e., slurs, staccato, marcato, slow spiccato.
To begin the study of third position.
To begin to develop a vibrato.

Tuning the Violin

Until this time the teacher has, in most cases, been tuning the violin for the pupils. This is done to save time and to be certain the instrument is in tune. Now it is time for the students to begin trying their own hand, and they should begin whenever they feel inclined. The teacher must bring judgment to bear in this matter. Students whose ability to handle the tuning process is questionable should not be encouraged. On the other hand, assistance and support should be given to those who are ready.

At first, tuning strings individually to the piano or a pitch pipe is enough. If the violin has regular pegs, the students should be shown how to turn and set them. At this stage, the violin should be held on the knee for support, and the strings plucked. The right hand works the A peg while the left thumb plucks the string. The left hand works the D and G pegs while the right thumb plucks the strings. This can be done either standing or sitting, but it is easier while sitting. Students whose instruments are equipped with patent pegs will have less trouble, since they do not have to worry about the pegs slipping.

After following the above procedure for awhile, the students will be ready to refine the process somewhat. They should now tune the A string to the piano, or another source, and then tune the other strings by fifths. They should first tune the A–E, then the A–D, then the D–G.

As the students' bowing becomes steadier and more reliable, the fingers stronger, and their ability to tune by the above method improves, they should begin to tune with the bow, using the following procedure:

Tune the A string to the piano, bar, or tuner.
Play the A and E separately and then together, tuning the E to the A. When the 5th is perfect, there will be no "waves" or pulses. If the E is quite sharp or flat, the pulses will be rapid. As it is brought in tune, the pulses slow and finally stop. The pulses are hard for some students to hear at first. The teacher should tune the violin, bringing out the pulses for the student to hear. Follow the same procedure on the A–D and D–G.

Several things need to be taken into account in regard to tuning. They are:

1. Pegs must be in good working order.
2. Pegs must be correctly oriented so the fingers can grasp them and turn them easily.
3. The upper half of the bow should be used, starting at the point and going up bow.
4. In turning a peg, always turn it toward you first. This reduces the tension on the string and lowers the pitch. Then raise the string to the correct pitch, pushing the peg *in* as it turns. Set the peg firmly.

The pupil should be shown how to hold the hand and fingers in tuning. (See Figures 7.13, 7.14.) Note the position of the hand while tuning the A peg and the position while tuning the D and G pegs. The E peg should rarely need to be touched;

Figure 7.13. Position of hand when tuning left pegs.

Figure 7.14. Position of hand when tuning right pegs.

it changes little, and the tuner can take care of most of the minor adjustments. If, however, the E slips badly, it should not be tuned with the violin on the shoulder. It is much better to put the violin on the knee.

Tone Development

(Refer to page 68 for a general discussion of tone production.)

In the early stages it is quite enough to expect the bow to be drawn parallel to the bridge at a point halfway between the bridge and the fingerboard. Even this objective is difficult for some children to reach. However, as the pupils gain increased control of the bow, they should be shown that the bow must move closer to the bridge when producing a louder and more intense sound, and should move toward the fingerboard when producing a quieter, more *flautando* sound.

An excellent way to achieve this concept is to draw the bow very slowly from frog to point and back, making a crescendo and diminuendo in the course of each stroke, as follows:

At the peak of the crescendo, which occurs in the middle of the bow, the bow should be close to the bridge. At the beginning and end of the stroke the bow should be toward the fingerboard. This stroke can be practiced on open strings, scales, arpeggios, or appropriate etudes. The exercise should be done very slowly, counting four or eight. The crescendo should peak at the mid-point, and both the crescendo and the diminuendo must be gradual and even.

The following variations on this exercise will develop even more tone and control and will create increased sensitivity in the bow hand.

Intonation, Dynamics, Facility

By this time the students should be able to play in tune in a variety of keys, including C, G, D, F, B♭, and E♭. They should be able to move easily from string to string. They should be able to read and perform rhythmic figures and note patterns of intermediate difficulty as well as a variety of bowings.

Intonation will continue to need constant attention, but if the students have ability, are conscientious and have good instruction, their intonation will be acceptable by now and improving all the time.

A true concept of dynamic range is usually difficult to acquire. Most students play neither pp nor ff. The actual possible dynamic range of a violin is not great. A string instrument can play very softly, but it is limited on the loud end of the scale. Frequently, students end up playing everything mf, thinking they are achieving a good range of dynamics, and must be coaxed persuasively to hear their dynamics objectively.

Left-hand facility comes from finger strength and resiliency. These are developed through the practice of scales and other technical studies and exercises. Practice with gradually increasing metronome rates is a good method to improve speed.

The bow should be capable of playing sixteenth-note runs, dotted-eighth-sixteenth figures, simple double stops and chords, staccato, marcato, and possibly spiccato at a slow tempo using the lower half of the bow.

Positions[7]

Most of the traditional violin methods, or schools, as they were often called, introduced third position after first, then fifth position. It was presumed that these methods would be used on a private lesson basis and that the teacher would see to it that second and fourth positions were introduced at the proper time (after fifth position had been sufficiently mastered), or that the student would learn these positions when needed. Recent increased awareness of the importance of second and fourth positions to even a moderately advanced playing level, has motivated some teachers to introduce these two positions earlier than was formerly done. Above all, it should be remembered that no position is more difficult than another. The same fingers are being used on the same strings. Learning a new position is simply a matter of learning to play a note with a different finger, and, in some cases, on a different string. The notes in positions I through V are shown on page 93.

THIRD POSITION

It is time for most students to try their wings now by moving to third position. Third position puts the hand a third higher than first position. The first finger moves up to where the third finger was.

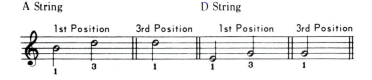

---

7. Refer to pages 55–59 for a general discussion of positions and shifting.

Third position extends the upper range of each string by a third—by a fourth considering the extension to the harmonic—and runs the high range to D or E above the staff.

In third position the lower part of the palm comes into contact with the upper bout. It does not necessarily remain in contact, but this is an excellent guide to third position.

The first finger should be the "guide" in third position. Playing naturalized notes with the first finger on the upper three strings, the 8va of the next lower string is sounded, thus affording a method of checking the placement of the first finger.

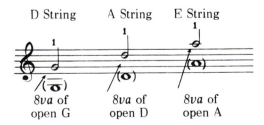

Smooth shifting, both up and down, are the product of careful, slow practice and faithful adherence to the principle that finger pressure must be eased while shifting. In the ascending shift, the hand and finger are relaxed and prepared, and the hand, forearm, and upper arm move together. In the descending shift, the thumb moves to first position and is followed by the hand and arm.

Shifting with one finger is accomplished as described above.

Shifting to a different finger uses the same technique. The finger playing the previous note is used as a "guide" finger. In practicing the shift this "guide" note is actually sounded. As the shifting technique improves, the intervening guide note can be eliminated.

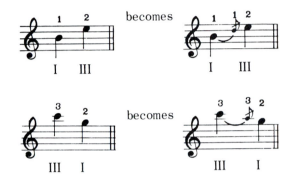

Figure 7.15. Hand in third position.

Vibrato

The general nature and purpose of the vibrato has been described earlier (see p. 55). On the violin the vibrato is produced by a back and forth rocking or rolling motion of the finger, which is generated by the hand moving from the wrist, first toward and then away from the player. This motion causes regular fluctuations of the pitch. Many violinists (and violists) use a certain amount of arm movement in the production of the vibrato. In fact, with some players the major impetus for the vibrato is in the arm, and the arm moves whenever a vibrato is produced. Still other players utilize both a hand-centered or wrist-centered vibrato and an arm-centered vibrato, and call one or the other into play depending upon the demands of the music. The great violin pedagogue, Carl Flesch, in his *The Art of Violin Playing,* Book 1, summed up his discussion of vibrato as follows: "*A perfect vibrato* is produced by the combination of the finger, hand and arm movements. The extent to which each of these factors participate is an individual matter; yet all the joints must be loosened and prepared to take an active part at any moment."

The easy, quiet vibrato is made with the finger, although the hand induces the motion. As the vibrato becomes more intense, the wrist comes increasingly into it; and at extremes the full arm will participate. An ideal vibrato is one that can be varied from softly rolling to very fast, depending upon the nature of the music.

In vibrato the finger must be held firmly on the string in order that no discernable pitch deviation will take place. The vibrato must not be too wide or too narrow, too fast or too slow.

By the time the students are ready to start third position, they are ready to begin learning the vibrato. To some students the vibrato will come easily. To others it will be a struggle.

A. Arm at side, palm forward.

B. Wrist bent.

C. Arm in front.

D. Arm in front, wrist bent.

Figure 7.16. Vibrato exercises.

Vibrato Exercises

The easiest place to get the vibrato started is in third or fourth position, with the first or second finger. Here the lower part of the hand can rest against the violin, making a hinge of the wrist. In this position the vibrato usually starts up rather easily. If it starts with the second finger, try the first finger, and then the third. Then move the hand to first position and see if the vibrato will continue.

If the vibrato balks in first position, rest the scroll of the violin on a mantle, dresser, or other object of suitable height. This frees the hand and arm and helps to get the vibrato going. Always work from third or fourth position back to first. If the vibrato still refuses to work, try one of the following exercises.

EXERCISE NO. 1 TO BE DONE WITHOUT THE VIOLIN

Phase 1—Arm lowered to side, palm forward.

1. Raise arm and touch shoulder with fingers.
2. Drop arm to side.
3. Repeat.

Phase 2—Arm lowered to side, palm forward (Figure 7.16A).

1. Bend wrist forward, bringing fingers up as far as possible (Figure 7.16B).
2. Drop wrist.
3. Repeat.

Phase 3—Arm extended to the front with elbow bent. Same as Phase 2 (Figure 7.16C and 7.16D).

Now take the violin.

Phase 4—Hold violin in playing position with the right hand.

1. Put left hand in first position. Do not grip the neck. (Figure 7.17).
2. With the arm retaining its position, bend the wrist forward until the hand touches the body of the instrument. (Figure 7.18).
3. Return wrist to first position.
4. Repeat.

All of the above should be done in an even rhythm, one motion per count, beginning slowly and gradually increasing the speed.

EXERCISE NO. 2 TO BE DONE WITH THE VIOLIN

1. Put the first finger on note B on the A string. First joint should be vertical.
2. With finger keeping point of contact with string, move the hand back slightly toward the scroll, flattening the first joint of the finger.
3. Return to original position.
4. Repeat.

This exercise should be done in an even rhythm with gradually increasing speed. It should be done with each finger and on each string. The movement of the hand is modified slightly for the 3rd and 4th fingers.

Additional information and assistance on the vibrato can be found in *The Art of Violin Playing* by Carl Flesch, in *Vibrato Method for Strings* by Gilbert Waller, and the Rolland-Mutschler *Teaching of Action in String Playing*.

Figure 7.17. Hand on neck, first position.

Figure 7.18. Hand on neck, wrist bent.

Common Faults of the Intermediate Stage

Carelessness in intonation.
Inaccuracy in shifting to third position.
Tone is still small and thin.
Vibrato is too fast or too slow.
Inadequate control of bow.
Limited dynamic range.
Limited reading ability.

THE ADVANCED STAGE

Objectives (All Appropriate Previous Objectives Continue)

To improve intonation and tone and musicianship generally, with a more mature concept of style and interpretation.
To increase and expand technique, including:
 Ability to play faster and more clearly both single note and double stop passages, chords, harmonics, trills.
 Skill in 5th, 2nd, 4th, and higher positions.
 Improved spiccato, staccato, ricochet bowings.
To play solo, ensemble, and orchestra literature of an advanced nature.

The Higher Positions

No single accomplishment typifies the advanced student more clearly than the ability to play in the higher positions. Moving from the third position stage to the fifth position stage is not a huge jump in terms of difficulty, but it is a big step in terms of the music which the student can perform. Fifth position is the threshold to the great literature for the violin. Reaching the fifth position stage opens new vistas and acts as a springboard to the other higher positions.

Figure 7.19. Hand in fifth position.

Fifth position is relatively easy for most students, since the notes in fifth position are played by the same fingers that play those notes in first position. The notes are simply played on the next lower string. For example:

But the glory of fifth position is that it extends the upper range by five notes, a third beyond the top note in third position.

After the students have gained facility in the use of the third and fifth positions, the second and fourth, and the higher positions should be mastered. The students will then be capable of undertaking more difficult music. Positions 1 through 5 are illustrated on page 93.

To improve technically, the advanced student should, of course, be studying privately with a good teacher. Each day scales in three octaves and in various rhythms, plus scales in thirds, sixths, and octaves, and etudes from one of the standard books should be practiced. Any particular facet of technique that is a problem should be analyzed and given special attention. The problem could be shifting, spiccato, trills, double stops, string crossing, bow changes at the frog, or any of a hundred things, any one of which can plague the violinist if not corrected.

The advanced player's diet should include concertos, sonatas, and solo pieces, all of which are available in a great variety of types, styles, and levels of difficulty. Hopefully, experience in small chamber music groups has been part of the string player's development. Playing duets, trios, quartets, and in larger combinations develops ensemble sense, concepts of balance, criticalness of intonation, and general musicianship. The violinist has achieved a very acceptable level of competence when he or she can participate satisfactorily with a group of matched players in playing the quartets of Haydn, Mozart, and early Beethoven, take part in the local college or community orchestra, and give an acceptable rendition of something from the standard solo literature.

A description of the advanced player must be extremely general; for this is the broadest and most indistinct of categories. It extends from the above average high school student to the concert artist. To understand "advanced," one must know the context in which it is used.

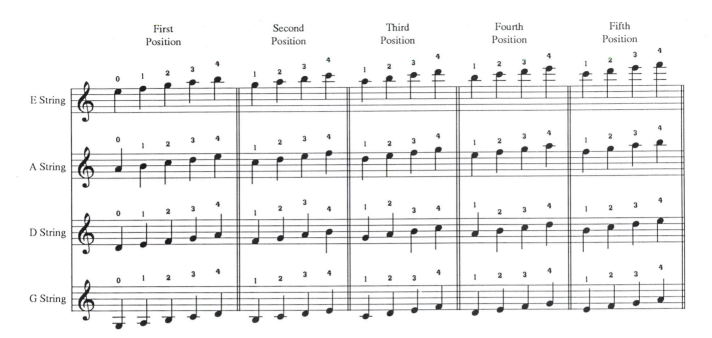

STUDY QUESTIONS

1. Describe one method used to determine the correct size violin for a child.
2. List five of the early steps involved in learning to play the violin.
3. Describe an accepted playing position for the violin.
4. List three or four common faults in holding the violin.
5. Give a brief description of the bow grip.
6. What are some common faults in holding the bow?
7. List several objectives of the beginning or "open string" stage of learning to play the violin.
8. What can be done for a child who is too small to draw the bow to the tip?
9. List several objectives of the intermediate stage of violin study.
10. Give several reasons for using third position.
11. Describe an exercise designed to help produce a vibrato.
12. What is the single most important accomplishment typifying the advanced stage of violin playing?

8 Chapter

Teaching the Viola

Basically, the approach to playing and teaching the viola is identical to that used in teaching the violin, and it is assumed here that all of the material in the previous chapter that pertains to the basic techniques of playing the instrument is applicable to the discussion of the viola. It is left to the student, therefore, to review the previous chapter and to apply the material therein to the present study.

This chapter on the viola, then, will concern itself mainly with the adjustments and modifications that must be made in various aspects of the playing apparatus to compensate for the larger dimensions of the viola. Comparing the viola to the violin is inescapable because, almost without exception, violists are former violinists. Essentially, therefore, this chapter is directed toward the student who is changing from violin to viola, which in no way lessens the applicability of the material to the student who actually begins on the viola. But it should be kept in mind that this chapter and the previous chapter should be studied together.

The viola is the alto of the string family. It plays harmonic and rhythmic accompaniments, countermelodies, and occasionally the lead. It has a rich, mellow tone quality, which complements the upper and lower strings and blends beautifully with french horns and woodwinds. The number of violas in a symphony orchestra ranges from eight to twelve, depending upon the size of the orchestra.

Until recent years a public school student who voluntarily started string instruction as a violist was practically unheard of. Ninety-nine out of a hundred violists began as violinists. Of those who reach professional status this is also the rule rather than the exception. There has been a little improvement in this situation in the last few years.

Of the hundreds of violinists who begin in elementary school, a few are persuaded by a teacher, dedicated to having a complete string section, to be individualistic and change to the viola. Some of the arguments that are used to bring off this coup are:

Being a member of a smaller section you will occupy a more distinguished position in the orchestra, and can take more personal pride in the achievement of your section.
(If applicable)
There will probably be less competition in the viola section than among the violins; so you should be able to earn a chair close to the front of the section.
The viola has a lovely mellow quality, and composers write interesting and beautiful parts for it.

Outstanding violists are rare. If you work hard, you should be able to earn a handsome scholarship at some college or music school. You will also have less competition in the professional world, if you decide to pursue that goal.

Another factor that should be considered in choosing between violin and viola is the physical makeup of the child. A large bone structure, including large hands and fingers, may eventually be detrimental to the violinist. Broad fingers add to the difficulty of playing in tune in the high register of the violin and consequently reduce facility. On the other hand, broad fingers are an asset to the violist, aiding in the production of the full, round sound, which is characteristic of the instrument. For these reasons an especially large child should be advised to try viola (or cello or bass) rather than violin.

If the teacher-candidate hopes to develop a complete string section, then something about alto clef and persuasive diplomacy must be learned.

SELECTING THE CORRECT SIZE VIOLA

Violas come in three basic sizes—junior, intermediate, and standard. Refer to page 13 for the measurements of all of these sizes in inches. The junior size is 13 1/4 to 14 inches in body length. A student who is playing a 3/4 violin should be transferred to the smallest available viola. If a small viola is not available, a small violin may be strung as a viola. This is not ideal because the small violin does not sound like a viola, and string length and tension are incorrect.

When fitting a viola to a child, select the largest instrument possible—within reason. It is not just the fact that a viola is tuned a fifth lower than the violin that makes it sound different from the violin. Chiefly responsible for the distinctive viola tone are the design and dimensions of the body. Therefore, a viola that is not much bigger than a violin will have little of the deep, rich tone that typifies the viola. The "real" viola tone can hardly be approximated in an instrument of less than 14 1/2–15 1/2 inches body length. This is not a criticism of the smaller violas. We need them. Just choose the largest one possible.

The same method of fitting child to instrument can be used for the viola as was demonstrated for the violin (Figures 7.1 and 7.2).

Figure 8.1. Viola, playing position.

Figure 8.2. Viola, rest position.

A Complete Outfit

The requirements for the viola are identical with those of the violin. (See page 80.)

FIRST STEPS FOR THE BEGINNER

The procedures detailed for the violin on page 80 are to be followed if the student is an absolute beginner.

Holding the Viola

The single point of variance is that the viola should be held slightly flatter than the violin. This can be accomplished by using a lower shoulder pad or by tilting the head a little to the left. The reason for the flatter attitude of the viola is to take maximum advantage of the force of gravity in the bowing process. The viola is larger than the violin; the strings are longer and larger in diameter; the bow is larger and heavier than the violin bow. To pull a big viola tone, all the help that can be realized will be needed if fatigue in the bow arm is to be avoided. In all other aspects the viola is held like the violin and the procedures outlined for the violin should be followed.

Learning to Read Alto Clef

The viola student, whether beginning on or transferring from the violin, will encounter the alto, or C clef, for probably the first time ever. Classroom instruction usually includes familiarization with the treble clef, and piano students

learn to read the bass clef, but seeing the alto clef prior to a musicianship course in junior high school is an extremely rare happening for all but the viola student.

The elementary students may know the syllables, and, if they are bright, the names of the lines and spaces of the treble staff. It is relatively easy for them to transfer what they know to the viola, or alto clef.

The relationship of the alto clef to middle C is the first thing to point out. Using the following visual presentation helps students to see this relationship.

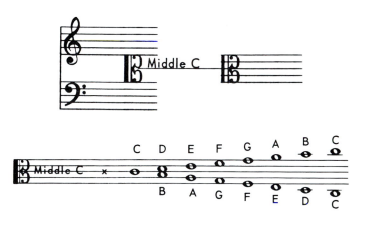

Use of the Janowsky *Viola Note Speller* or Rowe's *Music Workbook for Strings* (see Appendix III) will also help students learn the notes in this new clef.

HOLDING THE BOW

The similarities that apply to holding the violin and viola apply as well to holding the bow, but again there is a subtle difference. This difference is a matter of degree, and is as much in the "feel" of the bow on the string as it is in the actual grip and use of the bow. Nonetheless, the very fact that the viola bow is slightly larger in diameter, slightly longer, and, consequently, weighs more than the violin bow, is sufficient evidence that it will require a little huskier grip than the violin bow.

As stated above, the difference between the way the violin bow and the viola bow are held is a matter of degree. In very simple terms, the viola bow is taken into the hand a little more than the violin bow. The added weight, plus the need to employ more strength than the violin requires, compels the hand and arm to treat the viola bow less delicately than the smaller, slimmer violin bow.

An analysis of the difference described above would show that the thumb is inserted a fraction of an inch farther into the bow, and the first three fingers are extended over the bow a fraction of an inch more than in the violin grip. The little finger still rides on top of the stick and has to work harder because of the added weight of the viola bow.

OPEN STRING STAGE

The material on the violin should be referred to again. And again slightly different treatment of the bow is needed. The viola strings are longer and larger in diameter than violin strings. They are heavier. They require more weight and pull than violin strings do. The viola bow is larger and heavier than the violin bow. The frog is wider and the hair-spread is wider. This added weight, length, and width of hair is all intentional, and its intent is to help the violist draw a big tone.

To take advantage of these special characteristics of the viola bow, the bow should be flatter on the string, at less of a tilt than the violin bow. This puts more hair in contact with the string. To achieve this the following things happen:

1. The stick is tilted toward the bridge to a nearly upright position.
2. The wrist is dropped slightly.

Neither of these modifications should be exaggerated. Done in the right amount they will achieve the desired result.

Hopefully, the pupils will have begun orientation to the alto clef and will know the location of the open strings on the staff.

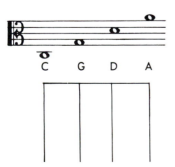

End Pin to Bridge Distance

If the viola is larger than the violin, the distance between the bottom of the instrument and the bridge will be greater than on the violin, since this distance increases proportionately with the size of the instrument. Pupils should be made aware of this factor; it can be the cause of bowing problems that they cannot account for.

A 3/4 violin measures 5.98 inches from the base of the instrument to the bridge. A 4/4 violin, which is about the same size as a junior viola, (13 1/4–14 inches) measures 6.42 inches. An intermediate size viola measures 6.97 inches.

If the viola is the same size as the violin, the change will present no problem in this respect; the distance will be the same. If, however, the change is from a 3/4 violin to a junior size viola, or from a 4/4 violin to an intermediate size viola, this increase of distance is considerable. It may appear insignificant in terms of inches, but it requires a definite adjustment in the elbow and upper arm. To reach the greater distance, the elbow will be bent less and the upper arm will be pushed forward. This is not a difficult adjustment and will be made automatically as the pupils put the bow on the string ahead of the bridge. But as they play, they will sense a difference, and the bow may ride up on the bridge. If they do not realize what is happening, they could become disturbed. If they understand what has happened, they can consciously correct the setting of the arm as needed.

LOCATING THE NOTES

The violinist who transfers to viola has found that the point of contact for the bow is farther away than on the violin. This is assuming that the viola is larger than the violin. If it is larger, there will be adjustments of the left arm that will be necessary too.

First of all, the left arm will have to extend farther to reach the neck of the viola. This alone can prove tiring for a young person, but adaptation to this difference is usually quick.

A more important difference, and one which most students adapt to more slowly, is the larger spacing between the fingers of the left hand, a consequence of the greater string length on the viola. On a 15-inch viola the distance between the fingers to produce whole steps in first position is about 1 3/8 inches—1/8 inch greater than for a 4/4 violin. This creates a 3/8 inch larger overall handspan. On a 16 1/2-inch viola a distance of 1 1/2 inches between fingers is required to form whole steps in first position.

The reason for documenting the differences in finger spacing is not to indicate specific places to put down the fingers, but simply to dramatize the fact that there is a diffference so that the teacher will understand the need to make this difference clear to the student. The bright student with a good ear hardly needs to have the above matter verbalized. Intuition will tell the fingers that they must behave differently and what they must do to achieve the results the ear commands. Furthermore, it is never really completely satisfactory to equate pitch with a visually identified place on the string. As pointed out in an earlier chapter, visual or tactile means to locate notes can bring results that are only approximate. The ear is the only completely accurate means to good intonation.

A

B

Figure 8.3. A. Correct position of the bow at the point.
B. Correct position of the bow at the frog.

But it cannot be assumed that the majority of pupils are either particularly bright or talented. It behooves the teacher, then, to make the violin-viola transfer a bit simpler and more understandable by pointing out that fingers need to be farther apart on the viola than on the violin. Half steps will, of course, find the fingers close together, but not as close as on the violin.

In playing the viola, the fingers of the left hand contact the string with the fleshier part of the finger tip. Thus, the finger will cover slightly more of the string. This creates a wider vibrato and a somewhat less intense or brilliant tone quality, which is, of course, typical of the viola.

THE INTERMEDIATE STAGE

The intermediate stage on the viola, as the violin, is typified by the study of third position. The techniques of learning and executing the positions are the same on both instruments. During this stage the violist is confronted with two additional tasks that the violinist is spared. The first is half position; the second is reading music that employs a mixture of the alto and treble clefs.

Half Position

Half position is located 1/2 step below first position. The term "half position" carries to its logical conclusion the practice that has evolved in designating positions, i.e., a position is established not so much by the longitudinal location of the hand on the neck as by the particular finger that is used to play a note occupying a given line or space on the staff, no matter how the note is altered chromatically. To illustrate:

is considered to be in first position. But the same notes written enharmonically, as follows, are considered to be in second position.

Similarly,

is considered to be in first position. When written in sharps, but played with the same fingers, it is regarded as half position.

Half position may be as useful to the violinist as to the violist, but, traditionally, violinists do not study it or commonly regard it as a position in its own right. This is not true of violists, who make extensive use of and frequent references to half position. The reason for this probably has something to do with the fact that the keys of C♯ Major and minor occur more frequently than does G♯ minor. These are the keys that utilize half position on the bottom string of the two instruments. Another factor is that composers and arrangers, in writing for the viola, favor the C string and the lower positions; for this is where the richest viola tone is to be found. And it is in this register that half position occurs most frequently. To the contrary, the high register of the violin is stressed; so positions three through five or higher get frequent use.

On the viola the following passage, for example, would be awkward if it were to be played sul. C. This would require the third finger to move from the E♯ to the F♯ in measure no. 1 and a stretch back to C♯ with the first finger in measure no. 3. If taken in half position, no shifting is necessary.

Simple orchestrations for young players will not require the use of half position. Those orchestrations intended for more advanced school use, which have been carefully edited by a string specialist, will contain half position indications for the violist where they are appropriate.

Reading a Mixture of Alto and Treble Clefs

The *tessitura* of viola parts includes frequent use of the notes that lie several ledger lines above the staff. Traditionally, music copyists avoid writing ledger lines when possible, and musicians are just as happy if they do not have to count ledger lines to identify a note. The solution to this problem has been to use the 8va sign or change clefs.

The use of the treble clef is not a factor until the music rises to third position on the A string. At that time the notes utilizing the third ledger line come into frequent use, and employment of the treble clef becomes a distinct convenience for the writer and for the player—when facility is gained in making the bridge between alto and treble clef.

The switch back to the treble clef would not appear to be a problem for a person who had played violin and knew the treble clef fairly well. But, it is surprising how completely oriented to the alto clef one may become in a short time, and how foreign the treble clef can appear to be when it suddenly appears in a line of viola music.

Orientation is the key word in this matter, and the student must learn to change orientation from one clef to the other in a fraction of a second. There is no shortcut or trick to learning to do this. The sequence of notes leading into and out of one clef or the other usually makes for a logical connection. The more thorough the student's musical background, the more readily clearing the clef-switching hurdle will be learned.

A few examples of the mixing of the alto and treble clefs are found below. They will illustrate the points made above. These illustrations encompass notes in fifth position, since the treble clef is particularly useful in writing notes in fifth position and higher.

Vibrato

The vibrato is made on the viola precisely as it is on the violin. Differences lie in its speed and width but not in its method. On the viola the vibrato may be wider than on the violin, although this is not always the case, vibrato being such an individual and personal thing. Generally, the viola vibrato will be somewhat slower and wider than the violin vibrato, due to the lower pitch of the viola, the longer string length, and the slower response to pitch fluctuation.

The vibrato exercises described in the chapter on the violin are applicable to the viola.

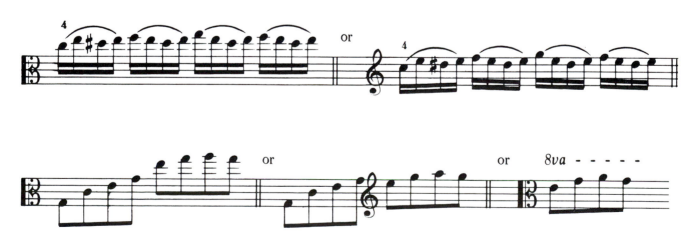

THE ADVANCED STAGE

Everything that is said in the comparable section of the chapter on the violin applies to the viola. By this stage the student who has transferred from violin is established as a bona fide violist. This is surely true of the student who began on the viola. The experience in orchestra and chamber music groups has developed a concept of real viola tone and has taught the player to assume a rightful musical role in these groups.

Through many years of the history of music the viola and the violist served only in a secondary or supportive role. The viola was an instrument to be taken up by second-rate violinists. It was rarely assigned a leadership position, musically speaking. The absence of viola concertos and sonatas by the early composers is ample evidence of the position the viola occupied in the hierarchy of instruments. A concerto by Teleman, the *Sinfonia Concertante* by Mozart, a concerto by Stamitz are some of the exceptions. Then Berlioz wrote "Harold in Italy" and a new era for the viola was launched. The viola began to emerge as an instrument capable of a sufficient range of expression and technique to justify a greater literature of its own. Violists such as Lionel Tertis, William Primrose, Emmanuel Vardi, and Walter Trampler, who developed their skill on the instrument to the heights of artistry, have done much to stimulate greater interest in the viola on the part of composers, performers, and listeners.

Largely due to the influence and impact of these artists, the viola has been elevated to a higher status than it had previously enjoyed. This has created new opportunities for the viola and at the same time, has imposed increased demands and responsibilities upon the violist. No longer can the violist be a converted second-rate violinist. To excel he or she must be a first-rate violist. This means developing all of the skills and techniques of the instrument to a high level of proficiency. It means mastering a varied and extensive repertoire. It means being prepared to assume a variety of responsibilities including orchestra member, chamber music performer, soloist, teacher.

The road to this level of achievement is built of the same material as the road to violin artistry. The titles may differ but the substance is the same. A balance of scales, studies, and solo literature is necessary. Private instruction and a great deal of hard work are essential.

The following illustrations of notes in first through fifth positions on the viola are provided for easy reference.

STUDY QUESTIONS

1. Discuss some of the ways in which playing the violin and playing the viola are similar.
2. What are some of the arguments in favor of playing the viola?
3. Are the violin and viola bow grip identical? Discuss.
4. In reading viola music what is the first problem encountered by the beginning student?
5. How do finger spacings on the viola differ from those on the violin?
6. Explain *half position*.
7. Who are some of the famous violists who have advanced the status of the viola as a solo instrument?
8. Write a brief melody in alto clef; transpose it to treble clef.

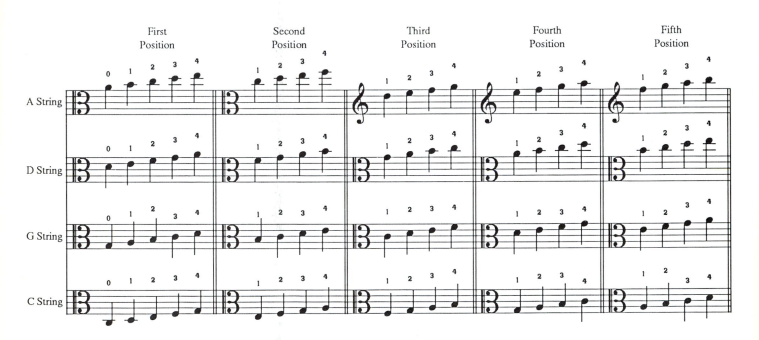

Teaching the Cello

The cello is the tenor of the string section. It has a range in excess of three octaves, has a large and powerful tone, and is capable of a broad range of dynamics. It is a magnificent solo instrument and lends great power and warmth to the string section of the orchestra. A symphony orchestra cello section numbers from ten to fourteen players.

In the music of the Baroque and Classical periods, the cello and bass parts were most often written as one line indicated as violoncello and basso. The sections played the same line but sounded an octave apart since the bass sounds an octave lower than written. However, in the Beethoven orchestral works, the cello and bass were treated as separate instruments. True, they frequently played the same line, but their individual capabilities and limitations were considered. When it appeared to be desirable to have the cello without the bass, this was done, or the cello and bass in unison, or the bass entering at a given moment to reinforce a chord or scale passage. Some composers after Beethoven gave the cello even more independence, using its full range in melody and countermelody.

A broad hand, or long fingers with considerable strength are an advantage on the cello. Just to stop the strings requires strength. But the stretching of the hand, the extensions of the fingers, and the speed and dexterity required of the player are much facilitated if the hand is large and strong. Especially important is the stretch between the second and third fingers, an asset that can be developed by proper exercise.

In first position the hand spans only the interval of a third, in contrast to a fourth on the violin and viola. This means that frequent changes of position are necessary to avoid awkward string changes. Cellists find themselves shifting constantly. The advantage that the cellist has over the violinist and violist is that the cello is anchored solidly on the floor via the end pin and is braced by the knees and chest. This completely frees the left hand and arm from supporting the instrument and gives the cellist absolute freedom to maneuver up and down the neck of the cello.

SELECTING THE CORRECT SIZE CELLO

Cello sizes range from 4/4 down to 1/8. Sizes ordinarily found in schools are 4/4, 3/4, and 1/2. (See page 15 for measurements.) Most elementary school children will require a 1/2 size cello, but one or two 3/4 cellos in each school is a precaution against the extra-large sixth grade pupil who shows up occasionally.

The cello is the right size if, when the lower bouts are correctly positioned between the legs, the lower right tuning peg is behind the left ear. The child's hand should be able to encompass the first position without stretching.

The Importance of the Chair

Graduated chair sizes for small cellists is a matter of the utmost importance but is frequently neglected. Most elementary schools have some small chairs in which a child is able to sit comfortably and touch the floor with the feet. The string teacher should have a supply of chairs of various heights from which to choose. While it is not desirable, the small violinist can get by in a standard chair by putting the feet on the rung; but in the case of the cellist, the knees are part of the holding apparatus, and being able to put the feet on the floor becomes an important item.

The importance of a chair with a straight back and flat seat has been discussed previously (see pages 38–39). It is highly desirable that these features be incorporated into the lower chairs if possible. An end pin holder of some kind is essential.

A Complete Outfit

Every cello outfit should be complete and in good working order. It should include the following:

1. A well-made cello with proper strings and tuners that work easily, strings at correct height and correctly spaced, an end pin that is sharp with a good wingnut set screw and a stop to prevent the end pin from slipping inside the instrument.
2. A bow full of good hair, properly rosined, a frog that fits properly and slides smoothly, a screw that works easily.
3. A satisfactory end pin holder.
4. A cake of rosin.
5. A cloth or hard case that fits the cello, has a bow pocket, a pocket for music and rosin, good zippers, snaps, or clamps, and a good handle.

FIRST STEPS FOR THE BEGINNER

Refer to this section in the chapter on the violin, all of which applies to the cello with the exception, of course, that the cello is never held and played like a guitar. If this technique is used with the violin and viola, the cello is held in a normal position and played pizzicato.

Holding the Cello

The following conditions must be met to achieve a satisfactory basic position for the cello:

1. A flat chair of the proper height, making it possible for the feet to rest flat on the floor. The left foot is forward, the right foot drawn back toward the chair. The body should be erect.
2. An end pin holder that makes it possible to position the end pin so that the cello is at an angle of between 55° and 65°.
3. The end pin should be adjusted so that the corners of the lower bouts are at knee level and the C peg is behind the left ear.
4. The top of the right side of the back of the cello contacts the body at the chest about at the lower center of the rib cage.
5. The cello should be held straight and flat.

Left Hand and Arm Position

The left thumb touches the back of the neck about 3 1/2 inches from the top of the neck. The fingers are over the string with the second finger opposite the thumb. The wrist and forearm are in a straight line. The angle of the upper arm varies according to the string on which the fingers are functioning. The fingers are slightly rounded, with the tips pointing down toward the string. The pads press against the string. The position of the thumb depends upon the string being played. The pad of the thumb lies flat against the back of the neck when playing on the A string and pivots to the left when playing on the lower strings.

The following pictures demonstrate the correct playing position and rest position for the cello.

Common Faults in Holding the Cello

The end pin is placed too close to or too far from the player resulting in the cello being too upright or too slanted.

The end pin is set so that it is too long or too short. This places the cello too high or too low in relation to the player.

No end pin holder is provided so the cello slips, making it necessary for the player to hold the cello in place with the legs and knees.

The tilt of the cello is insufficient to prevent the bow from striking the left leg when bowing on the A string or is exaggerated to the point that the bow strikes the right knee when playing on the C string.

The left arm is allowed to drop to the side of the body, putting the fingers, wrist, and forearm in incorrect position.

TIGHTENING THE BOW

To tighten the cello bow, hold the frog with the thumb and fingers of the left hand with the hair facing up, as shown in Figure 2.4. The cello bow is thicker and consequently stiffer than the violin and viola bows, so it will be slightly harder to tighten. If the bow has its original camber, the hair, when fully tightened, should be about 1/2 inch (+ or −) from the stick at its nearest point.

As in the case of the violin, the teacher should demonstrate each step for the pupil and then have the pupil repeat them. These steps should include tightening and loosening the bow and applying rosin. How often to rosin the bow and the importance of loosening the hair after each practice or rehearsal session should be stressed.

Figure 9.1. Playing position.

Figure 9.2. Rest position.

HOLDING THE BOW

The manner in which the cello bow is held is quite different from the way the violin and viola bow are held. The primary reason for this is that the bow arm is in a lowered position for the cello in contrast to the raised position of the arm for the violin and viola. While the positions differ, the concept of tone production is the same in that in both cases the natural weight of the arm is used.

To acquire the correct bow grip, the pupil should take the bow in the left hand, holding it by the screw button. The hair should face left. Held in this way the placement of each finger can be seen clearly. With the bow held as directed, the following steps should be followed in sequence:

1. With the first joint bent outward, the center of the thumb is placed on the frog; the right side touches the junction of the stick and the grip.
2. The first finger goes over the bow, resting on the wrapping between the first and second joint.
3. The second finger goes over the bow and down the side of the frog, contacting the ferrule (the silver mounting) where the hair enters.
4. The third finger, like the second, goes over the bow and down the side of the frog.
5. The little finger reaches over the bow about midway on the frog. The tip of the finger reaches down just to the right of the pearl eye.

After the position of the fingers is checked by the teacher, the bow may be turned over and laid on the strings.

In playing position the stick is tilted toward the fingerboard while the hair remains flat on the string. When the bow is on the string at the frog, the wrist will be slightly arched, providing a flexible hinge for changing bow direction. At the point the wrist will be straight or have a slight break, but it should not be dropped excessively.

Common Faults in Holding the Bow

The thumb is inserted too far through the bow.
The second, third, and fourth fingers wrap around the bottom of the frog, gripping the bow into the palm of the hand.
The hand slants too much toward the screw button or the tip.
The stick contacts the hand too far up on the first finger.
The thumb bends in instead of out.
The back of the hand falls forward placing the bow at the wrong angle to the string.

THE BEGINNING OR OPEN STRING STAGE

Objectives

To hold the instrument and bow correctly.[1]
To draw the bow parallel to the bridge.
To draw the bow on the proper string.
To draw the bow for the specified duration.
To make satisfactory bow changes from up to down and down to up.
To identify the strings by their letter names.
To know the signs for down bow and up bow and follow these directions.
To be able to identify the following parts: bridge, fingerboard, neck, tailpiece; bow—frog, point, hair, screw, upper half, middle, lower half.
To associate a printed note with the corresponding open string.
To know the names of the notes corresponding to the open strings.
To know how to count quarter notes, half notes, whole notes, and their corresponding rests in 2/4 and 4/4 time.
To keep one's place while playing a line of music.

Most method books spend several lessons on the open strings, so the pupils must learn their identity on both the instrument and the printed page. To review, they are:

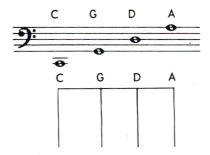

Figure 9.3. Correct position of thumb and fingers on the bow.

1. During the open string stage it is permissible for the left hand to rest on the right shoulder of the cello (left of the neck in playing position).

A

B

Figure 9.4. A. Correct position of the bow at the point.
B. Correct position of the bow at the frog.

Figure 9.5. Cello, left hand.

Using only open strings allows the pupils to concentrate on how they are holding the instrument and the bow, which is of paramount importance during this formulative period.

At the outset the pupils should not be expected to practice more than a few minutes at a time; their concentration span is short and the muscles in their bow arm will tire quickly. However, within two to three weeks it is not unreasonable to expect ten to fifteen minutes of steady practice.

Turn back to the section in Chapter 7, Teaching the Violin, for suggestions and exercises appropriate to the open string stage. Exercises spelled out for the violin are adaptable to the cello by the simple expedient of regarding the second string on the violin as the second string on the cello. In other words, if the violin A string is referred to in the exercise, regard it as the D string on the cello.

Beginning cellists will have the same problems other string players have; namely, they will have trouble keeping the bow on the designated string and parallel to the bridge. Cellists have an advantage over the violinists and violists in that they can sit in front of a full length mirror and observe the alignment of the bow.

LOCATING THE NOTES

First attempts at using the fingers on the strings will be on the A or D, depending upon the method being used. On a 4/4 cello the first finger will be about three inches from the nut to produce a note a whole step higher than the open string.

On a 3/4 cello this will be about 2 5/8 inches, and on a 1/2 size cello about 2 1/4 inches. As stated before, linear measurements are only approximate and are not completely accurate insofar as pitch is concerned. Only the ear can make a judgment in matters of pitch.

On the cello the left hand is held in such a way that the fingers are placed squarely on the fingerboard. The first joint of the first and second fingers are nearly perpendicular to the string, as they are on the violin and viola. The third and fourth fingers assume a somewhat flatter attitude.

The first finger is positioned about three inches from the nut. On the D string this produces an E natural. If the second finger is then placed a little more than an inch above the first, F natural, an interval of a half step is produced. The third finger produces F sharp, and the fourth finger G. The hand itself, from the first to the fourth finger, spans a minor third; from the open string it covers a perfect fourth. Thus, in first position, the cellist's range on each string is one whole step smaller than the range of the violin and viola. Without extensions, the cellist plays these notes in first position:

Whether the second finger is used at the outset depends upon the method being used. If it is a class method utilizing the D major approach, the finger pattern will be:

It is good pedagogy to always play the notes first so that the pupil can hear what he or she is supposed to produce on the instrument. It is in this way that the pupil begins to listen to and match pitch.

Cellists must be encouraged to place the fingers very firmly on the string in order to produce a clear tone and accurate pitch. The rather wobbly fingers of the nine or ten year old will gain strength rapidly if each practice period is a finger-strengthening effort. Long tones at full volume will aid this process. Also finger-strengthening exercises such as the following are beneficial.

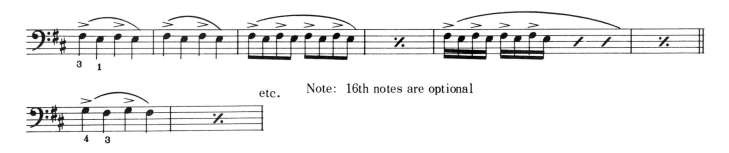

etc.　　Note: 16th notes are optional

In doing these exercises the fingers should be raised as high as possible and brought down onto the string with a forceful snap. These exercises should be done on each string.

During this stage the pupils will need to be reminded to keep the left elbow away from the body and at the correct angle. This requires some effort, and it is very easy for young children to resign themselves to the line of least resistance, letting the arm drop to the side. Correct arm position is extremely important in this respect since it controls the position of the fingers on the strings, the amount of strength that can be applied to the fingers, the vibrato, and shifting. The bow hand and the action of the bow must be watched constantly also. Weight, point of contact, and keeping the bow parallel to the bridge are three important concerns.

Common Faults During This Stage

The pupil is inconsistent in the placement of the fingers. In other words, the pupil is playing "out of tune."

The spaces between the fingers are not wide enough. Consequently the intervals are too small.

The fingers do not curve as they come down on the string. The first joint collapses.

The elbow is allowed to drop to the side of the body putting the forearm, wrist, and fingers in a faulty position.

THE INTERMEDIATE STAGE

Objectives (All Appropriate Previous Objectives Continue)

To play in tune.
To learn to tune the instrument.
To play with a pleasant tone.
To play with a range of dynamics from pp to ff.
To gain facility in backward and forward extensions.
To attain a velocity measured by slurred 16th notes at
♩ = 66–76 and bowed 16th notes at ♩ = 56–66.
To use the bow skillfully in a variety of bowings, i.e.,
slurs, staccato, marcato, slow spiccato.
To begin the study of the positions.
To begin to develop vibrato.

Tuning the Cello

Up until this time the teacher has, for practical reasons, tuned the student's instrument. In the first place, the pupil's ear is not developed sufficiently to do the job, and the muscles are usually inadequate for the job. If the instrument is equipped with tuners, a start may have been made to have the pupil attempt minor adjustments.

The first step is to tune each string individually to a pitch source. The piano is the most satisfactory. If the cello has tuners, show the pupil how to raise and lower the pitch of the string by turning the heads of the tuners to the right or left respectively. If gut-core strings are involved, have the pupils lay down the bow and turn the cello so that the strings are toward them. Of course he is seated. With the cello in this position, the A and D strings can be plucked with the left thumb while the right hand turns the pegs, and the G and C strings can be plucked with the right thumb while the left hand turns the pegs. The absolute importance of having tuning pegs that work well cannot be stressed enough.

When the A string is plucked, it will continue to vibrate for a short period of time. While the string is vibrating, the left hand should move quickly to the left side of the scroll providing a counterforce to the pushing of the right hand as it turns and sets the A or D peg. The hands reverse roles as the G and C strings are tuned.

After the pupils have become proficient at tuning each string to an individually given pitch, they should begin to tune one string to the other. This should begin with the A, which is tuned to a piano or pitch pipe. The D is tuned from the A, etc. Since considerable strength is needed to tune the cello, it is advisable to have the pupils continue to tune by plucking, unless the instrument has tuners or patent pegs. In the latter case, they can begin to use the bow.

When the bow is used in the tuning process, only the upper half is used. Begin at the point. Tune the A, then the D to the A, playing the two strings together. The phenomenon of the "waves" or pulses is described in the chapter on the violin,

Figure 9.6. Tuning the cello.

page 87. The greater length and sonority of the cello strings make these pulses more pronounced.

In the case of an instrument equipped with tuners, which is being tuned with the bow, the bow hand also adjusts the tuners. With gut-core strings the left hand turns the pegs while the bow functions on the strings. (See Figure 9.6.)

Extensions

Because of the length of cello strings, the fingers must be more than two inches apart to produce a whole step in the first four positions and nearly that far apart in fifth and sixth positions. This distance limits the interval the hand can span, without extending, to a minor third. This is, of course, extremely limiting technically and musically. To increase the range of the hand and expand the number of notes that can be played on each string, the cellist employs a technique described as "extension."

Extensions can be made in a backward direction and in a forward direction. In both cases the extension is made from the normal setting of the hand. It is very important in the backward extension that only the first finger moves, and in the forward extension that the first finger remains in place.

BACKWARD EXTENSION

The backward extension is accomplished by moving the first finger back one half step. In this position the side of the finger rather than the pad will contact the string. The rest of the hand and the thumb remain in position. This brings within the reach of the hand the note that is one half step above the open string. Example 1, below, illustrates this extension. (Note that the upper three fingers play the same notes they produce normally in first position.)

HALF POSITION

Closely related to the backward extension of the first finger is half position. Half position is realized when the entire hand, including the thumb, is moved backward one half step. In half position the fingers play the notes in Example 2.

This may, of course, be written enharmonically in flats.

FORWARD EXTENSION

In the forward extension the first finger acts as a pivot, becoming nearly straight, while the other fingers and the thumb move down the fingerboard one half step. The thumb should remain opposite the second finger. The forward extension brings the notes in Example 3 within reach.

Tone Development

The process of tone production is the same on all of the stringed instruments. While it is true that the arm is lower than the bow in the case of the violin and viola and is above the bow in the case of the cello and bass, the same principles are at work. Friction between bow hair and string created by the movement of the hair across the string is still the sound-producing element.

The ideal design of the cello, from the standpoint of string length and acoustical properties, contributes to the large volume of sound the cello is capable of producing. To get the most from the instrument, and to play it in the manner to which it is accustomed, the student must learn to apply strength and force, both of which depend upon the development of the arm and finger muscles along with sensitive balance and control. When called for, the cello can be attacked quite roughly and aggressively. The bow can strike the strings rather savagely without producing an unpleasant sound.

Note: Also refer to page 68 for a general discussion of tone production.

Shifting to the Higher Positions

Method books present the positions in varying order. After establishing first position some introduce half position, then second, third, fourth, etc. Others jump from first to fourth. It is difficult to debate the advantage of one over the other. Those who advocate a systematic coverage of the positions in succession feel that there is merit in the orderliness of this approach and that it prevents one position or another being slighted or omitted. The advocates of the quick jump to the fourth position argue that the fourth position extends the range of the player considerably. They feel that the fourth position is an easy position to find and be sure of because the thumb rests in the curve of the neck. It is also an advantageous place to establish the correct position of the left hand.

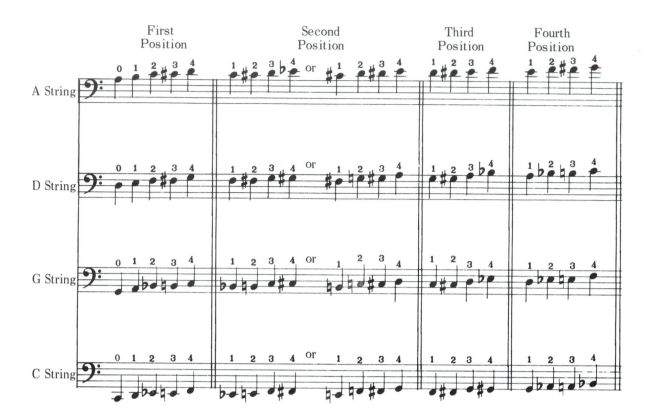

In shifting positions the arm does the shifting. The hand moves as a whole with the thumb retaining its position opposite the second finger. The normal setting of the hand prevails, although backward and forward extensions can be made from any position. The simplified chart above shows the notes in each of the first four positions on each string.

Vibrato

The general nature and purpose of the vibrato has been described earlier. (See page 55.) The cello vibrato is produced by a back and forth motion of the forearm. The forearm motion carries the hand and finger with it. It is the movement of the finger on the string that is the cause of the pitch fluctuation, which is the vibrato. It is because the finger is at right angles to the string that it must roll on the string to produce the pitch change, in contrast to the back and forth motion of the finger in producing vibrato on the violin and viola.

The hand can be placed at any position on the fingerboard for vibrato practice, but fourth position has some advantage. In fourth position the thumb can rest on the curve of the neck, which provides it with a kind of anchor. The second finger is placed on the D string and the forearm is rocked back and forth rhythmically. This should be done in various rhythms and at gradually increasing tempi.

The cello vibrato must be wide enough to create a genuine feeling of natural vocal-like tone. It must not be so small and quick that it sounds like a nervous tremor nor so wide and slow that it sounds labored. It must assist the bow to bring life to the music. It must project the entire range of emotions inherent in the music. To be fully effective it must be capable of a wide range of speed, width, and intensity. In the final analysis, it must respond to the emotional message of the music and project that message through the cello.

The mechanical exercises described above will not automatically create a vibrato. But they can condition the vibrato mechanism to function more readily than it otherwise might.

Common Faults of the Intermediate Stage

> Carelessness in intonation.
> Failure to retain basic hand position in extensions.
> Inaccuracy in shifting.
> Tone is too hard or too soft.
> Vibrato is made with hand or fingers rather than the forearm.
> Limited dynamic range.
> Limited reading ability.

THE ADVANCED STAGE

Objectives (All Appropriate Previous Objectives Continue)

> To improve intonation, tone, and musicianship generally, with a more mature concept of style and interpretation.
> To increase and expand technique, including:
>> Ability to play faster and more clearly both single note and double stop passages, chords, harmonics, trills.
>> Skill in fifth, sixth, seventh, and thumb positions.
>> Improved spiccato, staccato, and ricochet bowings.
>> Ability to read tenor clef.
> To play solo, ensemble, and orchestra literature of an advanced nature.

Figure 9.7. Cello, thumb position.

Most of the objectives of this stage are common to all the strings. But the thumb position is unique to the cello. Also unique is the need to play music in the bass clef, tenor clef, and occasionally treble clef.

Thumb Position

Thumb position extends the range of the cello and gives the cellist a great deal of facility in the upper register where the notes are close enough together that the cellist can utilize violinlike fingering. A sensible place to begin thumb position is at the octave harmonic on the A and D. The side of the thumb is placed on the two strings simultaneously. It acts as the open strings on the violin, the fingers functioning as they do on the violin—playing either half or whole steps.

The symbol for thumb position is ♀. Other fingers such as 1, 2, 3 may follow, but the thumb sign signifies that the notes following it are to be played in thumb position. The following passage is an example:

Thumb position also enables the cellist to play octaves.

Tenor Clef

The large range of the cello would, if it were not for the use of the tenor clef, require the use of many ledger lines above the bass staff. As stated earlier, this is an annoyance to both the composer and the cellist. To circumvent the use of ledger lines when the music goes above the bass clef, the tenor clef is used. It brings middle C down to the fourth line of the staff, a third higher than the viola. Thus, notes that would be written several ledger lines above the staff are brought into easy reading range. For example:

becomes

The students must master tenor clef as they did the bass clef. Showing the relationship of the clefs visually can help.

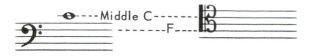

However, by the time the students are ready to play music that uses tenor clef, they should have enough theoretical background to comprehend the new clef fairly quickly. Once introduced to the clef, facility in reading it becomes a matter of repetition and experience.

Treble Clef

The use of treble clef is not unusual in advanced cello music. The reason for using it is to avoid using an excessive number of ledger lines when the music lies in the high register of the instrument. General practice in writing in the treble clef is to have it logically follow the tenor clef. When it occurs in this manner, the notes are written where they are to sound. Early practice, a practice still made use of by some composers, was to jump from the bass clef to the treble clef. When used in this way, the notes in the treble clef were meant to be played an octave lower than they were written.

The cellist's role in orchestra, chamber music, and solo is every bit as demanding as the violinist's. Consequently, the cellist must develop speed, agility, and accuracy. He or she must develop great strength in the fingers, hands, and arms, and be capable of moving about very quickly.

The cello is a key member of any chamber music group. It provides the bass and often has a major responsibility for the rhythmic solidarity of the ensemble. It is extremely important, therefore, that the cellist have a fine sense of rhythm and be sensitive to both the demands of the music and the needs of the ensemble.

Private instruction and a regular and well-balanced practice schedule are essential if the cellist is to reach an advanced stage and continue to progress. The player's diet should include scales, studies, and music selected from the standard solo literature. Experiences that include opportunities to play duets, chamber music, solos, and in orchestra are also essential.

STUDY QUESTIONS

1. Why is it important for the beginning cello student to have a chair that makes it possible for the feet to touch the floor?
2. The cello end pin is adjustable for the purpose of positioning the cello at the proper height for the player. What criteria are used to determine the proper height?
3. List several of the differences between the cello bow grip and the violin or viola grip.
4. What are some of the objectives of the beginning or open string stage of cello study?
5. What interval is spanned by the hand in the first position setting?
6. Discuss the backward and forward extension of the left hand.
7. What advantages are cited in learning fourth position at an early stage?
8. Draw the symbol used to denote thumb position.
9. What does the use of thumb position make possible?
10. Discuss and illustrate the clefs used in cello music.

Teaching the Bass

The bass is in some respects the most difficult to play of the stringed instruments. It is difficult because it is large and ungainly, with thick strings that are slow to respond. Intervals are far apart on the strings, requiring long reaches of the fingers. The pitches of its strings are so low it is very hard, at times, to discern the notes that are being played. Composers are aware of the problems and limitations of the instrument and write for it accordingly.

The bass is extremely important in its role as the foundation of the orchestra. In a symphony there may be from six to ten bases. Not only do they furnish the harmonic foundation for the orchestra, but they perform an extremely important function rhythmically. In many instances the bass is primarily a member of the rhythm section, providing the basic beat of the music. However, its ability to move freely to any pitch within its range and to produce a real sostenuto puts it in a special category among the rhythm instruments.

While speaking of the bass as a rhythm instrument, it is appropriate to mention the role it plays in the legitimate instrumental jazz combo. During the entire history of the dance band the bass has been regarded, along with drums and piano, to be one of the essential ingredients of the rhythm section. In this capacity the bass is almost always played pizzicato, most often supplying the basic beat, but occasionally surfacing to take a chorus.

In the large dance band complex the bass is more often than not lost behind the shining armor of the brasses and saxophones. When a rhythm solo is called for, the drummer usually takes over. But in the emergence of the small combo, the bass has assumed an increasingly important role. First of all it provides the foundation on which the rest of the combo builds its particular individual superstructure, and upon whom the others depend for the harmonic signals, which are essential to their ability to function successfully. And in the small combo the bass is often given opportunities to solo. "Taking a chorus" is not something new for the bass, but in the combo it happens with greater frequency. Furthermore, the combo puts the bass more "out-in-front" than it was in the big band. What this adds up to is that the bass player cannot be content with the ability to provide rhythm alone. If the bassist is going to excel, improvization is necessary; and to improvise well, technique must be developed. True, effective solos are more dependent upon imagination and creativity than upon technical skill, but the technical skill is what makes it possible for the creative bassist to bring his or her ideas to life.

THE ELECTRIC BASS

While on this subject, the current extensive use of the electric or "sit-down" bass must be mentioned. The electric bass is far more closely related to the guitar than it is to the bass viol. It has wire strings and frets, is played like a guitar, and plugs into its own or an available amplification system.

The electric bass emerged concurrently with the guitar-dominated rock groups. These groups required a bass line that was as percussive as the other instruments (amplified guitars and drums) and also would have the infinite range of volume characteristic of these groups.

The electric bass can be played by anyone who can play guitar. In fact, it is much easier than guitar in the sense that it does not involve chording.

Because it is relatively easy to play, can be picked up quickly by a guitar player, can plug into the sound system, and is much smaller than the bass viol (without all of the playing, shipping, and maintenance problems of that huge instrument) the electric bass has become very popular in the field of jazz and rock music.

THE BASS IN THE ELEMENTARY SCHOOL

In the elementary school it is as difficult to find pupils to begin on the bass as it is to find pupils to begin on the viola. It helps if the child who begins on the bass is larger than average and more developed physically. These are not essential qualifications, but they do provide an advantage. The small or delicate child, on the other hand, should, generally speaking, be steered away from the bass and toward one of the smaller instruments.

Transportation of the bass is a major problem and is often a serious deterrent to taking up the instrument. Some possible solutions to this problem are:

1. Provide practice time at school so the bass does not have to be moved.
2. Persuade the child's parents to provide transportation for the bass.
3. Furnish some kind of wheeled cart to carry the bass.
4. Supply a second instrument for use at home.

This discussion will be limited to 1/2 and 3/4 sizes, the sizes found most frequently in schools. Only the 1/2 size bass should be used in elementary schools. The 3/4 size is too large for elementary children and should be limited to junior and senior high school.

SELECTING THE CORRECT SIZE BASS

All elementary bass pupils should be started on a 1/2 size bass. The height of the bass can be regulated by adjusting the end pin. The bass can sit flush with the floor or it can be raised to about five or six inches above the floor. The end pin should be adjusted so the nut at the top of the fingerboard is slightly above eye level. It is better to have the bass too high than too low so that the right arm does not have to be strained to properly position the bow.

A Complete Outfit

A complete bass outfit includes the following:

A well-made bass of the correct size with proper strings and a machine head tuning mechanism in good condition, strings at the correct height above the fingerboard and correctly spaced, an end pin that is sharp, a good wingnut set screw and a stop to prevent the end pin from slipping inside the instrument.
A bow full of good hair properly rosined, a frog that fits properly and slides smoothly, a screw that works easily.
A satisfactory end pin holder.
A cake of bass rosin.
A cloth case that fits the bass, has a bow pocket, a pocket for music and rosin, with a good zipper or snaps.

A satisfactory and safe way to carry the bass is, in itself, a problem. The bass is large, rather heavy, and is awkward to handle. Small children should not be required to carry a bass any farther than from the storage locker to the middle of the room. The teacher should take responsibility for moving the bass between rooms.

When the student is large enough to be entrusted with the job of carrying a bass, a method such as that shown in Figure 10.1 is recommended.

FIRST STEPS FOR THE BEGINNER

See the statement in the chapter on the cello.

Holding the Bass

The use of a stool by the beginning bass student is optional. Of first importance is obtaining a satisfactory playing position. There is considerable difference in opinion regarding the exact setting of the feet; and, as with the other instruments, variations due to individual physical features are not to be frowned upon. The primary objective is to arrive at a position that is comfortable and practical. If the following directions are followed, a satisfactory position can be achieved.

1. The legs should be a shoulder-width apart, the left foot in front of the right for stability.
2. The knees are slightly bent and the weight evenly distributed.
3. The bass end pin is positioned eight to ten inches ahead of and slightly to the right of the left foot.

Figure 10.1. A satisfactory way to carry a bass.

4. The bass leans backward and tilts to the right. The lower right bout rests against the left knee. The upper right bout rests against the left side of the body, just below the rib cage.
5. Adjust end pin so that the first finger will be at eye level when playing A on the G string.

Left Hand and Arm Position

The thumb contacts the back of the neck opposite the second finger. The hand should be rounded as though holding a ball. The upper arm is well out from the body, only slightly lower than horizontal. The forearm is angled upward, and the wrist is bent a little so that the fingers are just above the plane of the strings.

The open and somewhat elongated position of the hand is important to the development of satisfactory finger action, vibrato, and shifting. A collapsed position, with the palm resting against the neck, should positively be avoided. This position looks bad, prevents correct finger action, makes a vibrato virtually impossible, and generally limits technique.

Common Faults in Holding the Bass

The end pin is placed too close or too far away from the player resulting in the bass being too straight or too slanted. If the bass is positioned too far ahead of the player, the player will more than likely lean forward. This is to be avoided.
The end pin is incorrectly adjusted resulting in the bass being too high or too low for the player.

Figure 10.2. Correct way to hold the bass, standing.

Figure 10.3. Correct way to hold the bass, seated.

No end pin holder is provided so the bass slips and the
 player feels insecure.
The bass is tilted too far to the left or right.
The arm is allowed to drop to the side of the body,
 putting the fingers, wrist, and forearm in incorrect
 position.
The left hand is allowed to collapse against the neck.

TIGHTENING THE BOW

To tighten the bass bow, hold the frog with the thumb and
fingers as shown in Figure 2.4, page 19. The bass bow is
stouter than the other bows and is considerably more rigid.
If the French bow has its original camber, the hair, when
fully tightened, should be from 1/2 to 3/4 inch from the stick
at its nearest point. The procedure described and the points
made on page 19 are applicable to the bass also.

Bass rosin is relatively soft and tacky. The bow hair does
not move freely across its surface. For this reason the bass
bow is always *drawn* across the rosin from the frog to the
point. It is never *pushed* in the other direction. The teacher
should demonstrate this procedure to the pupil.

HOLDING THE BOW

The French bow is held like the cello bow. The fingers may
be slightly more spread.

The German (Butler) bow is placed in the crotch of the
thumb, the frog pressing into the thick pad below the thumb.
The thumb hooks over the top of the stick. The first and
second fingers lie along the right side of the stick, contacting

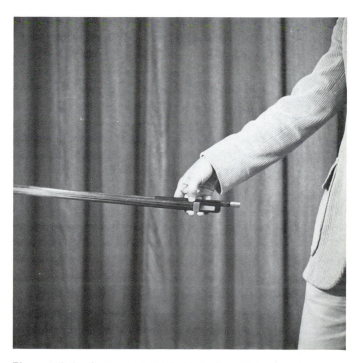

Figure 10.4. Correct way to hold the French bow.

Figure 10.5. French bow at the frog.

Figure 10.6. Bow at the point.

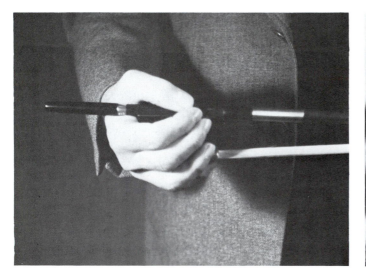

Figure 10.7. Correct way to hold the German bow.

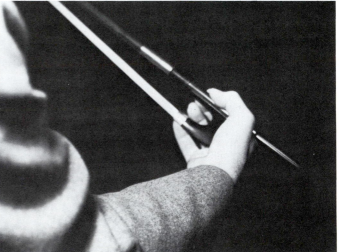

the bow at the leather part of the grip. The third finger is curved back into the frog opening, and the little finger is placed underneath the frog opposite the third finger. The Butler bow is often easier for young beginners to use than the French bow.

To acquire the correct grip, the bass bow should be taken in the left hand and placed in the right according to the above directions. After the grip has been checked by the teacher, the pupil is ready to use the bow on the strings. In playing position the stick is tilted toward the fingerboard. In the illustration above notice the attitude of the wrist at the frog and point.

Common Faults in Holding the Bow

French Bow
> The thumb is inserted too far through the bow.
> The bow is gathered into the palm instead of being held by the fingers.
> The hand slants too far forward or backward.
> The thumb bends in instead of out.

German Bow
> The second, third, and sometimes the fourth fingers are looped through the frog.
> The frog is pulled too far into the palm.
> The first finger is hooked over the top of the bow instead of lying along the stick.

Figure 10.8. German bow in playing position.

THE BEGINNING OR OPEN STRING STAGE

Objectives

To hold the instrument and bow correctly.
To draw the bow parallel to the bridge.
To draw the bow on the proper string.
To draw the bow for the specified duration.
To make satisfactory bow changes from up to down and down to up.
To identify the strings by their letter names.
To know the signs for down bow and up bow and follow these directions.
To be able to identify the following parts: bridge, fingerboard, neck, tailpiece; bow—frog, point, hair, screw, upper half, middle half, lower half.
To associate a printed note with the corresponding open string.
To know the names of the notes corresponding to the open strings.
To know how to count quarter notes, half notes, whole notes and their corresponding rests in 2/4 and 4/4 time.
To keep one's place while playing a line of music.

Most method books spend several lessons on the open strings, so the pupil must learn their identity on both the instrument and the printed page. To review, they are:

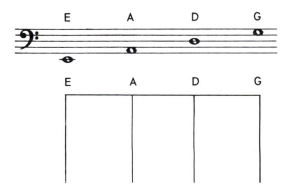

Notice that there is an interval of a 4th between the bass strings.

Turn back to the appropriate sections in the chapters on the violin and cello for suggestions for this stage.

Making the Strings Speak

The size of the strings on the bass presents a rather special problem in inertia. To overcome this inertia the bass player must apply more pressure to the string than is true of the other instruments. The trick is to apply the pressure at the beginning of the stroke, i.e., "bite" into the string with the bow, and then adjust the pressure to produce the desired dynamic level. It is sometimes incorrectly stated that this initial pressure is "released" once the tone is underway. But this is not quite accurate, especially when a f or ff dynamic is desired. The initial pressure may appear to be released for an instant as the bow begins to move, but it is immediately reapplied. The bassist should avoid using too much bow.

The beginning bass player should be taught to "bite" the string in a moderate dynamic. The "bite" will be achieved by gripping the bow more tightly and pressing down on the string. This should be practiced at the frog first, then at the point. Simply make a rote exercise of placing the bow on the D string at the frog and, beginning with a little accent, draw a very short bow. Repeat this until consistency is acquired.

Keeping the Bow Straight

Because the bow functions at considerable distance from the player's eyes, young bass players often are careless about keeping the bow parallel to the bridge. Also, they often fail to exert sufficient effort in the right arm to draw the bow between the bridge and the fingerboard, allowing it, instead, to ride up on the fingerboard, frequently in a see-saw fashion.

The teacher must give special attention to the beginning bass player's bowing if satisfactory results are to be achieved. If the bow functions at an angle, the string will not speak readily and the tone will be unclear. This is an especially acute problem on the bass because of the size of the strings and the difficulty in making them speak.

The exercises to orient the bow to the four string planes, which are described in the chapter on the violin, are adaptable to the bass. The bass bow, as the cello bow, should tilt slightly toward the fingerboard.

Common Faults of the Open String Stage

The bow is drawn over the fingerboard instead of halfway between the bridge and the fingerboard.
The bow is drawn at an angle to instead of parallel to the bridge.
The bow touches two strings at the same time.
The tone is fuzzy and notes are not started with a bite.

LOCATING THE NOTES

The difficulty of discerning pitch on the bass has already been mentioned. This problem, and the frequency with which young bass players completely ignore it, results in some appalling standards of intonation among bassists. It may appear to be heretical to say that visual finger placement aids, such as tape, are more practical on the bass than they are on the smaller string instruments. But the length of the bass strings allows a little more latitude in the placement of the finger for a given pitch than is the case with the violin, viola, and cello. Whereas a quarter or eighth of an inch movement of the finger on the violin makes a very apparent difference in pitch, this degree of deviation from "dead center" on the bass may not be intolerable.

In spite of what is said above, it is imperative that bassists learn to listen to themselves as carefully as do the players of the other strings. It must be understood that while measurements and visual aids can and may help, they are not the final answer. The ear is the ultimate authority.

Some methods start the bass player in half position. Others start with first position. If the string class is composed of all basses, half position is recommended. If the string class is heterogeneous, it is advantageous to start the basses in first position. Some approximate measurements are given to help in the location of these two positions on the 1/2 and 3/4 size bass.

Finger Placement Measurement
1/2 Size Bass

Distance from nut to 1/2 position	2 inches
Distance from nut to 1st position	3 3/4 inches
3/4 Size Bass	
Distance from nut to 1/2 position	2 3/4 inches
Distance from nut to 1st position	5 inches

When moving from half position to first position, the whole hand moves, including the thumb. The hand should maintain the same rounded shape. The length of the bass strings, and the consequent distance between notes, limits the span of the hand to a minor third in 1/2 position, including the open string (Example 1).

The third finger is used only to support the fourth finger until the hand reaches sixth position. At this point the third finger is put into active use. In general the first finger should assist the second by remaining on the string.

In first position the notes shown in Example 2 fall within the span of the hand.

The bassist must develop great strength in the left hand. Long tones at full volume on each finger and the finger-strengthening exercises in Example 3 are beneficial.

In doing these exercises, the fingers should be raised as high as possible and brought down onto the string with a powerful snap. These exercises should be done on each string.

During this stage the pupil will have to be reminded to keep the left arm out at the correct angle and the wrist curved. There seems to be a strong tendency for most young bass players to allow the arm to drop to the side and the wrist to cave in.

Common Faults During This Stage

The pupil is inconsistent in the placement of the fingers.
The spaces between the fingers are not wide enough; consequently the intervals are too small.
The elbow is allowed to drop to the side of the body putting all parts of the arm in a faulty position. In this position the palm of the hand is usually allowed to lie against the neck and the fingers are used collectively rather than independently. In this position it is impossible to gain any facility with the left hand.

THE INTERMEDIATE STAGE

Objectives (All Appropriate Previous Objectives Continue)

To play in tune.
To tune the instrument.
To play with a clear tone.
To play with rhythmic precision.
To play with a range of dynamics from pp to ff.
To attain a velocity measured by slurred 16th notes at ♩ = 60 and bowed 16th notes at ♩ = 50.
To play in positions II through V as well as the half positions.
To use the bow skillfully in a variety of bowings including slurs, staccato, and marcato.

Example 1

Example 2

Example 3

Tuning the Bass

As is the case with the other instruments, the teacher will have been doing most of the tuning up until this time. This is particularly true in regard to the bass because of the difficulty in hearing the pitch of the low strings.

The bass strings are tuned to G, D, A, and E on the bass staff. The actual pitch of the strings is one octave below where the notes are written on the staff. There are three ways to tune the bass. The bow is used in each case.

1. One way to tune the bass strings is to use the octave harmonic, which is located half way between the nut and the bridge. This produces a pitch one octave higher than the open string.
2. The harmonic located a fourth above the open string may be used also.

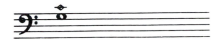

This harmonic produces a note two octaves above the pitch of the open string. Each of the strings may be tuned in this manner.

3. Still another method of tuning the bass is to use harmonics which produce unisons on adjoining strings. This is achieved in the following way:

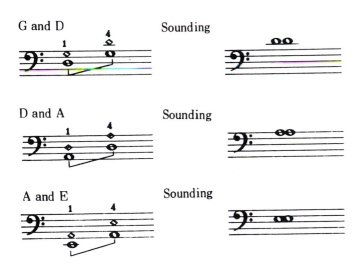

When tuning the harmonics, care must be taken to draw the bow evenly. Changes of speed, pressure, and point of contact may alter the pitch of the harmonic. The playing of harmonics is discussed in Chapter 6, pages 65 and 66.

Tone Production

Good tone production on the bass is achieved as it is on the other string instruments. The bow must be drawn evenly at a point between the bridge and fingerboard, which point will vary according to bow speed and volume. The left hand must depress the string firmly upon the fingerboard in order to completely stop the string. The length and diameter of the bass strings require that considerable strength be exerted by the fingers.

In playing staccato and marcato bowings, scratchy and rough attacks must be guarded against. Good tone quality can be achieved on the bass. It just takes work and care.

The Positions

The bass is tuned in fourths. The span of the hand is only a major second. Consequently, the overall range, without shifting, is extremely limited. When working with the bass in a mixed string class, this limitation poses a problem. Unless shifting is introduced early in the course of instruction on the bass, the bass will inevitably be omitted from some of the class exercises. It is for this reason that class methods introduce half position, first position, and third position relatively early. Third position extends the range on the G string to D and provides the flexibility that is needed for the bass to enjoy full participation in the group.

In shifting, the entire hand moves as a unit, the thumb retaining its place opposite the second finger. The chart on the following page shows the notes in positions I through III and the half positions.

Common Faults of the Intermediate Stage

Carelessness about intonation.
Poor left hand and left arm positions.
Bow is allowed to drift over the fingerboard producing a muddy, unclear tone.
Beginnings of tones lack precision, or bite.

THE ADVANCED STAGE

Objectives (All Appropriate Previous Objectives Continue)

To improve intonation, tone, and musicianship generally, and gain a more mature concept of style and interpretation.
To develop a vibrato.
To increase and expand technique.
To develop skill in the higher positions.
To develop a spiccato.
To play solo and ensemble literature of an advanced nature.

Most of the objectives of this stage are common to all of the strings. Attainment of these objectives implies the development of a good sense of pitch discrimination, a critical attitude toward tone and other aspects of performance, and a maturation of taste and musicianship in general. Private instruction from a good teacher is essential to the attainment of these objectives.

Vibrato

Bass vibrato, like cello vibrato, is produced by an up and down movement of the entire forearm. To produce a full and pleasant vibrato this movement must be fairly broad and unhurried.

To induce a vibrato, begin by removing the fingers from the strings and the thumb from the neck. With the hand freed, simulate the motion of the vibrato. When the correct action begins to appear, touch the thumb lightly to the neck while continuing the motion. It is possible in this way to develop the vibrato motion in the arm and condition the arm to respond to the vibrato impulse.

Higher Positions

The higher positions on the bass are achieved by moving the hand down the fingerboard toward the bridge. The thumb remains in its position opposite the second finger until reaching V 1/2 position at which time the thumb reaches the curve of the neck. It remains there until advancement down the fingerboard forces it to move.

Solo and ensemble literature for the bass is rather limited. Not very many composers have regarded the bass as a solo instrument, and in only a few cases is it included in small ensembles. Some solos have been transcribed for bass, however, and a number of contemporary composers are writing solos for bass; so there is material available for the enterprising bassist.

The bass is extremely important in the orchestra—chamber or symphonic. And to be an asset to these groups the bassist must have good intonation, a good tone, a steely sense of tempo, and an adequate technique. The latter implies good shifting, speed and dexterity with both the left hand and the bow, and the ability to read and play with authority.

STUDY QUESTIONS

1. What are some alternatives to transporting the bass that can be developed to alleviate this problem at the elementary level?
2. What size bass is preferred for elementary students?
3. List some of the principal points of body-instrument contact in the playing stance.
4. Name two faults of the left hand and arm common to beginning bass players.
5. Describe the bow grip for both the French and the German bow.
6. Discuss some of the special bowing problems as they apply to the bass.
7. In the lower positions, what use is made of the third finger?
8. In regard to bowing, what is one of the most common faults among young bass players?
9. Describe several methods used in tuning the bass.
10. What is the reason for introducing the positions early on the bass?

Part IV

Not all of the new thinking about and new approaches to the teaching of the string instruments is applicable to the public school music program. In some cases the innovations are too esoteric for general consumption and in other cases they require more time and individual attention than is possible in a system that requires certain minimum pupil–teacher ratios in order to exist. Nonetheless, teachers need to become acquainted with innovations in their subject field, and may, in the process, discover some concepts or techniques that are partially, if not completely, applicable to their program.

Chapter 11, "Some Recent Developments in Teaching Strings," provides a brief overview of some of the important recent contributions to string pedagogy and the people responsible for these contributions. Mention is also made of the rapid development in the area of music medicine. While it is not anticipated that teachers in the elementary and secondary schools will deal with students who have developed symptoms that can be classified as music-incurred (unless it is stage fright), this is a field of which they should be aware.

Chapter 12 attempts to deal realistically with some of the recent innovative technology and its application to teaching— specifically string teaching. "Technology In the String Class" lists some of the films and videotapes that deal with various aspects of string teaching and performance; it talks about the use of the video camera-recorder in the instruction program; it describes some electronic devices that help in the teaching of rhythm and pitch; and, finally, it discusses a number of computer programs that are designed to assist in the acquisition of note reading, rhythm, and pitch discernment skills.

The remaining two chapters of the book contain some very practical and important information and suggestions pertaining to the public school string program. Future teachers will do well to study this material carefully and to retain this book as a ready source of assistance in the teaching situation.

Some Recent Developments in Teaching Strings

In the first half of the 20th century probably the most important publication pertaining to string playing and teaching was *The Art of Violin Playing* by Carl Flesch. This extremely important two-volume work still holds a position of prime importance in this particular area of literature. No one before or since has done such a comprehensive job of discussing every facet of violin playing, examining and proposing solutions to literally thousands of problems in the violin literature.

In the second half of the century a number of significant and important publications and programs dealing with string teaching and playing have made their appearance. While it is not practical to discuss every new book or program, there are a few that have gained widespread recognition or have originated with famous personages and therefore justify mention.

A number of important books have been written on rather limited and specialized technical matters pertaining to one or another of the string instruments. These books are not general enough in their application to the broad field of public school string instruction to warrant discussion here. However, the works of Shinichi Suzuki, Rolland-Mutschler, and Samuel Applebaum are important to the school string program. Many aspects of these programs are innovative, and it is important for teachers to be familiar with them. A discussion of Yehudi Menuhin's *Six Lessons* is included because of the unique approaches proposed by this great artist. Also included is a discussion of Kato Havas, and the subject of music medicine is covered briefly.

SUZUKI METHOD

The Suzuki method is being singled out and explained because of the great amount of attention it has gained in this country since 1964 and the interest it has created among string teachers in this country, Canada, and England. No other innovation in the teaching of strings has motivated so much enthusiasm and activity. While the following account is brief, it touches upon the important elements of the method. Ample material and first-hand accounts are available for those who want to learn more about the Suzuki method. (See bibliography for Suzuki and others, *The Suzuki Concept*.)

Shinichi Suzuki is a Japanese violinist and teacher who has had phenomenal success teaching very young Japanese children to play the violin. Basic to the Suzuki concept is the belief that every normal child has talents, including musical talent. These talents must be allowed and assisted to develop. Suzuki believes that children should be able to learn to play the violin by the same process that they learn to speak their native language. While not every child is expected to become a great violinist, it is felt that the development of the ear, coordination of the hands and arms, cultivation of sensitivity, discipline, memory, and industry, more than justify the time expended in learning to play the violin.

Suzuki's method includes a close mother–child participation and a rote approach to learning the instrument. Imitation is a dominant aspect of the learning process, in regard to both playing position and execution of the bow and left hand. Repetition by the child of simple rhythm patterns introduced by the teacher is the basic format of the lesson. Emphasis is always placed upon good posture, good tone production, good bowing, and good intonation.

Suzuki first presented his students to the Japanese public in 1942. In 1947 the Talent Education Institute was formed. The first presentation of Suzuki students in America occurred in 1964, and there has been a rapid growth of interest in the Suzuki program since that time. Teachers from this country have gone to Japan to observe the Suzuki techniques and to study with Suzuki and his assistants. Seeing the nearly unbelievable results he achieves with Japanese children has instilled some teachers from this country with a kind of missionary zeal. They have returned home to talk and write about what they have seen and to try to find ways to make it work here.

Suzuki's success with teaching the violin in Japan has led to the establishment of the Early Development Association. The aim of this nonprofit organization is to apply the Suzuki concepts to other fields including drawing, calligraphy, the Japanese and English languages, gymnastics, and mathematics. The Suzuki method is now being applied to all of the string instruments and piano.

The Suzuki teaching materials are available in this country in the form of the *Suzuki Violin School* Volumes 1 through 10 for violin plus piano accompaniment and a recording of all of the material in the books. The books stress a relaxed hold for both bow and instrument and include photographs of children with ideal positions.

There has been a proliferation of Suzuki-based and Suzuki-inspired materials for the other string instruments, and recordings or cassettes are available for most of it. If you do not have the advantage of a music store from which to order, there are several mail-order sources. Among these are: Shar, 2465 S. Industrial Hwy, Ann Arbor, MI 48106; Ability Development, Box 4260, Athens, OH 45701-4260; Ithaca Talent Education, Inc. (ITE), 929 Danby Road, Box 669, Ithaca, NY 14851; and Summy-Birchard, 180 Alexander Road, Box 2072, Princeton, NJ 08540.

The Suzuki method includes a number of interesting concepts. One is the emphasis placed upon the "natural tone." The "natural tone" of the instrument is developed first by plucking the various strings and allowing them to vibrate freely. The student is then told to place the bow on the string and draw the bow producing the same tone quality as the resonating plucked string. This is described as "tonalization."

Another interesting concept (not necessarily original with Suzuki) is the use of the middle of the bow rather than the whole bow in the first lessons. A great many of the exercises are devoted to rhythm patterns played détaché or staccato in the middle of the bow.

In the *Suzuki Violin School* it is strongly suggested that the student listen repeatedly to the recording of the lesson material on a continuing basis. A fundamental precept of the system is that a parent will observe the lesson and will supervise the child's practice.

In the lesson called "Tonalization," which begins with alternating A string and E string played pizzicato, Suzuki says: "This should be taught at each lesson. Pluck the open string and listen to the sound of the vibrating string."[1] In the same lesson he lists five questions that teachers and parents must ask every day. They are:

Are the pupils listening to the reference records at home every day?
Has the tone improved?
Is the tonation correct?
Has the proper playing posture been acquired?
Is the bow being held correctly?[2]

Many teachers in the United States, both private and public school, are experimenting with the Suzuki method, often with modifications that make it fit the demands of their particular situation. Pilot projects are being conducted in many schools. In some elementary schools all or most of the children in the school, beginning with the second grade, receive instruction on the violin. Great enthusiasm is generated by these programs, and many talented youngsters are discovered who otherwise might never have begun the study of the violin.

It is too early to assess the long-range success of these efforts, although teachers who have employed the Suzuki techniques over an extended period of time claim that they have had as satisfactory a success rate with their "Suzuki" students as with students taught by traditional methods. This success also includes the student's learning to read music, which, many report, they learn to do very quickly. One of the questions that still needs to be answered is how and at what point some of the violinists are switched to viola, cello, or bass, since it takes more than violins to make an orchestra.

In 1966 John Kendall wrote the 32-page pamphlet, *The Suzuki Violin Method in American Music Education,* for the Music Educators National Conference (now available from the Birch Tree Group, see bibliography). In it, Kendall explains the Talent Education Program, attempts to correct some misconceptions about the program, and, briefly, addresses the question of integrating the system into the American music education system. Anyone interested in starting a Suzuki program should read as much as possible about the Talent Education Program, observe teachers who have had experience in the program, and attend workshops to learn, firsthand, how the Suzuki techniques are applied. A list of some of the books dealing with Suzuki and Talent Education follows.

---

1. *Suzuki Violin School,* Violin Part, vol. 1 & 2 (Evanston, Ill.: Summy-Birchard Company), p. 13.
2. *Ibid.*

Title	Author	Publisher	Date
A Parent's Guide to String Instrument Study	Lorraine Fink	Neil Kjos, San Diego, CA	1977
Ability Development from Age Zero	Shinichi Suzuki	Ability Development Associates, Athens, OH	1981
In The Suzuki Style	Elizabeth Mills & Parents	Diablo Press, Berkeley, CA	1974
Nurtured by Love	Shinichi Suzuki	Exposition Press, Smithtown, NY	1983
Shinichi Suzuki: Man Of Love	Masaaki Honda, M.D.	Suzuki Method International, Princeton, NJ	1978
Teaching Suzuki Cello	Charlene Wilson	Diablo Press, Berkeley, CA	1980
The Genius of Simplicity	Linda Wickes	Summy-Birchard, Princeton, NJ	1982
The Suzuki Concept	Several authors	Diablo Press, Berkeley, CA	1973
The Suzuki Violin Method in American Music Education	John Kendall	MENC, Reston, VA*	1978
The Suzuki Violinist	William Starr	Kingston Ellis Press, Knoxville, TN	1976
The Talent Education School of Shinichi Suzuki	Ray Landers	Exposition Press, Smithtown, NY	1984
They're rarely too young and never too old "to twinkle!"	Kay Collier Slone	Live Force Press, Lexington, KY	1982
To Learn with Love	William & Constance Starr	Kingston Ellis Press, Knoxville, TN	1983
Where Love Is Deep	Shinichi Suzuki	Talent Education Journal, St. Louis, MO	1982

*Revised and updated. Now available through Suzuki Series, Suzuki Method, International Div. of Birch Tree Group, Ltd.

THE TEACHING OF ACTION IN STRING PLAYING
PAUL ROLLAND ASSISTED BY MARLA MUTSCHLER

Paul Rolland is well known for his writings in American String Teachers Association publications and for his long affiliation with that organization. With financial assistance from the U.S. Office of Education, and staff and physical assistance from the University of Illinois, with which he was affiliated, and the professional and technical help of many prominent individuals, he has accomplished a huge and immensely detailed volume of work devoted to teaching strings. While the entire project is focused on teaching the violin, many of the principles and much of the pedagogy is adaptable to the other instruments.

Rolland's *String Research Project* produced fourteen color films, the book *The Teaching of Action in String Playing,* and wall charts, which are photographs of the basic techniques developed in the project, plus music and recordings.[3] Development of these materials took place over a four-year period and involved hundreds of hours of working with and filming groups of children at various stages of advancement in playing the violin.

The book and the films take the student from the very first lesson, and great emphasis is placed upon developing a comfortable, relaxed, and as nearly ideal position as possible for both the violin and the bow. Many pedagogical devices to accomplish this most important phase of study are to be found in the book and are illustrated in the films. A listing of the films will show the scope of the project.

Young Violinists in Action
Principles of Movement in String Playing
Rhythm Training
Establishing the Violin Hold
Holding the Violin Bow and Violin Playing at the
    Middle of the Bow
Principles of Left Hand Finger Action
Establishing Left Hand and Finger Placement
Extending the Bow Stroke
Developing Finger Movement and Basic Shifting
    Movements
Bouncing the Bow and Martelé and Staccato
Developing Flexibility
First Steps in Vibrato Teaching
Sustained and Détaché Bowing
Remedial Teaching

The 214-page book is a collaborative effort of Rolland and Marla Mutschler. It serves as a guide for teaching violin and viola and as a manual for the films. The text of the narration of each film is found in the chapter dealing with that topic.

The book demonstrates evidence of a very keen and creative imagination, as well as a grasp of child psychology and motivational techniques. Even if a teacher were not committed to a full use of the book, there are many ideas that can be extracted from it and techniques that can be applied to any method.

Typical of the approach taken in the book is found in chapter fifteen, "First Steps in Vibrato Teaching." First vibrato is explained— "It is the movement of the finger tip on the string that is the ultimate cause of vibrated sounds." Then there is a very brief discussion of how a vibrato is produced.

There are eleven subheadings in the chapter. They are designated as *Actions*.

Action I: Preparatory Relaxation Studies
Action II: "Tapping"
Action III: The Finger Vibrato
Action IV: The "Wrist" Vibrato
Action V: Developing Left Arm Balance (Arm Participation)
Action VI: The Intensity Vibrato
Action VII: "Tap and Hold"
Action VIII: Developing Flexibility of the Wrist and Fingers
Action IX: Regulating (Timing) the Vibrato Movement
Action X: Comparing Vibrato Speeds
Action XI: Controlling the Extent (Amplitude) of the Vibrato

Each action is discussed and photographed, utilizing a teacher and a student. There are eighteen photos in the chapter. Musical notations of some of the actions are also included, as are several graph-like portrayals of slow, average, and fast vibrato.

The actions are all designed to induce a vibrato. They range from whole arm motions to finger sliding action. The photos depict the teacher assisting the student in the particular action. The following instructions for the "Tapping" action indicate the approach and the imagination contained in the book.

Tapping movements are similar to vibrato movements. The tapping and immediate rebounding of the finger form one complete vibrato cycle. The fingernails must be short for this action.
1. Place the hand in the middle positions, thumb under the neck as shown. Keep the fingers curved.
2. Tap quickly with the curved third finger on the top plate of the instrument to the left of the lowest string. Use the thumb as a pivot support for whip-like motions motivated by the arm. Imagine that your finger is a ping-pong ball bouncing back from the table. Tap rhythms of your choice—tune rhythms, name rhythms, and the patterns on the right.
3. Tap rhythms on each string. *Throw* your finger and let it spring back as if touching a hot stove.
4. Combine Tapping with the Shuttle. Tap rhythms in the first, middle, and high positions.[4]

SAMUEL APPLEBAUM

Samuel Applebaum is a teacher-pedagogue who has turned out an immense amount of material. Applebaum's publications for strings range from simple to moderately difficult study material, from simple to advanced performance material, and include a series of films covering various aspects of string instruction. There are three ten-minute color films in the series. These are also available in half-inch and one-inch video tapes.[5]

3. Rolland String Research Associates, 404 East Oregon Street, Urbana, Illinois 61801.

4. Paul Rolland and Marla Mutschler, *The Teaching of Action in String Playing* (Urbana, Ill.: Illinois String Research Associates, 1974), p. 154.

5. Belwin Mills Publishing Corp., Melville, N.Y. 11746.

Program No. 1   *Rote-Games for the development of good playing position and control of the bow.*
Program No. 2   *Rote-Games to strengthen and develop facility for both hands.*
Program No. 3   *Developing an orderly mind through rote exercises for rhythm, sight reading, and intonation.*

Groups of children of various ages and stages of development are used in the films. These children become the "lab" group with whom Applebaum works. In an informal but positive way he goes through the various "rote-games" he has created to achieve certain desired results.

These films are designed primarily for use in the string class. It is a stimulating and challenging experience for children to see their peers try something and succeed. It is then perfectly natural for them to want to emulate what they have seen. The films are also extremely useful in teacher training programs where they can supply the prospective teacher with a wealth of teaching ideas and techniques.

The *Applebaum String Method* is a two-volume work with a third volume in preparation. It is published for violin, viola, cello, and bass, with piano accompaniment, and a teacher's manual. The method begins with a series of rote-games. (These are illustrated in the films.)

The instruments play together throughout the book. "Each book is a complete unit and may be used separately for class or individual instruction. The aim is to permit the student to memorize sensations that will help develop specific technical skills. These skills are analyzed and a series of exercises presented for their development."[6]

The method is supplemented by

Etudes for Technic and Musicianship
Chamber Music for Two String Instruments
Chamber Music for String Orchestra
Correlated Solos

In addition to the materials listed above Applebaum has produced a number of books that can be used to supplement this or any basic course of instruction. They are written for all the string instruments. Some are instructional in nature. Others are performance oriented.

First Position Etudes for Strings
Concert Program for String Orchestra
Duets for Strings, Vols. I, II, III
Orchestral Bowing Etudes
String Ensembles
Third and Fifth Position String Builder
Second and Fourth Position String Builder
Building Technic with Beautiful Music, Vols. I, II, III, IV
Scales for Strings, Vols. I & II
Beautiful Music for Two String Instruments, Vols. I, II, III, IV

Standard etudes, folk songs, and miscellaneous classical and semi-classical selections comprise most of the material in these books.

VIOLIN—*SIX LESSONS* WITH YEHUDI MENUHIN

Yehudi Menuhin, the mind-boggling child prodigy of the thirties who, at the age of seven, made his debut before disbelieving audiences, has, since 1963 when he founded the Yehudi Menuhin School in England, developed some unique and provocative concepts of teaching the violin, the instrument to which he has dedicated more than fifty years of his life.

A highly intelligent and sensitive person, Menuhin contends that matters of diet, general physical condition, breathing, exercise, and mental attitude are of vital importance in the study of "an instrument [I have known intimately for fifty years] which must surely be one of the most beautiful artifacts ever created by man and one of the most capricious to handle."[7]

Six Lessons complements six twenty-five minute films, which Mr. Menuhin has made over a period of years.[8] The films utilize students from his school, and in the films Menuhin conveys concepts of his approach to playing the violin. While the book and films deal exclusively with the violin, there are many ideas which are applicable to the other string instruments.

Lesson I deals with the general conditioning of the body, the breathing apparatus, muscles of the back, legs, and neck, stretching exercises for back and arms, balancing, etc. Some of these exercises are based upon yoga, which Mr. Menuhin practices.

The remaining lessons consist of directions for the physical manipulation of the fingers, arms, shoulders, and head, as they are used in playing the violin. The movements of the left thumb, the attitudes of its joints, and its relationship to the fingers are carefully described and detailed. A major consideration of Menuhin's approach is relaxation, lack of tension, and suppleness.

Lessons II and III deal with preparatory exercises for the right and left hands, Lessons IV and V with bow movements and left-hand movements, and Lesson VI with combined movements of the two hands. Appendix I contains a series of daily practice and warming up exercises, and Appendix II is a short commentary on care of the violin and bow.

A teacher in a public school string class could not conscientiously put a group of students through all of the exercises prescribed in *Six Lessons*. It is too time consuming a course for anything but an extended private class situation. However, it is possible to select key points and focus on them for general class use and select other exercises to be applied to special problems of individual students. Some of the exercises are of a rather advanced nature and would not be appropriate to beginning and intermediate level classes.

6. *A Guide to the Samuel Applebaum Course for Strings,* Belwin Mills Publishing Corp., Melville, N.Y. 11746.

7. Menuhin, Yehudi, *Violin—Six Lessons* (New York: Viking Press, Inc., 1972), p. 12.

8. Argo Record Company, 115 Fulham Road, London S.W.3., England.

Ideally, to get maximum advantage and understanding of the principles contained in *Six Lessons,* one would go through a course of instruction with Menuhin or with a well-trained exponent, or have access to the six films along with the book. The book has many drawings illustrating the exercises. Even so, a mature mind is needed to comprehend the execution of some of the exercises as well as their subtle purpose.

KATO HAVAS

Kato Havas has gained her reputation from giving workshops in many countries, writing books, and from her annual Summer School (The Twelve Lesson Course) in Oxford, England.

Havas was born in Hungary, and, according to her publicity, received the traditional virtuoso training as a child prodigy violinist at the Royal Academy of Music in Budapest. She made her debut in America at Carnegie Hall at the age of 17 after which she married and withdrew from professional life for many years. During this period away from public performance she developed what she calls "A New Approach to Violin Playing," which she describes in a 1961 book by the same name.

Many years and many workshops and lecture-demonstrations later, the Kato Havas Association for the New Approach (KHANA) was formed in 1985, with representatives in ten European countries as well as Canada, Australia, New Zealand, China, and the United States. The organization publishes a journal twice a year as a forum for the reinforcement of New Approach methods, testimony to its success, and exposure of new ideas related to the New Approach.

The New Approach focuses almost exclusively on the violin. Havas claims the New Approach is equally applicable to other instruments, but she is a violinist, her books are addressed to the violin, and the majority of students and performers who seek her help are violinists. Very briefly, her aim is to develop a relaxed, tension-free, anxiety-free method of playing which she says is the natural way to "just let it happen."

Kato Havas has written a number of books, all of which attempt to explain her theories of balance, freedom from tension, and expressive playing. The books are:

The Violin and I
The Twelve Lesson Course
A New Approach to Violin Playing
Stage Fright—Its Causes and Cures
Freedom to Play

A look at some of the things Havas says in *A New Approach to Violin Playing* will provide some insight to her theories. She contends first and foremost that the basic concept in playing a string instrument is one of balance, not strength. She also contends her theories are not new and "revolutionary" but have been derived from the great masters of the past. She has simply organized these teachings into a working system.

In speaking of tone production she says, "A warm and beautiful tone has nothing to do with talent or individual personality . . . nor hours of practise and perseverance. It is merely putting the right pressure on the right spot at the right moment."

Her approach is based on the assumption that the average violinist has faced frustration and misery (in practice and performance) most of his or her life. "I do not think there are as many neurotics in any other profession as there are among violinists." And then, in regard to the tendency many violinists have to blame their problems on their instrument, Havas assures us that the problem is not with the instrument but with the player. From the beginning we create one obstacle after another.

She likens the correct playing stance to the balance of a see-saw. When the ends are in balance, little effort is needed to put and keep the see-saw in motion. According to this analogy, bowing action should be just as effortless.

About holding the violin (which she again takes up at length in *Stage Fright*) she says it is of the greatest importance not to grab the violin with the chin. The head moves down onto the chinrest. The neck muscles relax. She advocates that the left elbow should point directly to the floor, never to the right. In holding the bow the primary objective is to achieve a light, effortless hold. "Tone is not produced by pressure, but by the friction of the hair on the string." And because of the differences in individual's physical make-up, it is not possible to prescribe an exact placement of the fingers on the bow.

Tone quality is dependent upon the free existence of harmonics. The fingers of the left hand must raise and lower from the base joints. Thus it is possible for the weight of the finger to produce pitch changes, not pressure on the string by the finger, and, thus, the string vibrates freely with all of its harmonics. Vibrato is a natural action from the base joints. "So, if the control is in the base joints, tone production, vibrato, and intonation are combined in one process originating in the same source." Bowing problems, such as spiccato, are usually due to tension in the left hand or arm, not to any malfunction of the bow arm.

Explaining her theory of teaching she says, "The secret of teaching the violin is not so much the question of imparting knowledge. It is the ability to make the road clear for the pupil both physically and mentally so that he can lose whatever constraint he has and, as a result, just 'to let it happen,' but not haphazardly trusting to chance and hoping for the best, but through the relaxed control of perfect physical co-ordination which releases the imagination."

In *Stage Fright—Its Causes and Cures,* Havas separates the causes of stage fright into three areas: physical, mental, and social. Havas starts with a short discussion of the shame attached to stage fright, describes the symptoms of stage fright, and the effect of the audience on the phenomenon. She then makes the case for the naturalness of the playing of the Hungarian Gypsy violinist, who, she maintains, is free of all of the symptoms of stage fright and the causative tensions.

"The Physical Aspects of Stage Fright" (Chapter 3) are analyzed as:

1. The Fear of Dropping the Violin
2. The Fear of the Trembling Bowing Arm
3. The Fear of Being Out of Tune
4. The Fear of High Positions and Shifts

"The Mental Aspects of Stage Fright" (Chapter 4) are analyzed as:

1. The Fear of Not Being Loud Enough
2. The Fear of Not Being Fast Enough
3. The Fear of Memory Lapse
4. The Power of Words
5. The Power of Imagination

Each category is analyzed with causes and cures listed, followed by specific exercises to implement the cures. While Havas declares that in the majority of cases the devastation of stage fright is merciless, leaving a wake of desolation, both physical and mental, in addition to the horrors of artistic frustration, she claims that "after years of constant testing and observation I feel justified in stating that with training, understanding and application, stage fright can be cured."

Having had the opportunity to observe Gypsy violinists during her youth, she claims that Gypsys seem to be *one* with the violin. They are relaxed, without rigidity. Their entire body moves with the music—a total interplay of motion and balance, through their rhythmic pulse. In drawing a conclusion from this, she says, "The mind and the body are so closely connected that complete release from tension and anxiety in violin playing can be achieved only through the combination of a certain mental attitude with an active physical balance."

Havas's "cures," in some cases, move into the realm of the metaphysical. When discussing the fear of dropping the violin, she states, "The cure is to establish a self-generating motion and balance (in the form of an organic rhythmic pulse) in the stance itself, without even thinking of the violin." This is a practice procedure done without the violin. "But to infuse it (the violin) with our own aliveness we must be able to envelop it with our own organic movements. . . . This is only possible if we can learn to make our arms feel as light as feathers and as full of motion and balance as the wings of a bird."

All of Kato Havas's writings have the same theme: free yourself from tension, find the "natural" way to play, develop an "inward-outward" rhythmic pulse, learn certain recommended ways to practice to best advantage, and you will be able to play at your optimum level of artistry.

With the abundance of teaching material available—traditional and proved, new and innovative—no teacher should feel at a loss for new ideas or new sources for ideas. Much of the new pedagogy comes from extremely reliable people in the world of string teaching, and is the result of years of experience or research. Therefore, teachers should familiarize themselves with these new concepts. An open minded attitude must be maintained, and the new ideas that teachers think they can use should be experimented with in a positive way. Too often we become very set in our ways and refuse to look at anything new because it might make us uncomfortable. Professional discomfort is really a very healthy thing periodically. The progressive teacher should welcome the opportunity that these moments present.

CARE AND MAINTENANCE OF THE STRING PLAYER (MUSIC MEDICINE)

There is no question that many musicians have for years suffered what can rightfully be called occupational disabilities—physical and emotional problems and stresses that are directly associated with their musical activity. Sports injuries, being more readily apparent and apparently more acceptable than those incurred in the arts, have spawned an entire field of specialized medicine—sports medicine! It is taken for granted that it is a necessary adjunct to sports, primarily because the bottom line is keeping the player on the field or the court.

Among dancers, injuries have been much more readily acknowledged and treatment and therapy sought. But among musicians the presence of pain, strain, or stress has been something the musician has not admitted readily. When the situation was bad enough, admission of it was usually limited to close friends, accompanied by the admonition that the information should not be repeated. It was almost as though, for a musician, a painful wrist or little finger was a social disease that was not discussed or admitted. It was as though the presence of a physical problem was an admission of failure or inadequacy.

There has been some reason for musicians to keep their music-associated pains to themselves; as Garry Graffman, the concert pianist, said about his incapacitating right hand problem, "Who wants to hire an injured pianist?" There has been the kind of pervading attitude among musicians that the overcoming of physical problems was part of the challenge in learning to play an instrument because the physical challenges of an instrument are there from the beginning. For string players, learning to draw the bow and place the fingers correctly are matters of physical manipulation that the player faces from the first time the instrument is picked up. Learning to stretch the fingers farther and quicker and move the bow in ever more rapid and intricate patterns is all an accepted part of the development of technique. If some part of the anatomy hurts once in a while in the process, that is considered normal and acceptable.

But the past ten years have brought about the recognition that *many* musicians suffer occupation-associated physical and emotional problems that go beyond the category of slight and occasional and can, and sometimes do, reach the point that they force a musician to retrain or even abandon his or her profession. As these kinds of problems have come increasingly into public view, the medical profession has begun to take the whole thing more seriously. Ten years ago a musician with an instrument-induced physical problem could either go to his personal physician, who might refer him to a specialist, or turn to an M.D. who specialized in sports medicine. The musician may have incurred considerable difficulty in trying to persuade the doctor that the problem might be caused by the demands of his profession.

The attention focused on musically induced physical and emotional problems during the past decade has brought about two pronounced changes. First, musicians are less reticent to admit that they may be having physical or emotional problems that are associated with their work. Second, the medical profession has accepted the fact that musicians have special problems that are caused by what they do, and more and better ways of dealing with these problems are being developed.

There is no intention here to treat this topic in any depth. That would require another book. There is little likelihood that any of the problems that afflict professional musicians will occur with the young children in a private or public school program. All of the research that has been done to date has been with adults who have studied and played their instrument over a long period of years, and there is no evidence to point to a problem of this kind with children and young students. Although it should be mentioned that stage fright, one of the ailments discussed at length in the various publications and symposia dealing with music medicine, is apparently no respector of age, occurring in young children as well as seasoned adult performers. But the effect that it may have on the young child can hardly be compared to what it can do to the person who must perform in public as part of his or her livelihood and who is repeatedly and predictably tormented by its debilitating symptoms.

But it is certainly possible that instrument-connected physical problems can begin to occur in the serious teenage student who practices several hours each day in addition to orchestra and ensemble rehearsals. If you are in a teaching situation that puts students of that description under your responsibility, you should become familiar with the range of problems that can occur and with the symptoms that accompany them. Publications and symposia dealing with the subject of music medicine are on the increase. Information about several follows.

Sforsando Music Medicine for String Players, Selected Proceedings from the Illinois–ASTA Conference, 1984, edited by Anne Mischakoff (see bibliography).

Medical Problems for Performing Artists, published quarterly by an editorial board of M.D.'s, Hanley and Belfus Inc., Medical Publishers, 210 S. 13th St., Philadelphia, PA 19107.

Annual Symposium on Medical Problems of Musicians and Dancers, Aspen, Colorado. Symposia have also been conducted in Chicago, Denver, and Minneapolis.

Often thought of and considered when dealing with the subject of music medicine is the Alexander Technique. Developed by F. Matthias Alexander, an English/Australian actor, the Alexander Technique is a system of psychophysical education that helps to eliminate musculoskeletal problems brought on by inefficient use of the body while practicing or performing. The Alexander Technique takes a comprehensive approach to the most efficient use of the body, including the attainment of posture that is conducive to freedom of movement and absence of tension. This is, of course, an oversimplification of a subject about which numerous books have been written and which people have spent extended periods of time studying in classes and workshops in order to understand and put to their personal use. For those who want further information about the Alexander Technique, addresses are provided below.

American Center for the Alexander Technique, Inc.
Abraham Goodman House, 129 W. 67th St., New York, N.Y. 10023.
931 Elizabeth Street, San Francisco, CA 94114.
1913 Thayer Ave., Los Angeles, CA 90025.

STUDY QUESTIONS

1. Name five prominent 20th century string pedagogues.
2. Discuss the significant contributions to string teaching of each of the above.
3. Do you find yourself in agreement or disagreement with the theories and practice advocated by these pedagogues? Discuss.
4. From your own experience, do you think that teachers need to be more aware of physical and emotional problems as they effect music students?

Technology in the String Class

For many years about the only teaching aids powered by electricity were the radio, the record player, the filmstrip projector, and the motion picture projector, and somewhat more recently, the tape recorder. Today we must add to this list television (along with video cameras, video tapes and videodiscs), and the computer. This entire array of equipment is now available in most schools. It is up to the teacher to determine how to make the best use of it.

The record player (including the compact disc player, which is an updated version of the record player with much greater sophistication), the filmstrip projector, the motion picture projector, and the tape recorder, their operation and their potential for use in the classroom, are no longer new and are sufficiently well known to everybody that it is needless to discuss them here. The material that follows will focus on information about and the use of video equipment and the computer.

Before discussing the valuable assistance that some of this equipment can provide, it should be stated that there is virtue in using a piece of electronic equipment only if it can provide a better way to help a child learn or achieve than a more traditional method. The use of any piece of equipment just for the sake of using it is foolish and unjustified. Remember, nothing can ever take the place of a good, well-qualified teacher!

Also, since some of this equipment may be new to some teachers, it is important that the teacher become familiar with its operation and learn as much as possible about its capability in order that the equipment and program content can be put to their best and most productive use.

THE VIDEODISC

The videodisc, or laserdisc, is a format that can be compared in a number of ways to the compact disc in sound recording. The videodisc is generally 12 inches in diameter, although 3-, 8-, and 10-inch discs exist. On its two surfaces, both sound and visual images have been recorded in much the same way they have been recorded on a compact disc, i.e., sound is recorded digitally in stereo and the visual images are also recorded digitally. The videodisc requires a special "player" that utilizes a laser beam, as does the compact disc player. The latest, most up-to-date players are capable of playing laser discs of all sizes and regardless of whether they are video/audio or just audio (compact disc). One drawback to the videodisc that should be mentioned is that at the present time it is not possible to record onto a disc as one can with videotape. The videodisc has only playback capability.

The videodisc has some laudable qualities, including excellent sound and picture fidelity, zero deterioration from use, and again as in the case of the compact disc, quick and easy access to the various sections of the recorded program. And, in the case of the interactive videodisc, it is possible to invoke the "freeze frame" capability or, in other words, stop instantly for a prolonged view or study of a particular moment of your choice. In addition, the user may randomly access sections of the disc or, with the help of a computer, preprogram the order in which the various sections will be played.

After this somewhat glowing account of the videodisc, it is regretful to have to say that, to date, no one has utilized it for string instruction materials at any level. There are many performance-type discs available, from solo recital to symphony, Broadway musicals, and opera; and there are instructional programs in a number of subject areas, including the broader aspects of music and music history. But, considering the desirable qualities that the videodisc offers, it is reasonable to expect that, barring the appearance of some newer and better technology, programs of instruction in various areas of music will be appearing on videodisc in the foreseeable future.

One videodisc program that deserves mention is *Music Is*. *Music Is* consists of ten thirty-minute television programs transferred to five videodiscs. Titles include:

Music Is	*Music Is Form*
Music Is Rhythm	*Music Is Composed*
Music Is Melody	*Music Is Conducted*
Music Is Harmony	*Music Is Improvised*
Music Is Tone Color	*Music Is Style*

The series is designed for upper elementary grades. No interactivity is built into the course. The producer is GPN, Great Plains National ITV Library, P.O. Box 80669, Lincoln, Nebraska 68501, 1–800–228–4630.

IDEAS PERTAINING TO THE USE OF FILMS AND/OR VIDEOS IN THE INSTRUCTIONAL PROCESS

There are several types of educational films or videotapes available. Some of them are:

Those that deal with a single instrument.
Those that deal with all of the strings.
Those that deal with a particular aspect of playing, such as vibrato.
Those that deal with some aspect of music, such as rhythm, a composer, or a historical period.
Those that focus on performance by an individual or group.
Those that deal with the history and construction or repair of string instruments.

When thinking of using a film or prerecorded video, you need to consider the time factor. Can the film/video be shown in the time available? This means, of course, that you need to know the length of the item. Ask yourself if you can afford to use your class time in this way, or is it more important that you spend that time in direct pursuit of your goals? Will the aid help you and the class toward that goal? Some visual materials seem to be more entertaining than instructional or, at least, the instructional elements are not closely enough aligned to what you are doing to justify their use. This is something to which you must give careful consideration in light of the time constraints of your overall program. If this sounds negative in regard to the use of film and video, it is not intended to be. Teaching aids should be used when they can do the job better than anything else, or can assist you in doing the job better.

You should always take care of the standard "housekeeping" chores in advance. Frustration on your part and disappointment on the children's part occurs when the equipment does not function properly, or the video or film has been improperly rewound or is broken, or when any of several other problems occur that can usually be avoided if you know and check out your equipment and preview the film or video beforehand.

A good piece of advice is that it is better not to use a film or video unless you have personally previewed it. You should be aware of its merits, its method, and the age group at which it is aimed. The suitability of the film or video to the group's stage of musical and technical development is another important factor to consider. Only then can you properly schedule it and prepare your class to view it with maximum benefit.

Sometimes, however, a film or video can be used as a "special treat." If your class has worked particularly hard and/or made especially good progress, you can reward them with an appropriate film or video. Thus, you provide a break in the routine, reward the class for good work, and, at the same time, expose them to something which is musically or technically instructive.

As stated previously, it can be assumed that the role of the video player purely as a substitute for the traditional film projector is such common knowledge that there is no need to discuss it in detail here. There are fine films with real educational merit that are not available on video, and there is now an extensive library of material on video that is not duplicated on film. Of course, there are a number of items that are available in either form. If it is available in both forms, the matter of the suitability of the screen size should be considered—the average video monitor screen is only a sixth to an eighth the size of the typical film screen. This becomes a factor in relation to the number of students who will be viewing and how near or how far they will be from the screen. Of course, this problem can be solved with the use of a video projector, by using several monitors "chained" together, or using one of the "super" television sets with an extra-large screen.

A brief, and recognizably incomplete, list of films and prerecorded videos pertinent to the string program follows. Videos, particularly, appear and disappear rapidly. Therefore, the list of sources may be of as much value as the items themselves.

Distributors and Their Addresses

AVIDI	American Video Institute
AITECH	Agency for Instructional Technology
	Box A
	Bloomington, IN 47402
BCNFL	No address available
EBEC	Encyclopaedia Britannica Ed. Corp.
	425 N. Michigan Ave.
	Chicago, IL 60611
FOTH	Films for the Humanities Inc.
	P.O. Box 2053
	Princeton, NJ 08540
GPITVL	Great Plains Instructional TV Library
	University of Nebraska
	P.O. Box 80669
	Lincoln, NB 68501
IU	Indiana University
	Indiana University
	AV Center
	Bloomington, IN 47405
KYTV	KY Educational TV Network Center
	600 Cooper Drive
	Lexington, KY 40502
MOHOMN	Morris Home Video
	413 Ave G
	Redondo Beach, CA 90277
PUBTEL	Public Television Library
	475 L'Enfant Plaza SW
	Washington, DC 20024
RADTV	Radio and TV Packagers
	9 East 40th Street
	New York, NY 10016
RHPSDY	Rhapsody Films Inc.
	30 Charlton Street
	New York, NY 10014
SHAR	SHAR Products Co.
	2465 South Industrial Hwy.
	P.O. Box 1411
	Ann Arbor, MI 48106
SWRTWT	Swartout Enterprises
	703 Manzanita Drive
	Sedona, AZ 86336
UILL	University of Illinois
	U of I Visual Aids Service
	1325 S. Oak St.
	Champaign, IL 61820
UWASHP	University of Washington Press
	1416 NE 41st Street
	Seattle, WA 98105
VINEVI	Vineyard Video Productions
	Elias Lane
	West Tisbury, MA 02575
U of Wisc	University of Wisconsin–Madison
	Dept. of Continuing Education in the Arts
	Room 726 Lowell Hall
	610 Langdon Street
	Madison, WI 53703

INSTRUCTIONAL FILMS AND VIDEOS

Film or Video Name	Content	Grade Suitability	Length	Type	Distributor
Auroscope Series, 10 Lessons	Notes, rhythms, scales	K–Adult	30 min	3/4&1/2" Video	AVIDI
Developing the Beginning String Quartet		Int–High Sch	15 min	16 mm film	AITECH
Expressing Note Values	Introduces music notation	K–Int	10 min	2" Video	SWRTWT
Learning to Read Music			29 min	2" Video	PUBTEL
Meter Reader		K–Int	15 min	3/4&1/2" Video	AITECH
Note Value		K–Int	15 min	3/4&1/2" Video	UILL
Playing the Cello		Jr. Hi–High	23 min	16 mm film	KYTV
Rhythm		K–Jr. High			
Role of a Cello in a String Quartet		Int–High Sch	15 min	3/4&1/2" Video	AITECH
Role of the Violin in a String Quartet		Int–High Sch	15 min	3/4&1/2" Video	AITECH
Role of the Viola in a String Quartet		Int–High Sch	15 min	3/4&1/2" Video	AITECH
Role of the 2nd Violin in a String Quartet		Int–High Sch	15 min	3/4&1/2" Video	AITECH
What Is a String Quartet		Int–High Sch	15 min	3/4&1/2" Video	AITECH
Basic Bow Strokes (Cello)		Jr. Hi–Adult	30 min	3/4&1/2" Video	IU
Basic Principles of Double Bass Playing		Jr. Hi–Adult	30 min	16 mm film	UILL
Bertram Turetzky Parts 1 & 2	New sounds of contemporary music	Int–Adult	30 min	2" Video	PUBTEL
Cello Sounds of Today, Fritz Maag, Ind. U.	Introduction, 6 in Series	Jr. Hi–Adult	30 min	3/4&1/2" Video	IU
Positioning the Player and His Cello	Part of Ind. U. series	Jr. Hi–Adult	30 min	3/4&1/2" Video	IU
Scales and Scale Bowings	Part of Ind. U. series	Jr. Hi–Adult	30 min	3/4&1/2" Video	IU
Basic Bow Strokes	Part of Ind. U. series	Jr. Hi–Adult	30 min	3/4&1/2" Video	IU
General Orientation of the Fingerboard—Left Hand	Part of Ind. U. series	Jr. Hi–Adult	30 min	3/4&1/2" Video	IU
The First Violin	Cartoon drama to encourage practice	Elem–Int	20 min	16 mm film	RADTV
Leroy Jenkins Solo Violin	Jazz solos		29 min	16 mm film	RHPSDY
Making Music—The Emerson Quartet	What makes a quartet work		28 min	3/4&1/2" Video	VINEVI
The Violin and Viola			25 min	3/4" Video	UWASHP
Bowed Instruments	History of bowed instruments		30 min	3/4&1/2" Video	FOTH
How to Play the Double Bass	Roger Scott of Phila. Orch.	Beg.–Adv.		1/2" Video	MOHOMV
Instruments of the Symphony Orchestra	Shows how strings make sounds	K–High Sch	10 min	16 mm,3/4&1/2" Video	EBEC
The String Family	Discusses the string instruments		15 min	3/4&1/2" Video	AITECH
Vibrant Strings Parts 1 & 2	Mus. Inst. Series	Jr. Coll–Adult	16 min	3/4&1/2" Video	GPITVL
Viola	Otto Erdesz creates a viola	Jr. Coll–Adult	29 min	16 mm, 3/4&1/2" Video	BCNFL
The Teaching of Action in String Playing	Paul Rolland demonstrates his method	Elem–Jr., Sr. High		9 ea. 1/2" Videos	Rolland String Research Associates
Guide to Orchestral Bowings through Musical Styles	Marvin Rabin & Priscilla Smith	Jr. Hi–Adult	52 min	Video	U. of Wisc
Rabin on Strings	Marvin Rabin and colleagues	Jr. Hi–Adult	3 hr 45 min	2 Videos	U. of Wisc

The following films are listed under the Consortium of University Film Centers. These films may be rented from the source indicated. The codes and corresponding addresses follow:

Name of Film	Content	Grade	Length	Distributor
Holding the Violin Bow	Mus. Perf. Improvement Series	Beg–Int	3 min	UWISC
Hand and Finger Bowing	Mus. Perf. Improvement Series	Beg–Int	5 min	UWISC
Martelé Family of Bowings	Mus. Perf. Improvement Series	Int–High Sch	6 min	UWISC
Mr. Goshu, The Cellist	Cartoon figure practices cello	Beg–Int	19 min	IFB
Remedial Teaching (Violin)	Summer orch. camp setting	Int–Adult	20 min	CLU/Theo. Pr
String Techniques	Playing and teaching	Jr. Hi–Adult	30 min	IU

UWISC	University of Wisconsin Bureau of AV Instruction P.O. Box 2093 Madison, WI 53701
IFB	International Film Bureau 332 S. Michigan Ave. Chicago, IL 60604
IU	University of Illinois, Film Center 1325 S. Oak St. Champaign, IL 61820
CLU	University of California, Los Angeles Instructional Media Library Powell Library Room 46 Los Angeles, CA 90024

The following set of nine videocassettes is available from Rolland String Research Associates, 404 E. Oregon, Urbana, IL 61801.

The Teaching of Action in String Playing	Paul Rolland Method Series	Beg–Adult

The ASTA Media Resource Center has a number of films dealing with string playing and instruction. For information write to: ASTA Media Resource Center, c/o Robert Gillespie, 110 Weigel Hall, 1866 College Road, The Ohio State University, Columbus, OH 43210–1170.

SHAR Products Company carries an interesting collection of performances and master classes on videocassette by the following and others:

Pablo Casals
Jascha Heifetz
Ivan Galamian
Donald McInnes
Josef Gingold
William Primrose
Perlman and Zukerman
Shlomo Mintz

For information write to: SHAR Products Company, 2465 South Industrial, P.O. Box 1411, Ann Arbor, MI 48106.

THE VIDEO CAMERA, RECORDER, AND PLAY BACK

Three pieces of equipment are required to make the video camera set-up complete: the video camera itself, a video recorder/player, and a video monitor, unless you are using a camcorder, which is a combination camera and playback unit.

If using a camcorder, only a TV or monitor is needed for playback. However, it is recommended that a separate "music quality" microphone be used with the camcorder in place of the built-in microphone.

The primary advantage of the video camera as a teaching tool is that it can provide the string student with the opportunity to see himself or herself in action from the visual perspective of the teacher or an observer. This solves one of the persistent and nagging problems in learning a string instrument—not being able to stand away and see one's playing position. Prior to the invention of the video camera, about the only thing a teacher could suggest to students who were having problems with bow direction or left hand position was that, periodically, they play in front of a mirror, hoping that in this way they could see their problem and correct it. But practicing in front of a mirror does not provide an ideal observation perspective for any of the string instruments, and, consequently, does not always lead to a correction of the problem.

The beauty of the video camera is its ability to photograph the student in action, from a variety of angles or perspectives, focusing on the bow arm or the left hand, if that is desirable, and instantly replay the photographed action for the student to see. Thus, the student is able to observe himself or herself in action, detect strengths and weaknesses, and determine what should be done to correct any obvious problems. Of course, this will work only if the student has been provided a good model—the teacher, another student, or an appropriate video or film.

One should not lose sight of the advantages of videotaping your entire group in both rehearsal and performance. Watching a videotape of themselves will allow the members of your class or orchestra to take "another look" at themselves; that is, see themselves as you and others see them. In the case of rehearsal or class session videos, the students will be able to hear your comments and hear and see how they responded. They will see how attentive they are in rehearsal, or what kind of distracting things they do—sometimes without being aware.

Being able to see themselves in actual performance can be extremely rewarding to the individual and collective ego and is the most effective possible reinforcement of your performance follow-up critique. From the standpoint of your own personal growth and improvement, can you think of a better way to evaluate your stage appearance and the job you are doing as teacher/conductor than to see yourself in action?

Usually you will be able to videotape class sessions without assistance. You will need a tripod for the camera and will need to position the camera and focus it to include the whole group or a particular group, depending upon your choice.

Then it is only necessary to turn the equipment on. If you want to move the camera about for special shots—special groups, close-ups, etc.—it would be better to have somebody to help out as camera operator. Then your concentration can be focused where it should be—on your students and the music.

Most certainly, in a performance situation, get help. Your attention is needed on other things, and, besides, this is more than a one-person job. Close-ups may be desired; lights will probably be necessary; some starting and stopping of the tape will be required; sound adjustments may be needed. Doing all of those things is a job in itself. It is far too much for someone to take on who is responsible for a stage full of students and a program of music.

COMPUTER-ASSISTED INSTRUCTION

The January 1983 issue of the Music Educators Journal, the official magazine of Music Educators National Conference, was devoted almost in its entirety to topics related to the variety of uses of the computer in the classroom and as an instructional tool. In that issue editor Rebecca Grier Taylor said:

> No matter how resistant to change you or your administration may be, the technological revolution will affect your classroom. You may be surprised at the enthusiasm and interest your students will show in a music class that is taught through the most modern methods. You, too, may be caught up in the computerization of America.

Within the short span of time since Taylor's prophecy, no one can deny its accuracy.

It is probably fair to say that in the interim the use of computers as an aid to instruction in the schools is moving, or has moved, into its second phase or generation. Phase one was innovative in every sense of the word. Computers were new. How they might help in the learning process had yet to be explored and proved. Systems were being developed and programs written. Schools were acquiring equipment and learning how to use it. The bright young men and women who understood computers were (are) the *wunderkind* of the time. They talked a new language that most of us did not understand and, consequently, made most of us feel inadequate and insecure in regard to computers.

Needless to say, the ranks of those conversant with computers and their terminology have swelled dramatically. More and more people have learned about bytes, ROM, RAM, MIDI, LOTUS, floppy discs, hard discs, soft copy, hard copy, printers, storage capacity, mouse, cursor, and much more. To provide some perspective, it should be noted that Thomas E. Rudolph, in his book, *Music and the Apple II,* has an eight-and-a-half-page glossary of computer terms and their definitions. Fred T. Hofstetter has provided a much needed service with his book, *Computer Literacy for Musicians.* But, while the glossary in Ruldolph's book is relatively practical, certainly the sophistication and extent of Hofstetter's book is designed to bring musicians to a much higher level of computer knowledge and expertise than is needed for ordinary, basic classroom instructional programs in the fundamentals of music. The computer is capable of functioning at levels of enormous complexity in the field of music, but it is also capable of performing relatively simple tasks with great efficiency. Our interest is in the latter.

Today, in what may be designated phase two of computer-assisted instruction (CAI), it no longer seems so necessary to learn all the terminology. Surely, there are some basic essentials and terms that computer users should know about and understand, but thousands of computer users have discovered that if they know where the on–off switch is, where and how to insert the program disc, if they have reasonable keyboard (typewriter) skills, and can read the instruction book that accompanies the program, they are quite capable of putting the computer to profitable use.

The computer itself, plus the monitor, the external disc drive (if there is one), the printer (if there is one), the game paddle or mouse, and any other piece of equipment that attaches to the computer, is known as hardware. What hardware you have to deal with depends upon what computer you have and what is needed for the programs you are using.

A few additional points should be made here. First, there are probably more Apple computers in schools than any other make, the reason being that the company that makes the Apple gave thousands of its computers to schools nationwide. As a result, there is probably more instructional software for the Apple than for any other computer. This is certainly true in the case of music, with music software for the Commodore coming in second.

A second point is that there are essentially two sizes of floppy discs for personal computers: 3 inch and 5¼ inch. One must select the right size disc for the computer. Furthermore, programs designed for a computer of one make will not operate on a computer of a different make. Even programs designed for certain IBM computer models will not work on other IBM models.

The computer has an internal disc drive (some have two). This is a slot in the body of the computer into which the disc is placed. Some computers are enhanced with an external floppy disc drive. This is an attachment (peripheral) to the computer that expands the computer's capability and increases its ease of use. It is possible to add a hard disc drive to the computer, thus increasing the storage capacity of the computer many times.

Some programs require additional hardware, such as external speakers, added memory cards, a joystick, a touchpad, or a keyboard. In considering purchase of a program, the peripheral hardware required to run the program must be taken into account.

Computers are useless without programs that instruct them what to do. Programs are referred to as software. Software must be designed for each specific brand of computer, although the same program may be, and often is, designed for several different computers.

Programs that are simple to operate and contain instructions in easy-to-understand language are now available. There are literally hundreds of programs designed to assist in music instruction. Finding the best one for your purpose may not be the easiest thing in the world, but not the most difficult, either. To assist in this process, some programs are described below.

Programs are written onto floppy discs (software); thus, one buys the floppy disc(s) (3″ or 5.25″ depending upon the computer involved) containing the program in order to get the program desired. Thomas E. Rudolph in *Music and the Apple II* says this about buying software:

1. Begin with one or two programs. Select, for example, a music theory program and a music game. Since students and instructors will need time to become familiar with the hardware and software, a limited amount of software will help reduce confusion.
2. Make the first purchases easy programs. Start with a program using the Apple II "as is" and then progress to more sophisticated programs by adding DAC boards and music systems.
3. Use microcomputer software as a supplement to classes one is already teaching, including instrumental instruction. Again, microcomputers work exceptionally well for drill and practice.
4. Initially avoid programs requiring a great deal of programming or specific computer knowledge. Programs should be user friendly and run merely by loading.[1]

Computer stores that handle software may have little of an educational nature and nothing in the particular area of your interest. To assist in this matter, some sources of programs are listed below.

It should be understood that, at this time, there are only one or two known computer programs designed specifically to assist in learning a string instrument, that is, in learning to manipulate the bow or place the fingers of the left hand. However, there are many programs whose purpose is to assist in the learning of the staff and its components, note values, provide rhythm practice, and improve pitch recognition and retention. These programs can, of course, assist a child (or older student) regardless of what instrument is being pursued.

The beauty of the computer is its capability to interact with one or several students on a one-to-one basis, at a level and speed appropriate for each, providing repetition where needed, encouragement, and evaluation of results, thus freeing the teacher to work with students on problems with which the computer cannot assist. Music reading and music fundamentals can be reinforced, and pitch discernment and melodic and interval recognition drills can be provided to improve aural skills, often such a problem with young string players. There is even a pitch discernment program available now that utilizes a graphic of a stringed instrument fingerboard.

Some computer programs, their descriptions, and their sources follow. But preceding these are the descriptions of two relatively new noncomputer teaching aids that are of great enough importance to be given prominent attention. They are Tap Master, a rhythm-teaching device, and Pitch Master, a pitch-teaching device.

TAP MASTER AND PITCH MASTER SYSTEMS

Temporal Acuity Products, Inc. (TAP) has produced two unique devices—Tap Master System and Pitch Master System, plus a number of very good software programs.

The Tap Master System is a self-contained device at which a student may work independently to improve rhythmic execution and reading of rhythmic figures. The system consists of the Tap Master II Unit, a set of stereo headphones, and a 9-volt adaptor. Rhythmic dictation is contained on cassette tapes, and a book accompanies each series. An acrylic book stand is available. A stereo cassette player is required but is not included with the system. The student performs each exercise by tapping on the Tap Master Unit's "Tap Button" and receives one point for each correct answer. There are three series of sequenced materials.

Elementary Series, age 3 through grade 4 (40 tapes and one book), progresses from no knowledge through all 8th-note concepts in duple meter.

Intermediate Series, grade 4 through university (40 tapes and one book), from no knowledge through all 16th-note concepts through duple meter.

Advanced/Professional Series, Parts I, II, & III (10 tapes per part and one advanced book), Part I compound meter, Part II cross rhythms, Part III mixed meters.

The Tap Master System has been used at various grade levels in a number of cities with good results. Research has been conducted with experimental and control groups, and in each case it has been found that the group using the Tap Master System has made significantly more improvement than the students receiving standard instruction with traditional techniques.

The second innovative device by TAP is the Pitch Master System. This system consists of the Pitch Master Unit, cassette tapes and accompanying book, stereo headphones, microphone, stereo cassette tape deck (not included), and optional acrylic stand for book. The tapes contain musical exercises with instructions to the student. When the student sings into the microphone as instructed, the student's voice is audible in one side of the headphone. If the voice is producing the correct pitch, a reinforcement tone will be heard in the other side of the headphone. If the pitch being produced by the student's voice is incorrect, the reinforcement tone disappears, alerting the student that there is a problem. A meter built into the Pitch Master Unit shows if the pitch sung by the student is sharp, flat, or in tune. A digital counter registers the score for each exercise. Supporting voices and accompaniments are provided on the tapes. There are three accuracy levels for every exercise—easy, medium, and hard. The two programs in the Pitch Master curriculum are:

Tune-up Series, grade 4 through adult (15 tapes). The objectives of this series are to:
Match pitch
Echo pitch
Sing in tune
Study independently
Diatonic Series, for anyone who has completed the Tune-up Series (15 tapes and one book). The objectives of this series are to:
Instant auditory and visual pitch recognition
Tonal awareness
Music reading skills
Effective study skills

With the purchase of the Fostex X-30 Multitracker, or an equivalent 4-track cassette recorder with a built-in mixer, it is possible for a teacher to produce his or her own Pitch Master tapes to meet special needs of the program or of the students. Research has also shown this program to be effective at various levels.

1. Thomas E. Rudolph, *Music and the Apple II* (Drexel Hill, Pa.: Unsinn Publications, 1984), p. 70.

COMPUTER-ASSISTED INSTRUCTION (CAI) PROGRAMS

In addition to the two noncomputer programs described above, TAP carries two series of CAI (computer-assisted instruction) programs, *Micro Music Software Library* and *Note Factory Software Library*. *Micro Music Software Library* is a series of programs designed for the Apple II series computers. Originally these programs required the Micro Music DAC Board, four-voice music card; but Version II of all except the harmonic programs in this library can now be used with the Apple's built-in monophonic speaker or with MIDI sound equipment. The Apple IIg's built-in sound chip provides the sound source for all Micro Music Version II softwear programs, including all four-voice programs. Version II also makes possible student recordkeeping for all the programs listed. *Note Factory Software Library* is a series of programs designed for the Commodore 64 computer and utilizes the Commodore's own system. Appropriate programs from each of these series are listed below with a brief description.

MICRO MUSIC SOFTWARE LIBRARY (FOR APPLE II COMPUTERS)

Melodic Dictation

Arnold	A challenging ear-training program that teaches tone recognition and melodic memory skills. Five levels of difficulty. Fourth grade–adult.
Doremi	A beginning ear-training program that teaches students to identify (by sound only) the individual degrees of a major scale using solfeggio responses. Fourth grade–adult.
Melodic Dictator	Teaches students to hear single-line melodies and then notate the pitches on the staff using a graphic representation of a keyboard. This program automatically adjusts to the individual's skill level.Fourth grade–adult.

Rhythmic Dictation

Rhythmic Dictator	Teaches students to recognize and remember rhythmic patterns. Jr. high–adult.
Rhythm Drills	Develops rhythmic memory through dictation. Fourth grade–adult.
Rhythm Machine	Gives practical experience in recognizing rhythmic patterns. Four levels of difficulty. Program can automatically adjust levels to match the student's performance. Records scores. Fourth grade–adult.
Rhythm Write	Develops reading and notational skills. The student writes isolated rhythmic sequences that the computer dictates. Ten levels of difficulty. Includes answer sheets, grading keys and record sheets. Fourth grade–adult.

Fundamentals

Theory Sampler	Five programs in one: scale and mode recognition, triad and 7th-chord recognition, scale and mode construction, triad construction, 7th-chord construction. Fourth grade–adult.
Pick the Pitch	Provides drill and practice for the recognition of notated pitches in the context of a staff, clef and key signature. Uses treble, bass, alto, and tenor clefs and grand staff. Options include working with or without accidentals or key signatures. In the game mode, the student's responses are timed. In the tutor mode, there are no time constraints. Fourth grade–adult.
Catch the Key	Drill and practice in the recognition of key signatures. Covers major and minor key signatures in treble, bass, alto, and tenor clefs and grand staff. Game mode timed; tutor mode untimed. Fourth grade–adult.
Sketch the Scale	Deals with scales. Comparable to the two previously described programs.

Error Detection

Sebastian II	Develops aural and visual discrimination through melodic error detection. Lessons may be customized. Fourth grade–adult.

Early Childhood

Magic Musical Balloon Game	First steps in melodic discrimination for the young child. Ages 3 and above.

Symbols

Music Symbols	Drills music symbols at beginning and advanced levels. Fourth grade–adult.

NOTE FACTORY LIBRARY (FOR COMMODORE 64 COMPUTERS)

Ear Training

Melody Race	Develops the student's ability to recognize and label notes correctly with letters, numbers, or syllables. Treble and bass clef. Students work against time. K–adult.
Pitch-u-lation	Develops melodic memory skills. Six levels of difficulty. Notes are displayed in scale form. The computer plays a series of pitches and the student is asked to identify the notes played. K–adult.

Rhythmic Dictation

Rhythmaticity — Develops rhythmic reading perception and performance skills. Students read the rhythm displayed on the computer screen and tap that rhythm using a computer key. Thirty levels of difficulty. K–adult.

Error Detection

The Music Detective — Develops students' ability to find pitch and rhythm errors. The mistake, if there is one, will be either a pitch or a rhythm. K–adult.

Tuning

Pitch Duel — Challenges pitch matching skills and harmonic tuning skills. Uses standard notation. Forty levels of difficulty, through triads, inversions, major and minor 7th-chords. K–adult.

Note: Temporal Acuity Products is continually adding new music software programs. The company should be contacted for its latest listings: Temporal Acuity Products, Inc., Building 1, Suite 200, 300 120th Avenue N.E., Bellevue, WA 98005, 800–426–2673, 206–462–1007 (Washington and Alaska).

Magic Piano

EduSoft, P.O. Box 2560, Berkeley, CA 94702 (800–EDUSOFT), handles a music learning system called Magic Piano by Alan Sagan. The program is for the Apple II series computers and is suitable for grades 2 and up. There is one disc, a user's guide, and music workbook. The catalog description reads:

> With this entertaining, easy-to-use program, every teacher can introduce music in the classroom. Kids spend hours of creative fun while learning music fundamentals. The Rhythm Game teaches note values and timing. In the Melody Game children play a computerized "Simon Says" to train their musical ears. The Magic Piano transforms your computer keys into piano keys. Beginners can compose tunes in minutes and hear their masterpieces played back. They'll be thrilled to see their songs magically displayed and printed in musical notation. With easy and difficult levels, everyone will find a challenge. A 64-page Music Workbook provides extra pencil and paper practice to support and reinforce learning.

Main Menu:
1. Magic Piano
2. Rhythm Game
3. Melody Game

Magic Piano choices:
1. to create a song
2. to hear a song
3. to edit a song
4. to save a song on disc
5. to load a song on disc
6. to load a song from disc
7. to delete a song from disc
8. to print a song

Choices are made by typing the desired number plus return. To create a song, a staff appears on the screen. Notes are selected by depressing the number key corresponding to the desired note. The melody can be edited, saved, heard, etc. A drawback is that no provision is made for meter signatures or bar lines.

RHYTHM GAME

There are ten levels of difficulty and six levels of precision. A meter and a rhythm appear on the screen. A metronome (visable) clicks two bars of pulse before the computer plays the rhythm. You copy the rhythm by pressing the space bar. The rhythm you play shows up below the given rhythm. If you are correct, you get positive encouragement in the form of such words as "excellent," "splendid," "wow," "bulls eye," "superlative." If you are wrong, you are told to try again. With any exercise, you can repeat, try again, or ask for help. Since you have typed in your name upon inserting the disc, your name shows up on the screen under a winner's ribbon. At the higher levels of precision, meeting the computer's demands can be frustrating. Instructions on the screen tell you how to get back to the menu and how to get help.

MELODY GAME

In the Melody Game you have choices of difficulty again. You can select melodies ranging from 2 to 19 notes. A melody is played and you are asked to repeat it using the keys as explained above. The key number of the first note is given. Encouragement, as well as repeated tries, is given.

Music Class Series

Wenger, 1401 East 79th Street, Bloomington, MN 55425–1126 (800–843–1337), handles Music Class Series by Frank Bradshaw and Virgil Hicks and produced by University of Akron. Programs are designed for Apple II, II+, //e, //c, IIGS, at least 64K of internal memory, one disc drive, and monitor.

Series has five programs:

Fundamentals: Learning the basics
Rhythm: Learning to feel the beat
Ear Training: Learning to hear
Music Symbols: Learning the language
Note Reading: Learning to see and understand

The complete package includes five guides and a set of ten discs, two for each program.

Fundamentals: Learning the basics

The *Fundamentals* program deals with the staff and notes and later with major and minor scales. Rhythm is introduced through Mr. Metro Gnome who taps his foot to set tempos while basic rhythms are played. There are tutorials explaining the chromatic scale ascending and descending, the whole-tone scale, and the major and minor scales. Treble and bass clefs are used. The computer plays each of the scales, then you have a chance to write them.

Rhythm: Learning to feel the beat

Mr. Metro Gnome introduces various notes. He sets tempo with his foot, plays a note or notes and asks you to play the rhythm on the space bar of the keyboard. A drawback is that notes are not sustained, giving a false sense of note lengths. You can then take a rhythm test or a written test.

Ear Training: Learning to hear

Melodies are written in both treble and bass clef. The melody is played for you with perhaps two pitches differing from what appears on the screen. The challenge is to determine which notes are not as represented and then to correct them using specified keys.

The remaining programs are similar.

Electronic Courseware Systems, Inc., 1210 Lancaster Drive, Champaign, IL 61821 (217–359–7099), has a number of music instruction programs for use with Apple, Commodore 64 and 128, Tandy 1000, 1200, and 3000, IBM PC, PC-Jr. and PS/2, and ATARI ST. A brief description of some of the programs follows. These programs are designed for young students grades K–8 who are beginning musicians. Several of the programs use a game format.

Tune-it by Fred Willman

Using a graphic representation of a stringed instrument fingerboard, this program gives students practice in matching pitches. Two pitches are played, with the second one sounding out of tune with the first. The student adjusts the second pitch until it matches the first. Pitch differences become finer as the level of difficulty progresses. Student scores are recorded.

Musical Stairs by Steve Walker

An aural-visual game designed to give the younger student practice in identifying intervals in bass or treble clef. Uses a graphic representation of a piano keyboard. Progressive levels of difficulty. Records students' scores.

Note Speller by Lolita Walker Gilkes

A drill and practice game designed to teach notes presented on the alto, treble, or bass staff. The user creates words, four to seven letters in length, by identifying notes on the staff. Four levels of difficulty. User chooses the clef. Scoring is based on speed and accuracy.

Ear Challenger by Chris Alix and Steve Walker

An aural-visual game designed to increase the player's ability to remember a series of pitches played by the computer. Seven levels of difficulty based on the number of pitches presented.

Super Challenger by Steve Walker

An aural-visual game designed to increase the player's ability to remember a series of pitches played by the computer. Uses a 12-note chromatic scale, an 8-note major scale, and an 8-note minor scale. Pitches are reinforced visually with a color representation of a keyboard.

Early Music Skills by Lolita Walker Gilkes

This program is a tutorial and drill program for the beginning music student. It covers four basic music reading skills—recognition of line and space notes, comprehension of the numbering system for the staff, visual and aural identification of notes moving up and down, and recognition of notes stepping and skipping up and down.

Elements of Music by John M. Eddins and Robert L. Weiss, Jr.

A three-disc set: 1) Note Names Drill, 2) Keyboard Note Drill, and 3) Key Signature Drill. May be purchased separately or complete.

An entry-level musical notation program for use by children or adults. Random drills, either timed or untimed, are provided for naming both major and minor key signatures and naming notes from a musical staff or keyboard. The complete set includes progress tests for each drill, and recordkeeping for the student and the teacher.

Tap-it by G. David Peters

A rhythm skills program teaching the concepts of beat and tempo through the presentation of rhythms and tapping drills. Students respond after either listening or reading rhythm patterns. Three skill levels with a quiz at the end of each level, plus a final quiz.

Music Flash Cards by Vincent Oddo

Important music material in a drill and practice format. Nine lessons, three diskettes. Disc 1: names of notes, rhythm values, and rhythm value equivalents. Disc 2: major scales, minor scales, modal scales, and key signatures. Disc 3: lessons on intervals and basic chords. Evaluation of student achievement displayed at the end of each lesson.

The Music Teacher's Assistant

We will close this coverage of computer music software with the listing of a program called *The Music Teacher's Assistant*. There are three parts to the series, but the most interesting to us is the *Orchestral String Teachers Assistant*. This program is a product of Swan Software, P.O. Box 3994, Eugene, OR 97403 (503–343–1893).

ORCHESTRAL STRING TEACHER'S ASSISTANT

The program is suitable for K–12. It runs on Apple IIc and IIe, Commodore 64 and 128, and IBM PC or compatibles.

This is a drill and practice program for note identification, string positions, and fingerings for violin, viola, cello, and bass. The student can choose from several levels of difficulty. The student also selects the instrument with which he or she wishes to work.

It should be kept in mind that the programs listed above do not, by any means, represent everything that is available. There are other companies and other programs. Established companies are constantly developing new programs, and new companies spring up each year and offer new programs. It should also be kept in mind that many of the programs listed, as well as many of those not listed, are not perfect. Drawbacks range from minor and forgivable to major and unacceptable. At the outset of this discussion of the computer as an aid to instruction, it was suggested that computer software is currently in its second generation. With each passing month, forward strides are made in computer technology. The same can be said for the software that drives them.

As computers become more common in the school setting, new and better programs will be developed to support them. Teachers will do well to be realistic about the capability of the computer to help children and students learn. They need to keep firmly in mind that the computers that are appropriate for school use are easy to use and so are the programs that have been and are being developed for them.

STUDY QUESTIONS

1. Describe the video disc and explain some of the advantages it has over videotape.
2. Is there very much string instruction material currently available on video disc?
3. List three prerequisites to showing a film or video in your string class.
4. If the same material is available on both film and videotape, name one factor that should be considered in making the choice.
5. Discuss ways in which you feel the video camera can be used to good advantage in the string program.
6. In what specific areas of instruction can the computer provide valuable assistance?
7. Is it necessary today to be a trained computer programmer in order to put the computer to use in the music program? Discuss.
8. List some of the additional hardware required for some programs.
9. Describe the Tap Master and the Pitch Master.
10. Describe three strong points of the computer as an instructional tool.

The School String Program

HISTORY OF INSTRUMENTAL MUSIC INSTRUCTION IN THE PUBLIC SCHOOLS

As stated in the section dealing with the history of the string instruments, exhaustive historical treatment is not the intent of this book. However, the students should have at least a minimal understanding of the relationship of the development of strings and the string program in the schools to those events in history that they use as guideposts. The following will provide that perspective.

Music in the Colonies

The early American colonists were too absorbed by the business of growing food and providing clothing and shelter to find time for the pleasures of music and art. Some groups actually opposed music, claiming it was sinful to indulge in the frivolous pastime of singing or playing an instrument. Only with the arrival of some of the wealthy aristocrats did music find a place in society.

Music in America at the Beginning of the 19th Century

At the end of the 18th and beginning of the 19th century, wars and revolutions in Europe caused many people to seek a better way of life in America. It was inevitable that musicians were among those who came to this country. As cities such as New York, Baltimore, Philadelphia, and Boston grew, cultural activities, including concerts, became an accepted part of the social structure.

The middle of the 19th century brought another influx of Europeans to America. A significant group was the Germania Society, a group of professional musicians. This group constituted a professional orchestra, which concertized in America for a period of six years. In 1854 it disbanded, its members settling in various cities about the country.

Thomas, Damrosch, Sousa

A man who was extremely influential in shaping the musical history of this country was Theodore Thomas (1835–1905). Thomas organized an orchestra with which he toured the principal cities. He brought good orchestra literature to the people and made a giant step in establishing a place for this kind of music in America. Thomas set the stage for the establishment of the Boston Symphony and the New York Symphony, the latter under the direction of Leopold and Walter Damrosch.

During this same period the concert band movement was making progress under the leadership of such conductors as Patrick Gilmore (1829–1892) and John Philip Sousa (1854–1932).

Music in the Public Schools

At the close of the 19th century, public school music consisted almost entirely of classroom singing. A prime objective was to teach children to read musical notation. But just before the end of the century a few high school orchestras were organized informally. Private instrumental study was becoming more commonplace, and a good many competent instrumentalists were being turned out by colleges and conservatories. These people often set up private studios, and, in turn, produced more instrumentalists. Players gravitated toward each other in schools and inevitably ensembles were formed. Formal instrumental instruction in the schools was slow to develop. But in the early 1900's a few dedicated and persevering musicians began to organize orchestras and instrumental programs in various schools.

It was in the period from 1900 to 1920 that instrumental music began to get a solid foothold in the public schools. Bands and orchestras were a part of the activity programs in many elementary schools and high schools. At first rehearsals were scheduled after regular school hours, but gradually these groups became an accepted part of the curriculum and their needs a part of the school budget.

The demand for formal preparation of teachers brought about appropriate courses in teacher training institutions. Class instruction in the schools became an accepted thing, and the public school instrumental music program was launched.

Subsequent development of school music programs has seen the development of highly structured regional and national contests, and the organization of state-wide and nation-wide bands, orchestras, and choral groups, many of these in conjunction with conferences of the Music Educators National Conference. Standards of instrumentation have been achieved, standards of excellence have risen to amazing heights, and the music program has become an accepted part of the curriculum.

In spite of widespread acceptance of music into the curriculum, when financial troubles occur, music is frequently one of the first subjects to be cut. Because of the important role music can play in fostering emotional health and personal well-being, in other words its therapeutic values, music may very well occupy an increasingly important position in our society in the future. True, it may not be music as we know it today. The sound source may be an oscillator instead of an orchestra; the composer may employ circuits instead of copy paper; and the listeners may push a button instead of purchasing tickets in order to select the kind of music they want at a given moment.

In the meantime, school programs demand well-prepared teachers who are expert in the orchestra, band, or choral fields. These teachers must have a thorough knowledge of literature, techniques of performance, and pedagogy, the ability to demonstrate, analyze, and inspire. They must be academician, musicologist, counselor, leader, press agent, concert manager, repairman, liason between school and public, idealist, and pragmatist.

The teacher who becomes absorbed in music will find teaching a most rewarding and gratifying experience; nothing can quite equal the thrill of hearing a group you have worked with for tedious hours play "over their heads," inspired by the strides they have made, and individually and collectively determined to do better than their best. Experiences like these keep music teachers going, each year trying to improve upon what was done the year before, searching for better ways of doing things, and never being quite satisfied with what has been achieved. The truly dedicated music teachers willingly and joyfully give of their time and energy far beyond the call of duty. The limits of the school day are inadequate for their purposes. They find themselves devoting time to students before and after school and in the evening, all of which increases the pleasure they derive from this role. Music teaching is not a job for a time-clock puncher. Teachers who think in terms of their jobs being finished when the last bell of the day has rung do a disservice to themselves and to music education.

HOW THE INSTRUMENTAL MUSIC TEACHER FUNCTIONS

In most school systems in the United States, instrumental music teachers who function in the elementary segment will be assigned to several schools. The number of schools to which they are assigned will depend upon the size of the schools involved, the number of students enrolled in the instrumental program in each school, the financial status of the school system, and the attitude that the administration and the community as a whole has toward the music program. School enrollment and the financial status of the school system can hardly be affected by the teacher (although the amount of money allotted to music can be), but the other factors can be influenced by the teacher.

Teacher enthusiasm and competence are far more important than buildings, equipment, and materials. There are many examples of thriving programs in small schools and in small communities that are the direct result of an enthusiastic, capable, and dedicated teacher. Such programs can be compared, to prove the point, with small, poorly run programs in schools whose size would justify a much larger program.

Teachers who move from one school to another are often referred to as traveling music teachers. In systems that have junior high schools or intermediate schools, the traveling music teacher is often assigned to the junior high school or intermediate school for a fixed number of periods each day and to elementary schools on a scheduled basis; i.e., two partial days at one elementary school, one partial day at another, to fill out the weekly schedule. A sample of a schedule for a traveling instrumental music teacher is shown on page 141.

In most systems senior high school music teachers are not assigned on a traveling basis, although exceptions to this practice do exist. The high school performance and activity schedule is generally full enough to keep the music teacher, or teachers, busy full time. A high school instrumental position is a demanding one, and dividing a teacher's time between two schools does not produce maximum efficiency in either.

Since many string teachers will be operating on a schedule like that described above, it is appropriate to point out some details of this kind of position that differ from the average teaching position, a knowledge of which may help the new teacher through the first year of teaching.

First of all the traveling teachers must realize that they are working for and are responsible to more than one person, namely, the principal of each school to which they are assigned. This is not always easy; each principal has the prerogative of determining how certain facets of the program will be handled in the school. The wise traveling teacher maintains an attitude of adjustability and adaptability and retains the philosophy that the ultimate objective is to establish the best possible program of instruction for children. The teacher's desire for uniformity and procedural consistency should be subjugated to the primary goal.

Teaching in more than one school poses problems in establishing rapport with teachers in the various buildings. The traveling teachers' schedules are sometimes so arranged that they are in and out of a school at times when teachers in the building are busy in their own classes. In a situation like this, it is possible for the traveling teachers to remain unknown for months unless they make a deliberate effort to make their presence known. A speaking acquaintance with the fourth, fifth, and sixth grade teachers is extremely important, and the traveling teachers must go out of their way to know them and become known to them. It is also strongly advisable to know the other instrumental music teachers who are a part of the same school program so that there can be a sincere atmosphere of cooperative interest in both orchestral and band instrument instruction.

The traveling teachers will do well to have a frank discussion with the principal at the beginning of the year about such matters as the reporting time to the school, leaving time, length of class lessons, method and time of reporting grades, handling of equipment, and programs for which they should plan. The teachers should realize that the purpose of this discussion with the principal is to arrive at a mutual understanding based upon the possible, and that the teachers' responsibilities to other schools must be taken into account when making plans for the year. The importance of a clear understanding on the points listed above cannot be stressed strongly enough, nor can the need for the teachers to carry out their side of the agreement be overstated. Good and fair administrators are much more prone to support and encourage a program when they know it is in the hands of a person they can depend upon than if they have to make adjustments because of a teacher's poor organization or lack of planning and follow-through.

Sample Schedule
Traveling Instrumental Music Teacher

		Monday	*Tuesday*	*Wednesday*	*Thursday*	*Friday*
A.M.	Jr. High	String Class Inter. Orch. Adv. Orch.	Same	Same	Same	Same
P.M.	Elem. Sch.	No. 1	No. 2	No. 3	No. 1	No. 2

RECRUITMENT FOR THE STRING PROGRAM

Generally speaking, in most parts of the country, and in most communities, bands have less difficulty recruiting and sustaining membership than do orchestras. Bands have shiny brass instruments, uniforms, parades, and other appealing activities to offer. And membership in a going, successful, accepted organization comes sooner for the brass, reed, and percussion player than it does for the string player.[1] But all of this has been said many times, and in far more detail than is necessary here. However, prospective teachers should be aware, at least, that if they plan to work with strings and orchestras, they are going to have to work harder at recruitment than their fellow band director.

When and Who

The recruitment program can be carried out in the last few weeks of the spring semester if this leads naturally into a summer program; otherwise it should begin in the first few weeks of the fall semester. The advantage of the spring timing is that the classroom teacher is thoroughly acquainted with and able to advise regarding pupil characteristics. The advantage to the fall timing is that everything is starting fresh after the summer vacation and interest in beginning a new activity comes more spontaneously.

Recruitment for the elementary string program should begin by the fourth grade, or the equivalent of the fourth grade in a nongraded school. If age is used as a criteria, nine is a reasonable age for most students to begin.[2] By this time children have adjusted to the school routine, are fairly well established in their study habits, are physically mature enough to meet the demands of a string instrument, and are intellectually and emotionally ready to assume the responsibility that the study of a string instrument imposes.

It must be recognized that all of the assumptions made in the preceding paragraph are generalizations, and that there can and will be exceptions to every one of them. There are the immature nine-year-olds who are not as ready as some seven-year-olds to take on the additional responsibility of the study of a string instrument. And there are those who are physically and intellectually mature enough, but who have emotional problems, which an additional task would not benefit. The converse to the latter is just as true, and many students with emotional problems have been helped by the achievement and satisfaction they have been able to realize from instrumental study.

All of this points up the need for the teacher to look carefully at each child who applies for admission to the string program. The teacher must assess the child's physical, mental, and emotional readiness for the program; and these factors should be discussed with the classroom teacher, principal, and parent.

What

DEMONSTRATION OF INSTRUMENTS

There are a number of things that can be done to stimulate the interest of children in the string program. Probably the best and most effective device is to play for them yourself—provided you are a proficient performer—or arrange performances by competent individual students, groups of students, or string players from the community. Caution should be practiced in this approach since a poor demonstration on an instrument, or a good demonstration by a person whose personality or manner might cause an unfavorable reaction among the children, can do more harm than good. By having some men or boys in your demonstration group, the psychological or status barrier that often exists between boys and string instruments can be dissolved. In any case, the demonstration should be short and of interest to the children.

USE OF FILMS, FILMSTRIPS, AND RECORDS

Second to the personal demonstration in effectiveness is the demonstration through the media of film or filmstrip and recording, several of which are available from producers of audio-visual materials. In the use of this technique, additional advantage can be achieved by having string instruments in the room to show to the children. Permitting the children to examine and touch the instruments increases their curiosity and interest.

PARENT MEETINGS

In some communities it is possible to arrange an evening meeting of parents and their children at which one of the local music dealers has a display of instruments. If the school does not own instruments, this may be a useful approach. A meeting such as this can be used to discuss the merits of the string program, point out the long-range advantages of learning to play a string instrument, make clear what will be expected of a child who enters the program, and explain the need for parental interest and support of a child who undertakes the study of an instrument.

The music dealer can discuss and display the various grades and qualities of instruments for sale and rent. Financial arrangements and questions regarding these arrangements can be explained. Teachers should avoid becoming involved in the financial phase of this procedure unless it is obvious that their professional judgment is needed to prevent a mistake or a poor decision.

---

[1]See "Strolling Strings" later in this chapter.

[2]Some successful experiments are going on in the lower grades using a Suzuki approach. This may be the wave of the future if success continues and acceptance is favorable.

MUSIC APTITUDE TESTS

Another device that can aid in recruiting students is the music aptitude test. This may sound like an odd claim when one considers that the basic purpose of the aptitude test is to assess native musical talent. However, the salutary effect of a good test score on both student and parent is well known, and several satisfactory tests are available. These tests are easy to administer and can be completed in a relatively short amount of time. A list of a few of these tests and their sources follows:

Name of Test	*Source*
Conn Music Aptitude Test Manual[3]	Conn P.O. Box 727 Elkhart, IN 46515
Farnum Music Test	Lyons Music Products P.O. Box 1003 Elkhart, IN 46515 219–294–6602
Leblanc–Musical Talent Quiz	Leblanc Educational Publications G. Leblanc Corporation 7019 Thirtieth Avenue Kenosha, WI 53141
Music Aptitude Test by Edwin Gordon	The Riverside Publishing Co. 8420 Bryn Mawr Avenue Chicago, IL 60631 800–323–9540

The Conn Music Aptitude Test. For grades 4–12. Estimated testing time 20–30 minutes. Comes with manual, test cards, and grading masks.

Farnum Music Test by Dr. Stephen Farnum. For grades 4–12. Testing time 40–45 minutes. Contains 4 subtests: Music Symbols, Notation, Tonal Patterns, Cadences. Package includes 16-page manual for instructions in using the test; scoring; a 12″ LP record with sample exercises, instructions and the test items; answer sheets for hand scoring (sold separately); and correction keys.

Leblanc–Musical Talent Quiz. Edited by E. C. Moore. Estimated testing time 30–40 minutes. Tests in six areas: Rhythm Patterns, Melody Retention, Interval Recognition, Chord Retention, Pitch Recognition, Chord Recognition. The teacher administers the rhythm test by tapping or clapping, and plays the remaining examples on the piano.

Music Aptitude Test by Edwin Gordon. For grades 4–12. Testing time 110 minutes. Contains seven subtests in three categories: Test T—Tonal Imagery, Melody, Harmony; Test R—Rhythm Imagery, Tempo, Meter; Test S—Musical Sensitivity, Phrasing, Balance, Style. Professional artists play 250 original short selections. The Complete Musical Aptitude Profile, with all materials for testing 100 students, consists of 3 cassette tapes, 1 manual with complete directions, information on scoring and using test results, and technical data; 100 MRC answer sheets; scoring masks; 100 record file folders; 100 musical talent profiles for students and parents; and two class record sheets. This is a more detailed, longer, more complete test than the other three.

These tests can be administered to an entire class, or to several classes, at one time. Children who do well on the test can be encouraged to begin an instrument, and their test score can be a persuasive argument with reluctant or neutral parents. The test can serve the additional purpose of indicating basic strengths and weaknesses in the child's musical makeup, thus making it possible for the teacher to give special attention to these areas in the student's lessons.

Selecting the Instrument to Fit the Child

The availability of 1/2, 3/4, and 4/4 size violins and cellos, small size violas, and 1/2 size basses makes feasible an earlier start for many children than would be possible if these small size instruments did not exist. These fractional-size, or junior-size instruments are exactly like their larger counterparts in every way, although the quality as well as the quantity of the tone they produce may, in some cases, leave something to be desired. To minimize this drawback, every effort should be made to acquire well-made small size instruments that meet minimum specifications. Acquisition should be from a firm whose reputation is reliable. Equip these small instruments properly with a well-cut bridge and strings of the correct length.

The small instruments are stepping stones. They are made to accommodate small hands and short arms, and they make it possible for the young children to begin instruction at a time when they are physically and mentally most adaptable and psychologically most eager to begin. The following chart gives the sizes of the various instruments most often needed to fit children at the grade levels indicated. These sizes are based upon children of average height. There will, of course, be exceptions in the case of unusually small and unusually large children.

The size of a child's hands, arms, and overall proportions are important factors to consider in choosing among the string instruments. The large, big-boned child is a better prospect for the bass than for the violin. The small, delicately proportioned child should be steered to the violin. Children of medium build can generally adapt to any of the instruments.

TABLE 13.1[4]

Recommended String Instrument Sizes
for Upper Grade Levels

	Grade 4	*Grade 5*	*Grade 6*	*Grades 7–9*
Violin	1/2, 3/4	1/2, 3/4, 4/4	3/4, 4/4	3/4, 4/4
Viola*	13 1/4″, 14″	13 1/4″, 14″	14″, 15″	14″, 15″ +
Cello	1/2, 3/4	1/2, 3/4	3/4, 4/4	3/4, 4/4
Bass	1/2	1/2	1/2	1/2, 3/4

*The 13 1/4-inch viola is referred to as the junior size. The 14-inch viola is referred to as the intermediate size. Some schools do not own these small violas. In such cases it is possible to string up a 3/4 violin, viola-style (C-G-D-A) as a substitute.

---

3. Test cards and grading mask are also available, in addition to a large assortment of materials dealing with music education.

4. For the lower grades use 1/8 and 1/4 violins, the smallest violas, 1/4 cellos, and 1/4 basses.

Need to Promote Cello, Bass, and Viola

One important aspect of the demonstration not mentioned before should be pointed out here. That is the need to promote each of the strings—violin, viola, cello, and bass—equally. Too often the only instrument that gets a real show is the violin. As a result, violin classes evolve rather than string classes, and the full potential of the strings cannot be realized. The teacher who has responsibility for developing and maintaining an orchestra at a higher segment level will keep in mind the need to foster interest in *all* members of the string family.

There is no magic formula that produces a beginning string class of just the right number of violins, violas, cellos, and basses. In fact, getting any student to show an interest in the cello or bass may be one of those "hardest of all jobs" for the teacher. It may very well call for salesmanship and horse trading. An assisting and controlling factor may be the number and kind of instruments owned by the school. Some districts purchase only basses and cellos on the assumption that parents will provide violins. Another practice is for the school to supply the small size violins and cellos as well as basses, on the assumption that parents will provide the full-sized instrument when the proper time comes.

The initial opportunity to stimulate interest in the larger string instruments is in the demonstration. It is important, therefore, that the bass and cello be demonstrated as effectively as the violin and viola. The need to develop an interest in the lower strings is stressed here because a balanced instrumentation in the secondary program is completely dependent upon the achievement of a representative instrumentation in the beginning program. Remedial action can be taken, of course, such as bringing in a pianist to play bass or persuading a sousaphone player to double on string bass. But these measures are usually makeshift at best, and the need for resorting to them can be avoided by careful planning and the diligent use of persuasive techniques in the lower segment program.

A clinching argument in favor of the bass—to the practical-minded parent whose thinking takes in this dimension—is that the bass is the first of the string instruments to become a money-earner. With a good ear, the ability to keep a steady beat, and a reasonable amount of practice, the bass player can handle jobs in combos and dance bands by senior high school.

The viola probably falls into the "least wanted" category more often than not. In communities that do not benefit from contact with a metropolitan area's cultural resources, and even in some that do, there may be widespread ignorance about this member of the string family. People cannot be expected to want something they know nothing about; it follows that the viola falls into sad neglect. Another reason contributing to this neglect of the viola is the relatively unspectacular role it plays in the orchestra. It is like the second violins: not apparent until missing. This lack of built-in salability creates the need for the teacher to point out the advantages and attractive qualities of this instrument—that it has a deep, mellow tone quality; that it does not have the shrillness sometimes associated with the violin; that its music is generally somewhat less demanding than that of the violin; and that since fewer people take up the viola, there is less competition and more opportunity to excel on it than on its more popular cousin, the violin.

CLASS ORGANIZATION

String instruments can be grouped in two ways for class instruction: like instruments (homogeneous) or unlike instruments (heterogeneous). Arguments can be made in favor of each of these kinds of grouping, for each has its merits. However, it is not always a question of which is best as much as what is possible. An insufficient number of a given instrument to meet an administratively set class minimum may require the addition of other instruments even though the instructor feels that a homogeneous grouping would be preferable. These two methods of grouping are discussed below.

Homogeneous Grouping

At the beginning stages of instruction homogeneous grouping is desirable for the following reasons:

With just one kind of instrument to deal with, the teacher needs to be conscious of only one set of problems.

Small children will find less to distract them if all the instruments in the class are the same kind.

Children will learn more readily by example if they have only one example to follow.

With only one kind of instrument in the class, everything the instructor does and says, and everything that takes place in the class is pertinent to each child.

Mixed instrument grouping will inevitably result in some lost time for some students while the teacher is giving attention elsewhere. Furthermore, there are few method books that are written in such a way that all instruments receive equally effective treatment at all times.

Heterogeneous Grouping

As students achieve sufficient competence and maturity, heterogeneous grouping becomes not only feasible but desirable. The reasons are:

Heterogeneous grouping relieves the monotony of a single tonal quality and limited range of pitch, which are qualities of like grouping.

There is much more music available for a mixed group than there is for a like group.

In a mixed group bonafide four-part harmony is possible. The addition of harmony to the string sound brings about a new level of interest for the student.

In a heterogeneous group students will begin to listen to other instruments analytically. They begin to hear themselves in proper perspective in the tonal spectrum and in the relationship they will ultimately assume in the string orchestra.

The greater sonority of the full string section and the fullness of harmony which it is capable of producing will stimulate the development of a fuller tone. At the same time the students will begin to be aware of the need for balance among the instruments. They will begin to know when to subdue and when to predominate, and what they must do to achieve these two results.

OPTIMUM CLASS SIZE

An ideal beginning string class should not exceed six to eight students. More than this number makes it difficult for the teacher to give individual attention, which is so necessary during the beginning stages. With more than eight in the class the tuning process absorbs a disproportionate amount of instructional time, and the general progress of the class will be slowed down because of the teacher's inability to get around to each student and to handle all of the details and problems that need to be taken care of.

PHYSICAL ARRANGEMENTS

The Rehearsal Room

Much has been written about the design and arrangement of orchestra and band rehearsal rooms. The reader is referred to the *MENC* publication, *Music Buildings, Rooms, and Equipment,* a book containing a good deal of practical information on the subject. Junior high schools and senior high schools usually are built with special rooms for instrumental and choral music classes. This is rarely done in elementary school construction, since the instrumental teacher is seldom scheduled in an elementary school more than three days a week, and in most cases less frequently than that. As a result, instrumental music classes are superimposed upon the regular daily classroom schedule, and students who take instrumental music are taken from their regular classroom to report to the multipurpose room, stage, or an available classroom designated for instrumental instruction.

Planned rehearsal rooms should receive attention in the following areas:

Lighting
There should be a minimum of 100 foot-candles distributed evenly over the seating area including the teacher's station.

Acoustics
A reverberation time of 1 second per 24,000 cubic feet is recommended for orchestra.

Ventilation
The contemporary trend is the windowless rehearsal room. The argument is that a closed room minimizes both in- and out-transfer of sounds. The problem lies in the failure of architects to understand that a rehearsal room is not like an office building or the administrative wing of the school, or an ordinary classroom, all of which contain normal amounts of activity. The rehearsal room houses an activity in which the students develop an abnormally high quantity of BTU's. Whether bowing or blowing, they put out a great deal of energy. To keep the room fresh requires a larger than normal air exchange system.

Arrangement of Stands and Chairs

The way stands and chairs are arranged in the room, or on the stage, will depend upon the size and shape of the room, the number of students in the class, and what instruments

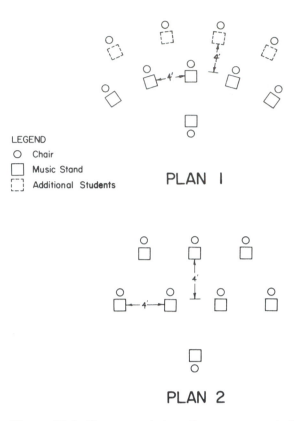

LEGEND
○ Chair
▢ Music Stand
⬚ Additional Students

PLAN 1

PLAN 2

Figure 13.1. Recommended seating arrangements for string classes.

they play. Regardless of these factors, however, there are three conditions that should be achieved in the physical setup.

1. Each student must have sufficient room to bow without the threat of hitting another student's music stand, instrument, or bow.
2. The teacher must have a clear and unobstructed view of each student in the class.
3. The teacher must have free access to each student in the class without having to wind through the music stands, bows, cellos, or chairs.

Practically, this means that each student must have his or her own music and stand, opposed to having two students reading from a single piece of music. Physical arrangements like those discussed above and shown below are necessary for beginning classes so that the teacher may quickly get to any pupil in the class to adjust the position of the instrument, bow, or fingers, or to point out something in the music. The need for this kind of help from the teacher decreases as the students become more proficient. Two possible seating arrangements are shown above. Places for the recommended number of students are shown with solid lines. Places for additional students are shown with dotted lines. Some teachers may prefer to have all students in a single line when the size of the class and the room make that possible.

A Place for Music Cases and Books

If the room has been specifically designed as an instrumental rehearsal room, provision should have been made for storage of instruments and music, with shelves upon which instrument cases and books may be placed while rehearsals are going on. Without these built-in facilities, movable storage cabinets can be substituted, and chairs or tables may serve as a place to put cases and books. Without the benefit of a planned place for cases and books, the teacher will find that these items are put in the only place remaining for them—the floor, and more often than not on the floor next to the chair the student occupies. This results in a disorganized classroom, which is messy to contemplate and dangerous to navigate.

If permanent instrument storage cabinets are supplied, the floor of each compartment should be covered with a rubber matting or a short-nap carpeting. Without this seeming luxury, case hinges will be damaged. If the cabinets are constructed of metal, the metal to metal abrasion will damage both the case and the cabinet. If the cabinets are constructed of wood, the metal hinges on the cases will soon make splinters of the front lip of the compartment floor at the same time that the instrument case and its hinges are damaged.

Straight Chairs for Cellists

A string rehearsal room must be equipped with straight chairs with flat seats for the cello players. Cellists must sit on the front edge of their chair to play; they cannot comfortably maintain good playing posture on a chair with a sloping seat. It was pointed out earlier that in the elementary segment, chairs of varying heights should be available so that the small, short-legged children can touch their feet on the floor. (See Figure 3.39.)

Cello and Bass End Pin Holders

An end pin holder of some kind is a necessity for each cellist and bassist. Without the benefit of a holding device, cellists and bassists will have a constant problem keeping their instrument in the correct position, and they may become discouraged because of the frustrations that they feel and the insecurity that the situation causes them. (See Figures 3.32 and 3.34.)

BEGINNING STEPS

The nine-year-olds who have passed the music aptitude test, who have shown a desire to start lessons on a string instrument, whose parents have indicated willingness for them to enter the program, enter the room for the first lesson with interest, eagerness, and aspiration. Frankly, their chief desire is to get their hands on an instrument and begin drawing the bow across the strings.

At this point the teacher's forebearance and sense of perspective are put to a critical test. The pupils' eagerness to make sounds on the instrument must not be summarily dampened. But still a sense of respect for the instrument, for the teacher, and for fellow students, and a realization of the standards of behavior expected of them in the class must be conveyed quickly and clearly.

Most children respond positively to reasonable sets of controls, particularly when the reasons for the controls are apparent to them. Stepping into a new situation such as the instrumental rehearsal room, they will quickly respond to the standards that are set for them. The teacher should explain that string instruments and bows are fragile, that there are certain ways in which they are to be treated and handled, and that anyone who is unable to conform to the rules of the class will have proved that they are not yet ready to assume the responsibility that membership in the string class imposes.

At this point no detail is too trivial or insignificant to cover. Following is a list of some of the procedures and precautions that should be conveyed to the pupils at the first lesson.

How to take the instrument and bow from the case.
How to tighten the bow, and how much.
How to rosin the bow.
How to affix the shoulder pad.
The importance of always returning the instrument and bow to the case and securing the case after each practice session.
The importance of keeping the instrument out of the reach of smaller brothers and sisters.
It goes without saying that as much time as possible should be devoted to how to hold the instrument and bow.

Elementary children respond more favorably to specific assignments tailored to their attention span than they do to general suggestions. At the outset, lessons assigned should be short. Four to six lines of music is ample. They should be encouraged to practice for about ten minutes twice a day, giving careful attention to the way in which they hold the instrument and the bow.

In some elementary schools, a very effective beginning string program has been realized by having the young string students report for string class every day for fifteen minutes on a rotating schedule for the first six weeks of study. The instruments remain in the instrumental room, where they are tuned before class. This kind of arrangement provides daily supervision by the teacher and can successfully eliminate many of the problems that occur with the prevalent weekly instruction schedule.

The amount and kind of material assigned will depend upon the approach used in the class. If a rote approach is used, perhaps the equivalent of only one line of music will be assigned. The background of the children and the kind of music program they have had in the classroom must also be considered.

Most recent string class methods have been prepared with an aim to presenting material that will immediately interest the young pupil. Piano accompaniments are often supplied for open string exercises, and as soon as possible, simple tunes are introduced.

Motivation is extremely important. The teacher must give some attention and praise to each student and keep the class, as a whole, progressing at an acceptable rate. The string group needs opportunities to perform for peers, parents, and teachers. Seasonal programs provide an ideal opportunity for the group to appear.

C and D Approaches

At this point something should be said about the two key approaches used in string method books. They are the C approach and the D approach. The C approach requires the young violinist to adjust the hand to three different settings. On the G string the half-step falls between the 2nd and 3rd fingers.

On the D and A strings the half-step falls between the 1st and 2nd fingers.

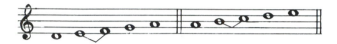

And on the E string the first finger must be extended backward to reach the F natural.

Comparable adjustments must be made on the other instruments.

The constant resetting of the finger position is considered by many to be too taxing for the beginning string students considering that they are having to think about how they are holding the instrument and the bow, how they are drawing the bow, and what notes they are supposed to be playing. With a bright student and plenty of individual attention, the added problems inherent in this approach can be overcome.

As school instruction in the strings became more prevalent, teachers searched for ways to reduce methods to the simplest terms, to produce results faster, and to bring the realization of accomplishment to the student at an earlier point in his study. One result of this search was the so-called D major approach. Literally, this method starts the students in the key of D major when they begin using fingers. First lessons are on the A string, then the D, then the G, where the key is changed to G. When the time comes to move to the E string, the key of A is introduced. This procedure makes the finger setting the same on all four strings, the half step coming between the 2nd and 3rd finger in each case. This is the only finger pattern used for an extended period of time.

This approach has its proponents and opponents. The advantages have been pointed out. The disadvantage is that the students do not learn to adjust the fingers to different settings early enough. "They do not know the fingers can go any other way" is a complaint often expressed. This method also delays putting the strings together with the winds.

SOME IDEAS FOR BUILDING AND SUSTAINING INTEREST IN THE STRING PROGRAM

It is not enough today just to be a good teacher, even though you know and love music and love to teach. There are simply too many things competing for the student's attention. To mention some of the more obvious there are television, sports, homework, jobs, and career preparation.

In the face of this competition, you can be the finest teacher in the world only to find that you are not attracting and holding students. You are not building the kind of program you want. And you may begin to wonder if the problem is in your teaching. You may begin to think that you are missing some important quality necessary for success in instrumental music education.

That may not be the problem. You may be a very good teacher, keeping current on pedagogy and materials, giving a full amount of energy to your teaching, and loving what you are doing. But perhaps you have not come to realize that there are many things in competition for the students' time and attention, and, like it or not, the music teacher, to succeed, must become a competitor in that arena, imbuing teaching with something more than enthusiasm for the subject.

This new essential ingredient is called *selling your program.* And it may have to permeate every facet of your professional activities and be always present in your thinking and teaching. You may have to revise some of your ideas and approaches and adopt some new techniques and new sets of values.

For some of you this may not be difficult. You may possess innate qualities of salesmanship and may routinely sell your program, in which case we are talking about manner and degree—how, how much, how well. To others this whole idea may be anathema.

Some ideas follow, some of which have been touched upon before, that, if used properly, could help to make a string program more attractive to students and possibly gain support for and strengthen the program. These suggestions are based upon the assumption that you are or are becoming a well-trained and well-qualified teacher. You know the strings well enough to feel comfortable teaching them. You have given a lot of thought to the matter of teaching strings to the age groups you will work with. You have examined a great deal of teaching material and continue to do this regularly, and are qualified to select materials that meet the criteria you have established. If you feel inadequate in any of the areas just mentioned, you need to do whatever you can to remove those inadequacies. For competence and preparedness are essential ingredients to success.

Recruiting Techniques

TESTING[5]

Most teachers who use them will admit that an aptitude test given to all fourth grade students is as much an interest-building tool as it is a talent-discovery tool. But this does not in any sense discredit the use of aptitude tests. If you are not able to find an appropriate test, design one of your own. Pitch

5. See additional remarks about testing on page 142.

recognition and discrimination should be the main things to test. When you have identified the children with the best ears, you may want to check with the classroom teacher to see how they are doing generally—scholastically and socially. But a word of caution—if a child is eager to learn, do not keep him out of the program because of a poor test score. Tests can be wrong.

SONG FLUTE

Another approach is to teach the entire third or fourth grade class the song flute. Ability will show up, and also some note-learning and rhythm-learning will take place. This is an excellent way to discover students with musical ability and an interest in learning.

INSTRUMENT DEMONSTRATIONS[6]

Play or have the instruments played for the children. Get advanced students or friends to perform. Do this during the day for full classes or at night when the parents can be there. If you make a night presentation, try to have an instrument dealer there with instruments to talk about rental or sales. If you cannot have actual instrument demonstrations, use recordings and/or films.

At meetings with parents, such as this, it is important to build a good case for playing a string instrument. For instance, you can explain that

1. A string instrument can eventually be the most beautiful of all the instruments.
2. A string instrument can be played for a lifetime. It is a healthy activity.
3. Playing a string instrument provides a good social entree now and later. Participation in school orchestra can be great fun. It can lead to a sense of pride and accomplishment and can be a source of good and lasting friendships. Later on in life it can do the same thing.
4. While it may not become the major source of income for many, for those who have the ability and decide to become professionals, it can be a means to make a respectable living. Members of orchestras such as the New York Philharmonic, the Boston Symphony, the Philadelphia Orchestra, the Cleveland Orchestra, and others make a comfortable annual salary, and there is prestige connected with playing in one of these orchestras.

SUZUKI APPROACH[7]

Another approach that some teachers have used is a modified Suzuki concept. Start the entire class on violin, using some of the Suzuki teaching techniques or devise your own. At some point in time this will stop. At that point try to persuade the better students to continue.

ADDITIONAL SOURCES OF INFORMATION ON RECRUITING

The new teacher can get help and ideas on recruiting from a number of sources, not the least of which is his or her own intuitive and acquired principles of dealing with people and the desire to promote what he or she fervently believes in. Another valuable source will be successful teachers whose

programs have endured over time in size and quality. Recently a very practical guide to recruiting was produced by the Music Achievement Council and funded by the National Association of Music Merchants. The 25-page pamphlet is titled *A Recruiting Guide for Band and Orchestra Directors* and is available at a modest cost from: Music Achievement Council, 5140 Avenida Encinas, Carlsbad, CA 92008. The guide offers general advice on recruiting and retention of students and specific, programmed steps for the teacher to take to achieve the desired results. Many of the ideas suggested in the preceding paragraphs on recruitment will be found in this *Guide* plus many others, including sample letters to parents and a Director's Recruiting Checklist.

Parental Interest and Support

We all know that parental interest and support of their child in the music program is worth a great deal. We also know that you are lucky to get one out of two parents to take an active interest. But even that is worth working hard for. However, you will need to devise ways to do this. Here are some ways:

1. Practice records: This is an easy form to devise. Basically, it should indicate the name of the child, the instrument played, and how much daily practice is expected. There should be a statement regarding the importance of daily practice, what is good practice and what is bad, conditions that enhance practice, a request that the parents support the children in their efforts, a place for a daily record of practice done, and a place for the parent to sign vouching for the amount of practice done. An example of a weekly practice record is shown on the following page. It is an easy matter to convert this form to cover a month or even a longer period of time.

The practice record is good in elementary school but is of dubious value after that as students start to feel "grown up" and resentful of too much parent involvement.

Some teachers still use the gold star, red star, blue star system of reward for a good, fair, or poor lesson. The stars are only symbols, but they are visible symbols that represent the child's accomplishment. A "happy face" sticker or stamp can also be used to indicate a job well done.

2. Notes to Parents: It is very satisfying to you, the teacher, to see children make progress. When they do, you should let them know that you are pleased. In fact, singling out before the whole class for special recognition those students who have made special progress can do much to make them feel good about what they have done and can stimulate other members of the class to work harder. But don't forget the parents. You have to assume that they will be as pleased as you are with their child's accomplishments. A phone call or a note is an easy, but a very nice gesture, and can pay big dividends.

You don't need to keep a constant flow of paper going. But your informal communication should be at least as often as report cards, and for better results, more often.

You could develop a form that has items you can check to provide the information you wish to convey. But better yet is a brief, personal note stating what the child is doing especially well and what needs extra work.

---

6. See page 141 for more on this topic.
7. See pages 121–122 for a discussion of the Suzuki method.

Scarsdale Elementary School
Instrumental Music Practice Record

| Student's Name | Instrument |

Minutes Practiced:

| Monday | Tuesday | Wednesday | Thursday | Friday | Saturday |

Parent's Signature

OVER

Reverse Side

Regular and careful practice is the key to progress on a musical instrument. We recommend 15 minutes each day at the beginning, increasing to at least 30 minutes. A quiet place where your child will not be disturbed is the best place for practice. Positive, cheerful support of your child's efforts will do much to build his or her interest and confidence.

3. Certainly urge parents to attend performances that are for the public. Most parents take great delight in seeing their children perform. These occasions provide a great opportunity to invite grandparents, aunts, and uncles.

Materials for Study and Performance

Next to teaching ability, the selection of teaching materials is probably the most important thing you will do to determine the success or failure of your program. Select materials that the students can grasp, that they can play, understand, and enjoy. This does not mean programs made up exclusively of show tunes and television themes.

There is plenty of good music at all levels of difficulty. The nearest music store that handles printed music is the place to start. If there is not such a store in your town or city, locate the nearest one and establish a good working relationship so that you can take out music or scores on approval, and get quick service when it is needed. (There is nothing more frustrating than waiting for a piece of music that arrives too late for it to go into preparation for a program as planned.) If your situation is so unique that nothing satisfactory can be found to suit your needs, then write or arrange something yourself, even to the extent of designing parts specifically to meet the ability of each student.

It seems almost too obvious to mention, but other, more experienced teachers can be a very valuable source of information about materials. Also, attend as many programs as you can so that you can hear firsthand music that other teachers are using. Try always to use good taste and good judgment and do not fall in with each fad that comes along. The music you select should be of good quality, should have some worth, and you should be able to give acceptable reasons for having chosen it.

Have a variety of music in the folder: tuneful things, rhythmical things, familiar things, unfamiliar things, cute and catchy things, things that are fairly easy and can be learned and played with a minimum of effort, and things that make the students work, think, and try.

Do not limit yourself (in elementary school) to the keys of G and D for the first two years. While this practice will surely develop proficiency in these keys, it will come as a shock to the child when he finds that in some music the half step is between the first and second fingers instead of always between the second and third.

Also, of course, much beginning music for full orchestra is in flat keys to make things easier for the winds. So, after completing Book I, or after a year of instruction, whichever comes first, begin to sneak in a line or two in C or F. Or transpose a piece the students know into another key. This procedure has several advantages. It teaches students that a piece can start on different notes, and that with minor adjustments it will sound the same. It also teaches them to think, to use their ears, and make adjustments in the finger setting patterns. It also gives you a chance to stress again and again and again the importance of the half step—a real half step.

Do not neglect scales. When students at the University of Southern California auditioned for lessons with Heifetz, they naturally prepared the concerto or piece that showed them off to best advantage. After listening to them display their most brilliant playing, Heifetz stopped them and said, "Now lets hear some scales."

If one of the greatest violinists of our time insists that his students exhibit competence in scale playing, there must be something to it. Scales train the mind, the ear, and the fingers. But, of course, they must be played with care and attention. Simply going through the motions in a routine fashion, with no concern for right notes and correct intonation, is a waste of time and energy. This can be said about practice in general.

Start scale work early, and to keep scales from becoming a bore, use different bowings and rhythms. Repeated notes and slurs are excellent for the bow, as are dotted rhythms. Scales are a good way to introduce staccato, martelé, slurs, and later spiccato.

Nearly every method book has an assortment of finger and bow exercises. Select those that you feel are best and use them in each class session or lesson. Again, for maximum benefit vary the key and speed. For each exercise explain its purpose so the children understand why they are doing the exercise. Also, keep reminding them so that they do not fall into mindless repetition. Above all, constantly insist on good intonation. Even the children with the best ears need to develop the ability to discern the most minute pitch discrepencies, and this is doubly hard in a group where pitch is ignored by some and goes unrecognized by others.

Perform for Peers and Parents

There is nothing more stimulating than performance. And most children love to perform. As teachers, your job is to direct this nearly universal and innate trait into channels that will be satisfying, productive, and completely viable from an educational point of view. The teacher must have a good attitude about performance and be able to convey that attitude to the students. While the children are young and cute, their natural cuteness should be left alone. They should be permitted to be themselves, unless their behavior is excessive in some way and might cause embarrassment to themselves and others. As they grow older and become more mature, they need to assume some of the dignity and behavior norms that are expected of their age group.

Performance should be a normal outgrowth of the instructional program. Preparation for a performance should be unhurried and unworried—without pressure and without fear. Performance should be carefully planned for, with each student being urged to maximum achievement.

It is up to the teacher to set a tone of controlled excitement in building toward a performance. The children should look forward to playing, and the teacher should help them to feel good about what they are doing.

How you deal with the children after the performance is just as important as building the right attitude and level of preparation beforehand. Nervous, shy children must be handled gently. If they did not perform very well, they still must be encouraged for what they did do well. The cocky, self-assured ones sometimes have to be made to feel a little modesty. You must learn to know each child and deal with each one in what you perceive as the best possible way.

Uniforms

We string teachers often cite the band's uniform as one of the reasons some students select a band instrument instead of a string instrument. There is probably some validity to this claim. Children and young people like to dress up, and putting on a uniform satisfies that desire. A uniform adds a certain glamor to an organization.

There is no reason for an orchestra not to have a uniform, too. Even at the elementary level you can probably find an inexpensive, distinguishing sweater that parents would be willing to buy. Or convince the PTA that providing a uniform for the orchestra would be a good project for them. Or get an orchestra parents club going and let them take on the project.

In junior high school the uniform needs to be a bit more elaborate, such as a jacket with pants or skirt. If the school has spent money on band uniforms, there is no reason for it not to spend some on the orchestra.

Awards

Awards and recognition for achievement are also important. This does not refer just to the end of semester grade and the occasional "pat on the back," although those are important. Rather, reference is made to tangible, physical symbols—certificates, medals, trophies, and emblems. These are things that students can see, feel, wear, and display. Awards can help instill a sense of pride and accomplishment, qualities that are very important when a decision is being made whether or not to continue in a program and/or with lessons. A letter, a pin, or a sweater are often highly treasured possessions which for many years after they were awarded evoke strong feelings of pride and loyalty.

STROLLING STRINGS

One answer to the problem of attaining more visibility for strings and making the string program more appealing to students is a relatively new concept, strolling strings. The idea is exactly what the name implies: your players stroll. But there is more to it than just strolling. To make it work requires some re-thinking of traditional ways of doing things. But the end result could very well be worth the effort.

Among professional string players, the idea of strolling is nothing new. Many small professional string groups have used the strolling technique to advantage for years. What separates this kind of "performance" from the traditional seated performance is the relaxed atmosphere that it creates, the personal contact that it establishes between the musician and his "audience." In fact, one could say that the audience becomes individuals with whom the players develop a personal (even if it may be fleeting) relationship.

It was Mr. James "Red" McLeod who, after many years of arranging for a professional strolling strings group, saw the potential of the Strolling Strings idea for string programs in the schools. The first need was, of course, for suitable arrangements. The music had to be appealing to students and their "audiences," within the student's ability to play well, and not too long or involved to be memorized relatively easily, since memorization is one of the key precepts of the Strolling Strings idea. Mr. McLeod proceeded to arrange a number of appealing musical selections that met these criteria which he assembled into programs. Published by Neil A. Kjos Music Company, there are now two complete Strolling Strings programs available: "A Musical Buffet of All-Time Favorites," and "A Night in Vienna." Each program is about 25–30 minutes in length. Preceding the musical selections are ten "Strollogisms" (a kind of Ten Commandments for the stroller). Then follow a suitable show opener and a collection of nicely arranged and appealing musical selections. In addition there are presently available two separate selections called "ShowStoppers." They are "Salute to Freedom," a medley of patriotic tunes and "Themes from *The Nut-cracker*," a medley of three parts of that famous ballet by Tchaikovsky. Either one of these can be inserted into one of the previously named programs or used independently.

To supplement the two Strolling Strings collections, Kjos has published *Strolling Strings, An Introduction*, an eight-page overview of the program. In addition, they have available a videotape that shows Strolling Strings groups in action along with helpful comments by several string teachers who have developed successful Strolling Strings programs.

A few quotes from *Strolling Strings, An Introduction* will help to answer some questions about this program and provide a better understanding of it.

As long as you have a pianist, bassist, and at least one violinist, you have a strolling group! Of course, the more strollers, the merrier.

Not only is Strolling Strings versatile from an instrumentation perspective, it is suitable at any secondary level of instruction. Simple coordination is all that is required for strolling, along with a fundamental familiarity with each instrument's basic positions. Of course, walking while playing initially presents a challenge to any instrumentalist; but with a little practice, strolling literally becomes second nature to violinists, violists, and even cellists. . . . After building endurance, a cellist can stroll with ease by positioning the C-peg so that the angle of the peg allows the instrument to rest comfortably on the nape of his or her neck.

The essential rhythmic drive and harmonic foundation are provided by the pianist and bassists anchored on stage. Countermelodies and obligatos, the icing on the cake, are played only by strollers clustered around melody players. . . . The art of strolling necessarily involves mobility, and the positioning of the musicians throughout the room. Such a dispersion consequently develops a highly trained ear and a keen awareness of intonation and sectional unity. These skills are crucial to symphonic playing at the high school level and beyond. Moreover, the logistics of strolling require that each musician memorize his or her music. Constructive memorization techniques (not merely mastering by rote) emphasize the students' learning their particular part within the context of the piece as a whole. Many students will begin to sense that musicianship is an art, not simply the mechanical execution of notes and rhythms. Music becomes a form of communication. Strolling Strings builds confidence and self-esteem by making all of your players soloists. [There are no "last" chairs in Strolling Strings groups.][8]

Most Strolling Strings groups adopt some kind of distinguishing uniform. It may range from something as simple as all-white clothes with a red sash to something resembling a tuxedo or tails. Budget limitations, the socioeconomic makeup of the school, and simply a question of taste can influence the decision about what is appropriate. An enterprising teacher will find any number of ways to get help on this, as well as other aspects of the program, once a presentable group is ready to function.

Strolling Strings is the strings' answer to the marching band, the stage band, and the swing choir. It provides an opportunity for string players to participate in the show-business side of music. This whole idea may be resisted by those with long-established, successful traditional string programs. In fact, teachers in that situation may not need any infusion of new ideas. But there are many string programs that are in need of help. Strolling Strings may be able to provide that help. As a supplement to your regular orchestra or string orchestra program, it is one answer to the present-day demand for light music in the popular vein that can be readily enjoyed by a wide segment of the public while offering worthwhile musical and social experiences to the student.

In summary, you must build a quality program; you must give recognition to students for their achievement and see that they receive wider recognition as well. And you must keep in mind the need to constantly sell and promote your program in a society where the study of a string instrument must compete with sports, studies, TV, chores, etc., for a share of the child's time and attention.

From this point forward in the teaching process, the teacher must adapt the suggestions contained in this book on teaching the string instruments to the method book they have chosen to use. They must then apply the best of what they know about group teaching, control, and motivation. It is important that each student be presented increasingly challenging but achieveable goals, and that he or she realize success and satisfaction as a result of their effort.

STUDY QUESTIONS

1. Name three 19th-century American musicians who were influential in shaping the musical history of this country.
2. At about what time in history did instrumental music get started in the public schools?
3. Why does a string teacher have to work harder than a band teacher to recruit elementary students?
4. Discuss some techniques that may be used to recruit students for the string program.
5. What size string instruments are needed for a beginning elementary program? Violin _____ Viola _____ Cello _____ Bass _____
6. Discuss the pros and cons of homogeneous and heterogeneous grouping.
7. What is an optimum class size figure for a beginning string class?
8. Name three particularly important aspects of design to consider when planning a rehearsal room.
9. List some factors to keep in mind when planning storage for instruments.
10. What are some of the important concepts to convey to the student in the first lesson?
11. Discuss the C approach versus the D major approach.
12. Why is it so important today to "sell" your string program?
13. Name three or four specific techniques that you can adopt to stimulate interest in the string program.
14. Describe a few ways to build parent interest in your program.
15. What are a few ways to develop a favorable image for the string program?

8. From *Strolling Strings: An Introduction* by Neil A. Kjos Music Company. Used by permission.

14 Chapter

Selecting Instruments, Bows, and Cases

QUALITY CATEGORIES

String instruments can be grouped roughly into two quality categories—artist and student. It must be understood that these terms are broad and overlapping. Student instruments are available in several grades, and artist instruments range from poor to magnificent.

In overly simplified terms, a student instrument is one intended for use by a person in the beginning stages of development. This could be interpreted to mean students between the ages of nine and fifteen years of age. For the talented student who makes rapid advancement this may mean moving into the artist quality bracket at a relatively early age.

An artist instrument is any instrument that can be rated superior to those instruments generally considered to be of student quality. It will surely be a handmade instrument. It will have carefully selected wood throughout and will reflect the artistry of the maker. Grain of wood and appearance of the varnish will be distinctive.

SELECTING AN ARTIST CALIBER INSTRUMENT

When accomplished string players set out to find an instrument for their personal use, they look for one with the following qualities:

The potential to produce a variety of tone qualities.
Even tone quality from string to string.
Even tone quality throughout the range of each
　　individual string.
Carrying power.
Responsiveness to the bow; ease of playing.
Freedom from flaws such as wolfs (distortions of tone),
　　loud spots, soft spots.

In addition to the above named playing features of the instrument, the physical features looked for are:

Good choice of wood, with good grain.
Fine varnish, which brings out the grain of the wood.
Fine workmanship, which is apparent from the way the
　　wood is carved and assembled.
Correct proportions, and a "right feel" in the hands.

Cost is not mentioned here because it is only important in relation to the individual. Good instruments can be purchased for prices ranging from $200.00 to $20,000.00 and more. Therefore, when shopping for an instrument, it is only

practical and reasonable to inform the dealer of the price bracket you have established. On this point, if you are inexperienced, it is advisable to discuss with the dealer how you intend to use the instrument—orchestra, chamber music, solo, etc., and whether you are a professional or amateur. The dealer can then advise you as to the quality instrument you should have, what is available that is suitable, and the price range you should consider.

The artist or collector looks for all of the qualities mentioned and then brings in the added dimension of the instrument's pedigree. Of first importance is the maker. All makers of any reputation are known and their instruments are a matter of record. The name of the maker is not an absolute indication of quality, or price; since every maker passes through various stages of development. But it is a consideration of utmost importance. Then comes the question of whether the instrument has undergone any major repairs such as replaced parts, large cracks, or severe damage. In the case of the extremely rare and valuable instruments, the line of ownership will play an important part; for the reputation and importance of the people who have possessed the instrument is in large measure a determiner of its value.

SELECTING AN ARTIST CALIBER BOW

To fine players, the bow is equal in importance to the instrument. It must suit their manner of playing and be satisfactorily matched to the instrument. Bows vary in weight, strength, and balance. When accomplished string players set out to find a bow for their personal use, they look for one with the following qualities:

Weight and balance suited to their manner of playing
　　and to the instrument.
Weight distributed so that the bow "clings" to the
　　string in the upper half.
The bow bounces easily and produces a satisfactory
　　spiccato.
The stick is strong enough to produce a big tone and
　　supple enough for sensitive shadings of tone and
　　volume.

In addition to the above named playing features of the bow, the physical features looked for are:

Good choice of wood with good grain.
An artistically carved tip.

A frog that fits securely on the bow and moves easily in
the tightening process.
A suitable grip.
Absence of splits or breaks. (The tip should be
examined particularly. This is the delicate part of the
bow. If it should become cracked, the value of the
bow is severely impaired. In repairing cracks at the
tip, repairmen sometimes insert metal pins, which
alter the balance of the bow.)

SELECTING STUDENT CALIBER INSTRUMENTS

For many years there was a wide and very discernible gap
between even the best student-grade instrument and a
medium quality handmade instrument. Fortunately, this situation has been almost completely corrected as a result of
the self-imposed standards of some of the string instrument
dealers, and the impetus toward improvement brought about
by the "Minimum Standards" adopted some years ago by
the Music Educators National Conference.

String instruments are made of wood and glue, and wood
cannot be standardized. Consequently, it is not possible to
make two instruments that will be exactly alike in tone
quality. All other things being equal, then, the final selection
of an instrument must be based upon its individual tone
quality, its response to the bow, its evenness from string to
string, and the volume of sound it is capable of producing.

This very individuality of tone quality of each string instrument contributes to the beauty of sound of the string section, blending many different timbres into the several voices
of the string choir in the way a choral group blends the voices
of its members into a unified whole.

Because of the improvements in standards of construction, school orchestra directors and their students no longer
need to be frustrated by poorly made, poorly equipped, and
poorly adjusted instruments. By dealing with a reputable
supplier and insisting upon a satisfactory product, it is possible to obtain quality instruments and avoid the problems
caused by substandard instruments. If some oversight has
produced a flaw in the instrument, these dealers, being reputable, will remedy the complaint.

In spite of quality controls and good intentions on the supplier's part, you, the purchaser, should put every instrument
to some kind of a test. If you are in a small system and only
a few instruments are purchased, you can probably accomplish this inspection yourself. If a number of schools are involved, and a large number of instruments, ask some
experienced teachers to assist.

A systematic approach, with the use of a checklist, will
help to assure thoroughness. The instrument, bow, and case
should be completely checked. The primary objective, of
course, is to make certain that the instrument you put into
the students' hands will not present problems over which they
have no control. Tuning pegs that slip or cannot be turned,
end pins that will not hold where they are set, or bows that
cannot be tightened are things to watch for. These faults, and
others, can discourage students, retard progress, interrupt
class procedures, and generally cause frustration. Many of
these problems develop as instruments are used. Preventing

problems from developing is a matter of maintenance. To
avoid starting out with such problems is a matter of checking
new equipment carefully.

Use of checklists such as those on pages 154–155 will provide a way to make a careful and thorough examination of
instrument, bow, and case. It is recommended that this procedure be followed whether it be for one or one hundred instruments.

Every item on the checklists can be evaluated objectively.
Unfortunately, tone and playing qualities cannot be. It follows, then, that instruments must be evaluated and accepted
on the basis of objective criteria unless arrangements are
made whereby they are handpicked from the dealer's stock.
Even if this latter procedure is followed, the equipment should
be scrutinized to determine the degree of compliance with
the items on the checklists. Although it is not common, it is
possible for an instrument to produce a beautiful sound but
have so many problems that a student cannot handle it readily.

Another point that should be kept in mind on this matter
is that young children, generally, find a shiny, new instrument much more attractive than an older one, even though
the older one may be superior tonally. This is mentioned because string teachers frequently find their program in a com-
petitive situation. With many children the decision to begin
(or continue) a string instrument is weighed against one or
any combination of the following: band; grades in mathematics, English, social studies; choir; recess; sports; television; and other attractions, ad infinitum. So the appearance
of the instrument and the case take on importance out of proportion to what they should. But if a shiny, new violin or cello
is what it takes to win a convert, then shiny and new they
should be.

All of this is said with full realization that new violins do
not stay that way very long, and budgets do not allow for
replacement as often as it is needed. The alternative is to
enforce strict rules in regard to the use of instruments and
have them checked, cleaned, and polished by a competent
repairman on a regular schedule. This kind of maintenance
will extend the youth and life of the instrument as well as its
attractiveness.

PURCHASING INSTRUMENTS FOR SCHOOLS

Determining what instruments to buy for school programs, and in what quantity, depends upon several factors.
The first is the basic philosophy of the administration regarding the kind of equipment the school should furnish, to
whom it should be loaned, for what purpose, and for how
long. In regard to this matter there are two extremes.

One point of view is that the school should furnish only
the instruments that parents normally would not purchase.
The school that follows this line of thinking would limit its
inventory to basses in the elementary and junior high schools,
the conclusion being that all students should be able to furnish their own instrument by the time they are in senior high
school. It is obvious that the success of such a program is
completely dependent upon the ability and willingness of
parents to spend their money for instruments for their children.

The other point of view is that the school should furnish some instruments. These instruments are for beginners who need a period of experimentation to help them decide what instrument they will stay with. For this purpose, instruments are loaned for a period of six months or one year. At the end of this time, the students are expected to make a decision and buy their own instrument.

Schools should furnish string basses at all levels since the purchase of a string bass imposes a hardship upon a family, and furthermore, regularly transporting a bass to and from school is a great deal to expect.

Junior and senior high schools should own some instruments in order that students can try instruments in addition to their "main" instrument. Violinists should have the opportunity to become acquainted with the viola, cellists with the bass, etc. The school's basic inventory of instruments also makes it possible for the teacher, with the above mentioned "switching" process, to achieve a complete string section. Violinists can be asked to play viola for a set amount of time. This gives them the experience of playing the viola and, at the same time, fills out the section. Pianists or cellists may be given a stint on the bass for the same reasons.

If a school, or a school system, adopts the policy that it should furnish a basic inventory of instruments, the degree of affluence and the nature of the community must be considered when determining what to purchase. Recommendations in Table 14.1 are for new schools in an average community.

TABLE 14.1

Minimum Number of String Instruments to Buy for New Schools[1]

Elementary[2] (Enrollment 400)	Junior High (Enrollment 1,000)	Senior High (Enrollment 2,000)
Violins 4½ 4¾	Violins 6¾ 6⁴/₄	Violins 10–12⁴/₄
Viola 2 Junior	Viola 4 Intermediate	Viola 2 Intermediate 4 Standard
Cello 1½ 1¾	Cello 2¾ 2⁴/₄	Cello 6⁴/₄
Bass 1½	Bass 2½ 2¾	Bass 4–6¾

[1]Quantities recommended here represent a compromise between the "Basic Program" and "Quality Program" equipment suggestions in *The School Music Program: Description and Standards*, Music Educators National Conference, 1974, pp. 36–41.

[2]If there is to be a string program in the lower grades, some of the smaller sizes must be purchased.

SHOP ADJUSTMENTS

Many school-quality instruments arrive in this country unfinished. They are in a rough, incomplete condition. Putting the finishing touches on these instruments is called "shop adjusting." A "shop adjusted" instrument has had the following things done to it:

1. *Bridge*—precisely fitted, feet graduated, top arched.
2. *Soundpost*—scientifically measured as to diameter, height, arch.
3. *Pegs*—properly set for string clearance and ease of tuning.
4. *Fingerboard*—dressed for correct dip, accurate measurements.
5. *Fingerboard nut*—proper height and string spacing.
6. *Edges*—checked and glued where necessary.
7. *New strings*—good quality and matched for gauge, correct length.
8. *String adjusters*—where needed for metal strings.
9. *Tailpiece gut*—correct length, efficiently secured.
10. *Chinrest*—new, correctly placed.
11. *Instrument*—cleaned and polished.
12. *Bow inspected*—stick straight, screw and screw-eye operational, suitable bow grip.
13. *End pin*—properly aligned, operational.
14. *Machine head*—operational.
15. *Case*—good quality and correct fit.

When string instruments are ordered for schools, they are usually ordered as "outfits." An outfit includes the instrument, a bow, and a case. Criteria for instruments have been pointed out. In examining bows the following should be checked:

The stick
  Is it straight?
  Does it have sufficient curve?
  Is it strong enough?

The frog
  Does it conform to the shape of the stick, and does it move easily?
  Does the screw turn easily?

The hair
  Is there enough of it?
  Is it straight?
  Are there loose hairs at the frog or tip?
  Can it be tightened and loosened sufficiently?

Cases should be sturdily made of tough material. Hinges and clasps should work easily and be durable. The case should have a carrying strap. The interior should be lined with a soft, durable material, and should contain dependable bow holders and accessory compartments.

On pages 154–155 and 163 are checklists, which can be used in examining new equipment. These lists may also be used for periodic maintenance examinations.

CHECK SHEET FOR NEW STRING INSTRUMENTS

Note: If an item is checked as satisfactory, none of the
discrepancies listed is found to be present.

Instrument

Strings
_____ Satisfactory
_____ Poor quality (   )
_____ Wrong length (   )
_____ Loose wrapping (   )
_____ False (   )

Fingerboard
_____ Satisfactory
_____ Uneven
_____ Warped
_____ Too low
_____ Too high

Bridge
_____ Satisfactory
_____ Too low
_____ Too high
_____ Notches too shallow
_____ Notches too deep
_____ Notches incorrectly spaced
_____ Feet too thick
_____ Feet do not conform to top
_____ Warped

Pegs
_____ Satisfactory
_____ Too tight
_____ Slip
_____ Too long
_____ Too short
_____ Do not conform to holes in peg box
_____ String hole too far to left or right

Tuners
_____ Satisfactory
_____ Wrong size
_____ Thumb screw hard to turn

Tailpiece Adjuster
_____ Satisfactory
_____ Too long
_____ Too short

Neck
_____ Satisfactory
_____ Improper alignment
_____ Rough or sticky

Glue Joints
_____ Satisfactory
_____ Seams open (   )
_____ Neck loose
_____ Fingerboard loose

End Pin (Cello and Bass)
_____ Satisfactory
_____ Improper fit
_____ Set screw hard to turn
_____ Set screw does not hold
_____ No device on peg to prevent it from slipping into
            instrument

Machine Head (Bass)
_____ Satisfactory
_____ Not screwed tightly to scroll

Bow

Wood
_____ Satisfactory
_____ Insufficient arc
_____ Lacks strength

Hair
_____ Satisfactory
_____ Too sparse
_____ Too long
_____ Too short
_____ Large number of hairs crossed or broken
_____ Hair loose at frog or tip

Frog
_____ Satisfactory
_____ Does not conform to stick
_____ Too large
_____ Too small
_____ Loose, wobbles
_____ Eyelet improperly adjusted
_____ Frog movement stiff

Screw (Button)
_____ Satisfactory
_____ Hard to turn
_____ Threads stripped
_____ Threads do not match eyelet
_____ Head loose or off center

Tip
_____ Satisfactory
_____ Loose
_____ Incorrect fit

Violin and Viola Cases

Fit
_____ Satisfactory
_____ Too small for instrument
_____ Too large for instrument

Hinges, Snaps, Lock, etc.
_____ Satisfactory
_____ Poor quality
_____ Too light
_____ Snaps do not hold tight
_____ Top does not close properly

Outer Cover
_____ Satisfactory
_____ Not durable

Lining
_____ Satisfactory
_____ Not durable
_____ Not well glued

Fittings
_____ Satisfactory
_____ Compartments not securely glued
_____ Bow-holders weak

Cello and Bass Bags

Fit

_____ Satisfactory
_____ Too large
_____ Too small

Material

_____ Satisfactory
_____ Too light-weight
_____ Not well sewn
_____ Seams not bound

Snaps or Zipper

_____ Satisfactory
_____ Hard to work
_____ Snaps do not hold

Bow and Music Compartments

_____ Satisfactory
_____ Poorly stitched
_____ No fasteners

THE COMPLETE STRING GUIDE: STANDARDS, PROGRAMS, PURCHASE, AND MAINTENANCE

At this point, previous editions of this book have included a copy of the 1957 MENC *Minimum Standards for Stringed Instruments in Schools.* This document was innovative at the time it was prepared by the MENC String Instruction Committee, and served as the standard for public schools and for the music industry for nearly thirty years. Much of the credit for the improvement in school string equipment can be attributed to it.

However, over the years, materials, processes, and instructional programs have changed. In some cases man-made products have proved superior to formerly used natural products. Modern technology and machinery have made possible the large-scale production of instruments, bows, and accessories of improved quality. Changes in the nature and emphasis of instructional programs have nurtured the development of new products and new instructional techniques. This constant process of change has gradually made parts of the *Minimum Standards for Stringed Instruments in Schools* out-of-date or obsolete.

Thanks to a collaborative effort on the part of the American String Teachers Association, Music Educators National Conference, and National School Orchestra Association, a new and up-to-date set of standards is now available. The publication, dated 1988, is *The Complete String Guide: Standards, Programs, Purchase, and Maintenance.* It is available from MENC, 1902 Association Drive, Reston, Virginia 22091. The fifty-two page *Guide* ranges from broad philosophical statements providing a rationale for the string program to illustrations and measurements of bridges and soundposts. There is also a chapter dealing with the writing of specifications for the purchase of string instruments and equipment. The *Guide* is clear, concise, and contains a wealth of valuable information and advice for the new as well as the experienced string or orchestra instructor. Every individual involved with string instruction should own and study this *Guide.*

STUDY QUESTIONS

1. What are some of the playing characteristics associated with a fine instrument?
2. When choosing a string instrument, what are some of the physical aspects that should be considered?
3. What are some of the playing characteristics associated with a fine bow?
4. What are some of the physical aspects that should be considered when looking at a bow?
5. What is the name of the publication that replaced the 1957 MENC *Minimum Standards for Stringed Instruments in Schools?*
6. Discuss the importance of the instrument's appearance in the case of a young, beginning student.
7. Formulate an opinion on the question of whether a school's inventory of string instruments should be large or small, and state the reason for your opinion.
8. List as many of the procedures involved in shop adjusting an instrument as you can.
9. When new school instruments are received, what are some of the important things to check?

    Instruments

    Bows

    Cases

Appendixes

APPENDIX 1

Glossary of Symbols and Terms Used in String Music

BOWING TERMS AND SYMBOLS

Symbol or Term	Meaning	Explanation or Execution
⊓	Down bow	The bow moves in the direction of frog to point.
V	Up bow	The bow moves in the direction of point to frog.
Fr.	Frog	To be played near the frog.
Pt.	Point	To be played near the point.
(notation)	Détaché	To be played with separate bows, not slurred.
(notation)	Slurred	Two or more notes played smoothly while the bow moves in one direction.
(notation)	Staccato	Notes are played with abrupt beginning and ending. Length of note is shortened.
(notation)	Slurred staccato	Two or more notes played in one bow with stops between the notes.
(notation)	Martelé	Heavily accented notes played with staccato qualities.
(notation)	Spiccato	A bouncing bow stroke in which the bow leaves the string after each note.
(notation)	Ricochet	The bow strikes the string, rebounds, and, while moving in the same direction, strikes the string again to play the second note under the slur. Bow direction is changed to play notes not included in the slur. The number of notes played in one bow is variable.
(notation)	Spring bow arpeggio	The bow is bounced across the strings striking each string in sequence.
(notation)	Tremolo	Very rapid up and down bow, usually toward the point.
am steg (Ger.)		The bow contacts the string near the bridge.

Symbol or Term	Meaning	Explanation or Execution
a meta l'arco (It.)		To be played with half the bow.
a punto d'arco (It.)		To be played at the point of the bow.
archet (Fr.)	Bow	
arco (It.)	Bow	Used after a pizzicato passage to indicate the bow is to be used again.
au chevalet (Fr.)		The bow contacts the string near the bridge.
au milieu de l'archet (Fr.)		To be played at the middle of the bow.
au talon (Fr.)		To be played at the frog.
avec le dos de l'archet (Fr.)		To be played with the back (wood) of the bow.
battuto coll'arco (It.)		To strike the string with the wood. Same as *col legno*.
bogen (Ger.)	Bow	
bogen mitte (Ger.)		To be played at the middle of the bow.
col legno (It.)		To be played with wood of the bow.
colla punta d'arco (It.)		To be played at the point.
coup d'archet (Fr.)	Bow stroke	
détaché (Fr.)	Detached	Not slurred.
en jetant l'archet (Fr.)	Thrown bow	As in *ricochet* or *flying staccato*.
flautando (It.)	Flute-like	The bow contacts the string near or over the fingerboard with little pressure.
flying staccato		A series of staccato notes played up bow with the bow leaving the string between notes.
frog, abbr. Fr.	Frog, nut, or heel of the bow	Used to indicate that the portion of the bow near the frog is to be used.
heel	Frog or nut	
jeté (Fr.)	Thrown	As in *ricochet* or *flying staccato*.
jeu ordinaire (Fr.)		Normal use of the bow after a special bowing instruction such as *jeté* or *au chevalet*.
L.H.	Lower half of the bow	From the middle to the frog.
lange bogen (Ger.)	Long bow	
louré (Fr.)		Written ♩̲ ♩̣ ♩̣ . Played in one bow but lightly pulsed or separated.
M	Middle of the bow	To be played in the middle of the bow.
marcato (It.)	Marked	Accented, separated bow stroke.
martelé (Fr.)		A heavily accented stroke with staccato qualities.
martellato (It.)		Same as *martelé*.
mit dem bogen geschlagen (Ger.)		To strike the string with the bow.
nut	Frog or heel of the bow	

Symbol or Term	Meaning	Explanation or Execution
ponticello (It.), abbr. pont.		The bow contacts the string near the bridge.
portato (It.)		Same as *louré*.
position naturelle	Natural position	Bow normally after *sur la touche* or *au chevalet*.
Pt.	Point of the bow	
saltando, saltato (It.)		Slightly ambiguous terms indicating a bouncing bow.
sautillé (Fr.)		Rapid *spiccato* in which the bow barely leaves the string.
spiccato (It.)		An up and down bow bouncing bow stroke in which the bow leaves the string between notes.
spitze (Ger.)	Tip of the bow	
springbogen (Ger.)	Springing bow	A bouncing bow stroke in which the bow leaves the string after each note.
sul tasto (It.)		See *flautando*.
sulla tastiera (It.)		See *flautando*.
sur la touche (Fr.)		See *flautando*.
sur le chevalet (Fr.)		See *au chevalet*.
talon (Fr.)	Frog, nut, or heel	
tip	Point of the bow	
tout l'archet (Fr.)	All the bow	To be played with the whole bow.
U.H.	Upper half of the bow	From the middle to the point.
W.B.	Whole bow	

OTHER SYMBOLS AND TERMS

Symbol or Term	Meaning	Explanation or Execution
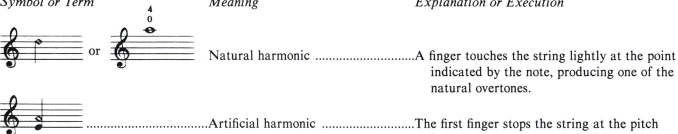 Natural harmonic	Natural harmonic	A finger touches the string lightly at the point indicated by the note, producing one of the natural overtones.
	Artificial harmonic	The first finger stops the string at the pitch indicated by the lower note. The fourth finger (sometimes the third) touches the string lightly at the interval indicated by the diamond shaped note producing a harmonic of the lower pitch. The example produces

Symbol or Term	Meaning	Explanation or Execution
(staff, high note with +)	Left hand pizzicato	The string is plucked with the finger(s) of the left hand.
(staff, tr)	Trill	A rapid alternation of the principal note with the note one half or one whole step higher.
(staff, finger tremolo)	Finger tremolo	The two notes are alternated in rapid succession. They are slurred.
(staff, portamento)	Portamento	A subtle, expressive slide to or from a note.
á²		In orchestral music. Indicates both players on a stand are to play the same part after *divisi*.
avec la sourdine (Fr.)	With mute	
con sordino (It.), abbr. con sord.	With mute	
divisi, abbr. div	Divided	In orchestra music when two or more lines exist in one part. This tells the players to divide the lines.
glissando (It.) abbr. gliss.		The finger slides on the string. The starting and ending points are usually indicated by notes. Sometimes a glissando is written chromatically as follows:

(musical example)

gliss.

Other times it is indicated by a slanted line as follows:

(musical example)

gliss.

Symbol or Term	Meaning	Explanation or Execution
mettez la sourdine (Fr.)	Put on the mute	
molto vibrato (It.)	Much vibrato	
non divisi (It.)	Not divided	In orchestra music where there is more than one line on a part, this indicates the player is to play both parts in the case of double stops or all the notes in the case of chords.
non vibrato (It.)	No vibrato	
otez la sourdine (Fr.)	Take off the mute	
pizzicato (It.), abbr. pizz.		The string is plucked with a finger of the right hand.

Symbol or Term	*Meaning*	*Explanation or Execution*

portamento (It.) ....Akin to a glissando. Produced in the course of shifting between two notes of different pitch. The audible glissando may be from the first note (1) or may precede the second (2).

(1)   or   (2)

restez (Fr.) ....Remain in position.

sans sourdine (Fr.) ....Without mute

senza sordino (It.) ....Without mute

senza vibrato (It.) ....Without vibrato

sordino (It.) abbr. sord. ....Mute ....*Sord.* is often used by itself to indicate the mute is to be used. *Senza* or *senza sord.* indicates the mute is to be removed.

sourdine (Fr.) ....Mute

sulla corda (It.) ....The passage is to be played on one string. *Sul. G.* or *Sulla C* is another way to indicate the same thing.

APPENDIX II

String Instrument Inspection Record

Prepared by Dr. Paul Van Bodegraven, Chairman, Department of Music, New York University

Published by Educational Division of Scherl & Roth, Inc.

To help you determine if your instrument is in best possible playing condition.

	Yes	No
A. PEGS		
1. Do they fit snugly in both peg hole openings?		
2. Do they turn smoothly and silently?		
3. Do they hold in position with <u>slight</u> inward pressure while tuning?		
B. FINGERBOARD NUT		
1. Do all strings clear fingerboard without buzzing when playing open or stopped strings?		
2. Are the string grooves in the fingerboard nut shallow?		
C. FINGERBOARD		
1. Is it smooth with no grooves?		
2. Is it glued securely on to the neck?		
3. Is it free of excess glue along edges?		
4. Is it the proper height?		
D. BRIDGE		
1. Is it the proper height?		
2. Do the feet fit perfectly with the top contour? ...		
3. Is the E string on low side of bridge (violin) A string on viola and cello, G string on bass?		
4. Is it set opposite the inside notches on the F holes?		
5. Are all string grooves shallow?		
6. Is it perfectly straight, not warped?		
7. Does it lean slightly towards the tailpiece?		
8. Is there sufficient arch so the student does not have difficulty playing from one string to the other? ..		
E. TAILPIECE		
1. Is the small end of tailpiece almost even with the outside edge of saddle?		
2. Is there some space between it and top of instrument?		
3. Is there a clearance between tailpiece and chinrest?		
F. STRINGS		
1. Are all perfectly smooth, without kinks?		
2. Is the metal winding tight?		
3. Are the adjusters on all metal strings working smoothly?		
4. Are the strings free of caked rosin?		
5. Do you have an extra set of strings in your case? .		
6. Are your reserve strings sealed from dryness?		
7. If you have any steel strings on your instrument, are they equipped with adjusters?		

	Yes	No
G. INSTRUMENT BODY		
1. Is it free from open cracks?		
2. Is the top clean and free of caked rosin?		
3. Are the front and back thoroughly glued to the ribs?		
H. THE SOUNDPOST		
1. Is it directly behind the right foot of the bridge? ..		
2. Is it perpendicular to top and back?		
3. Is the soundpost setter slot facing the right F hole?		
I. THE BOW		
1. Can it be loosened and tightened freely?		
2. Does it have enough hair?		
3. Does the hair extend the full width of the frog ferrule?		
4. Has it been rehaired in the past year?		
5. Is the bow stick free of caked rosin?		
6. Does it have real wire winding and leather thumb grip?		
7. Is the bow arch noticeable when it is tightened ready to play?		
8. Is there a protective facing, ivory or metal, on the tip?		
J. CHINREST		
1. Is the chinrest securely attached to instrument? ...		
2. Is the chinrest free of broken edges?		
3. Is it of proper height for correct posture and comfortable playing?		
K. ROSIN		
1. Do you have a full size (unbroken) cake of rosin? .		
2. Do you have a clean cake of rosin?		
3. Are you using rosin for the individual bow, i.e. (violin, cello, bass rosin)?		
L. MUTE		
1. Do you have a mute attached to your instrument ready for instant use? (Sihon mute)		
M. CELLO AND BASSES		
1. Is the adjustable endpin in proper working order?..		
2. Do you have a cello or bass endpin rest that prevents instrument slipping while playing?		

ALL ANSWERS SHOULD BE "YES"

Instructions to correct faults of your instrument are found in repair manual,
"YOU FIX THEM," published by Scherl & Roth Inc.

INSTRUMENT_____ SERIAL NO._____ DATES INSPECTED _____

1st quarter   2nd quarter

_____ _____ TEACHER _____ STUDENT NAME _____

3rd quarter   4th quarter

ADDRESS _____ TELEPHONE NUMBER _____ GRADE _____

SCHOOL _____

List of Teaching Materials for Strings

There is a great deal of string teaching material available. By far the greatest amount is for the violin with the cello coming next. Neither the quantity nor the variety has been written for the viola and bass. A good deal of material has been written for string classes; conscientious directors should not have difficulty finding material that is suitable for their group. It should not be necessary to stress the importance of using a variety of materials. This keeps up interest and more nearly assures the teacher that none of the important techniques will be omitted.

The best up-to-date sources of information about publications are publisher's catalogs. These can be seen at most music stores that handle music and where, in fact, it is often possible to see new scores and sets of parts.

The American String Teachers Association publishes a list of string teaching and performance materials in the *ASTA String Syllabus*. This publication, under the chairmanship of Margaret Farish and an excellent group of subcommittees, was revised in 1986. It contains separate listings for each of the instruments plus a category for ensembles of all kinds, from duets to full groups. Methods, studies, and repertory listings for each instrument are categorized and graded as follows: Elementary A and B, Intermediate A and B, Advanced, Young Artist. Ensemble music is separated into three categories—Elementary, Intermediate, Advanced. The *Syllabus* and other ASTA publications may be obtained from Theodore Presser, Bryn Mawr, PA 19010.

A number of mail-order houses maintain extensive listings of string music. Among them is SHAR *Sheet Music Catalog* which has a comprehensive listing of single solos, collections of solos, duets, trios, and quartets for like instruments and standard combinations. The address is: SHAR Products Company, 2465 S. Industrial Hwy., P.O. Box 1411, Ann Arbor, MI 48106.

Selective Music Lists (1978) for Full Orchestra and String Orchestra, compiled by Music Educators National Conference and the National School Orchestra Association is still available from MENC. Although these lists are now ten years old, they are still a valuable resource. Write to MENC, 1902 Association Drive, Reston, VA 22091.

A number of state organizations publish graded lists of performance materials. One of these is the University Interscholastic League, the organization that draws up the list of music for competitions within the state of Texas. Published by the University of Texas at Austin, this list of prescribed music is revised every four years. The list presents graded music for each instrument and voice, and all types of ensembles. It is available for a modest price from the University Interscholastic League, Box 8028, University Station, Austin, TX 78713–8028. You should also check with your state association to determine if it publishes lists of performance materials.

STRING CLASS METHODS

AUTHOR	TITLE	PUBLISHER	DESCRIPTION OR COMMENTS
Anderson, Gerald and Frost, Robert S.	All for Strings	KJOS	Books 1 and 2. Comprehensive string method. All, piano acc., score and manual includes excellent fingering charts and photos of playing positions. Also available: Theory workbooks coordinated with method. Book 2—new fingering patterns, scales, bowings, shifting for cellos and bass.
Applebaum, Samuel	Applebaum String Method	Belwin Mills	Books 1, 2, and 3. For class instruction or individual tutoring. All strings, piano acc., teachers manual. Book 3 presents 3rd position and double stops.
Applebaum, Samuel	Belwin String Builder	Belwin Mills	Books 1, 2, and 3. Piano Acc., teacher's manual.
Applebaum, Samuel	The Young String Student	Belwin Mills	String books with piano acc. and teacher's manual. A conceptual approach designed to inspire creativity, technique, and musicianship in the younger beginner. The book contains a number of photos showing good and bad positions followed by a number of brief pieces selected to utilize a particular left hand or bow technique.
Bornoff, George	Bornoff's Finger Patterns Fun for Fiddle Fingers	Big 3	A basic method for strings.
Dasch and Bennett	The Aeolian String Ensemble Method	Fitzsimons	Books 1, 2, and 3. For group or individual instruction. String books and condensed score.
Dilmore, Herman	The Breeze-Easy Method for Strings	Warner	Books 1 and 2. Teacher's Manual, Piano Acc.
Etling, Forest R.	Solo Time for Strings	Highland/ Etling	5 Books. All, Piano Acc., Teacher's Manual.
Etling, Forest R.	String Class Method	Etling	String books 1 and 2. Piano Acc.
Fletcher, Stanley	New Tunes for Strings	Boosey and Hawkes	String books, teacher's book with piano acc. with an instructional design by Paul Rolland and assistance of advisory editors, Margaret Rowell (cello) and Edward Krolick (bass), this book serves as a supplement to *PRELUDE TO STRING PLAYING* but may be used with other methods. All pieces are playable in a variety of instrumentations.
Gordon, Beckstead, and Stone	Visual Method	Highland Music Co.	For class or private instruction for beginners on all string instruments.
Green, Elizabeth	Teaching String Instruments in Classes	Prentice Hall	Step-by-step approach for the first ten lessons.
Havas, Kato and Landsman, Jerome	Freedom to Play	ABI/A. Broude, Inc.	This is a step-by-step method based upon and demonstrating the concepts of relaxation and focus espoused by Kato Havas.
Herfurth, C. Paul	A Tune a Day	Boston Music Co.	Books 1, 2, and 3 for violin and viola; 1 and 2 for cello, 1 for bass. Piano acc. for books 1 and 2, teacher's manual. Books 1 and 2 for some wind instruments.

AUTHOR	TITLE	PUBLISHER	DESCRIPTION OR COMMENTS
Hohman-Green	For the String Class, a 2nd Book	Carl Fischer	All, score. A follow-up to any first method book.
Isaac, Merle	String Class Method	M. M. Cole Pub. Co	Two books for all strings. Piano Acc. with score.
Johnson, Sheila (Ed.)	Young Strings in Action	Boosey and Hawkes	Vol. 1, Paul Rolland's approach to string playing. All. Teacher's book.
Kafka, Irving	Building Strings Together	Belwin Mills	2 vols., piano acc.
Kievman	Introduction to Strings	Kelton Pub.	A 12-week string course for individual or group practice.
Klotman, Robert	Action with Strings	Southern Texas	String books with piano acc.
Maddy and Giddings	Universal Teacher for Orchestra and Band	Willis Music Co.	A method adapted for class or private lessons containing ensemble pieces for any combination of string or wind instruments or any three instruments of the same kind. Piano Acc.
Matesky and Womack	Learn to Play a Stringed Instrument	Alfred	2 vols. piano acc.
Müller, Fred and Weber, Fred	The Belwin Orchestra Builder	Belwin Mills	Part 1. All.
Müller, J. Frederick and Rusch, Harold	Müller-Rusch String Method for Class or Individual Instruction	KJOS	Books 1, 2, and 3. For violin, viola, cello, and bass, score. Books 4 and 5 advanced positions.
Pernecky, Jack	Growing with Strings	Cole	2 vols. with piano acc.
Pinkston, Patricia T. and Moore, Miltona	Champion Strings	KJOS	Violin, viola, cello.
Washaw and Smith	Work and Play String Method	Theo. Presser	Two books for violin, viola, cello, and bass, plus teacher's book.
Wisniewski and Higgins	Learning Unlimited String Program	Hal Leonard	An orchestral and individualized beginning method with supplementary cassette tape. All, teacher's manual, score. Acc. book includes piano, guitar (optional) and drums (optional).
Zwissler, Ruth	First Lessons for Beginning Strings	Highland	Start by Rote. Books for all Strings.

Note: Most string class methods may be used satisfactorily for individual instruction.

OTHER MATERIALS FOR STRING CLASS INSTRUCTION

Anderson, Gerald	Essentials for Strings	KJOS	All, Score. A systematic approach to technical development.
Applebaum, Samuel	Building Technic with Beautiful Music	Belwin/Mills	4 Vols., Piano Acc.
Applebaum, Samuel	Early Etudes for Strings	Belwin	All strings with piano acc.
Applebaum, Samuel	First Position Etudes	Belwin	All strings with piano acc.
Applebaum, Samuel	Orchestral Bowing Etudes	Belwin	All strings with piano acc.

AUTHOR	TITLE	PUBLISHER	DESCRIPTION OR COMMENTS
Applebaum, Samuel	Scales for Strings	Belwin	Supplementary studies to develop the string ensemble. All, teacher's manual, piano acc.
Applebaum, Samuel	String Builder	Belwin	3 vols., piano acc.
Applebaum, Samuel	3rd and 5th Position String Builder	Belwin	A continuation of the Belwin string builder or any other standard string class method. Piano acc.
Applebaum, Samuel	2nd and 4th positions	Belwin/Mills	All, Piano Acc.
Applebaum, Samuel	The Young String Student	Belwin/Mills	All. Possible substitute for Applebaum string method.
Applebaum, Samuel	Etudes for Technic and Musicianship	Belwin/Mills	All, piano acc., teacher's manual.
Best, George	Early String Shifting	Varitone, Inc.	All.
Bornoff, George	Bornoff's String Reader	Carl Fischer	All. An instructional primer for heterogeneous, homogeneous, or individual instruction.
Brunson, Theodore	Daily Intonalization Studies for Strings	KJOS	All. For eliminating pitch indiscretions and enhancing tone production.
Cowden/Muegel	Bowing for Better Sound	Elon College, Box 865, N.C.	
Dawe, Margery	New Road to Scale and Arpeggio Practice	Cramer	
Dawe, Margery	New Road to String Playing	Cramer	3 vols., all, piano acc.
Dawe, Margery	More Travel Tunes	Cramer	Violin, viola, cello, piano acc.
Etling, Forest	Intermediate String Techniques	Etling	All, teacher's manual. This book contains scales, scales in rounds, rounds, bowing exercises, rhythm studies, and technique building exercises.
Flor, Samuel	I Like to Play the Violin, Viola, Cello, Bass	Elkan	
Froseth, James O. and Johnson, Robert E.	The Individualized Instructor	G. I. A. Publishers	Solos and ensembles. A book of supplementary songs for self-initiated and self-directed instruction.
Fussell, Raymond C.	Exercises for Ensemble Drill	Schmitt, Hall, and McCreary	A series of warming-up exercises, technical studies, and rhythm drill for daily practice by any group—large or small. Arranged for band or orchestra.
Gordon, Philip	Orchestra Warm-ups for Orchestra or String Orchestra	Carl Fischer	Progressively arranged melodius warm-ups in keys most commonly used in orchestra.
Gordon, Philip	String Debut	Shapiro, Bernstein	All strings with piano acc.
Hudadoff, Igor	A Rhythm a Day for Strings	Pro Art/ Belwin	All strings.
Hutton, Truman	Basic Bowings for the String Section	Highland/ Etling	All, score (piano). Legato, spiccato, staccato, special bowings.

AUTHOR	TITLE	PUBLISHER	DESCRIPTION OR COMMENTS
Isaac, Merle and Weber, Fred	Orchestra Rehearsal Fundamentals	Belwin Mills	Full orchestra.
Johnson, Harold	The Positions for All Strings	Fitzsimons	A class method for studies in the positions. All strings, condensed score.
Knechtel, A. Baird	27 Studies for Strings	Thompson Music	All strings with piano acc. and teacher's manual. A few of the etudes are original, but most are abbreviated adaptations of etudes by Romberg, Lee, Wohlfahrt, etc. Most are in unison. Catchy titles. Specific objectives set for each etude.
Martin, Pauline, M.	The Funway to Fiddletown	Seraphic Press	A string readiness program. Rote and note studies.
Martin, Pauline, M.	The Runway to Fiddletown	Seraphic	Second book of above.
Matesky, Ralph	The Well-Tempered String Player	Alfred Pub. Co.	All strings with piano acc., teacher's guide. A collection of 50 etudes selected from the standard literature (several by Matesky), organized by key.
Miller, L.	The Advancing Strings	M. M. Cole Pub.	Supplementary studies and technical development. 7 Units, each emphasizing a different aspect of string instrument technique development.
Müller, J. Frederick	Etudes for Strings	Belwin	All strings with piano acc.
Müller, J. Frederick and Rusch, Harold W.	Basic Scales and Two-Part Inventions	KJOS	All strings with piano acc.
Müller, J. Frederick and Rusch, Harold W.	Etudes and Ensembles	KJOS	All strings with piano acc.
Müller, J. Frederick and Rusch, Harold W.	Intermediate Etudes and Ensembles	KJOS	All strings with piano acc.
Müller, J. Frederick and Rusch, Harold W.	Rhythm and Rhythmic Bowings	KJOS	All strings with piano acc.
Pernecky, Jack M.	Growing with Music	M. M. Cole Pub.	All, piano acc. easy solos, may be played singly or in unison.
Preston, Herbert	Direct Approach to the Higher Positions for String Classes	Belwin	All strings, teacher's manual, and score with piano acc.
Reese, Wendel	22 Studies for Strings	Belwin	For individual or class instruction. Unison or ensemble. All, piano conductor.
Sanfilippo, Margherita	Basic Class of Individual Position Studies for Strings	Highland Music Co.	All strings with piano acc., score. Interval patterns (major and Minor 2nds) within a four-note span duplicated on each string, ranging from first through fifth position.
Whistler and Hummel	Elementary Scales and Bowings for Strings	Rubank	For individual and class instruction. All, piano acc., score.
Whistler and Hummel	Intermediate Scales and Bowings	Rubank	All strings with piano acc.
Whistler and Hummel	The New Hohmann-Wohlfahrt Method	Rubank	

AUTHOR	TITLE	PUBLISHER	DESCRIPTION OR COMMENTS
Whistler and Hummel	Pre-Ensemble Folio for Strings	Rubank	All strings with piano acc.
Young, Phyllis	Playing the String Game	Univ. of Texas Press	Strategies for teaching cello and strings.
Young, Phyllis	The String Play	Univ. of Texas Press	The drama of playing and teaching strings.

VIOLIN METHODS

AUTHOR	TITLE	PUBLISHER	DESCRIPTION OR COMMENTS
Alshin, Harry	The Sounds of the Violin, Bk. 1	Frank	
Auer, Leopold (Gustav Saenger)	Graded Course of Violin Playing	C. Fischer	A complete outline of violin study ranging from pre-elementary grade to virtuoso accomplishment, with prefatory and incidental text, additional exercises and duets, and systematic grading of all material. Eight books.
Bang, Maia	Violin Method Based on the Teaching Principles of Leopold Auer	C. Fischer	In seven parts. Part I—Elementary Rudiments, Part II—More Advanced Studies, Part III—3rd and 2nd Positions, Part IV—4th and 5th Positions, Part V—6th and 7th Positions, Part VI—Higher Art of Bowing, Part VII—Piano Accompaniment.
Barbakoff, Samuel	Fiddling by the Numbers	C. Fischer	A rote method.
Carse	New School of Violin Studies	Augenour	6 Vols.
Dancla, Charles	Conservatory Method (Elementary and Progressive Method)	C. Fischer	2 Vols.
de Beriot, Chas.	Violin Method	C. Fischer	
Doflein, Erich and Elma	The Doflein Method	Schott	5 Vols. Vol.1—The Beginning, Vol. 2—Development of Technique, Vol. 3—2nd and 3rd Positions, Vol. 4—Further Technique in Bowing and Fingering, Vol. 5—The Higher Positions.
Gardner, Samuel	School of Violin Study	C. Fischer	2 Vols. Book 1—Elementary, Book 2—Intermediate.
Givens, Shirley	Adventures in Violin Land	Sees	Book 1, a, b, c, d, e, f.
Havas, Kato	The Twelve Lesson Course	Bosworth & Co.	Detailed information and guidance in the application of the "New Approach" by Havas.
Hohmann-Wohlfahrt (Whistler)	Beginning Method for Violin	Rubank	2 Vols. A compilation of two famous methods, entirely revised, re-edited and restyled to meet the demands of modern education.
Johnson, George	Violin Method	Kjos	
Laoureux, Nicolas	A Practical Method for Violin	Schirmer	Four Parts. Part I—Elements of Bowing and Left Hand Technique, Part II—Five Positions, Part III—School of Bowing, Part IV—Virtuosity of the Left Hand. With supplements.

AUTHOR	*TITLE*	*PUBLISHER*	*DESCRIPTION OR COMMENTS*
Langey, Otto	Celebrated Tutor for the Violin	C. Fischer	
Menuhin, Yehudi	Six Lessons with Yehudi Menuhin	Viking Press	A detailed analysis of the motions of playing and the application of the principles of relaxation to technique and performance.
Polnauer, Dr. Frederick F.	Total Body Technique of Violin Playing	Presser Co.	A pictorial method of portraying body positions for various playing requirements. Based upon "Sensomotor Study and Its Application to Violin Playing" by Polnauer and Marks. (ASTA)
Potter	Rubank Elementary Method	Rubank	
Riegger, Wallingford	Begin with Pieces	Schirmer	Elementary method of individual or class instruction using short pieces. Piano accompaniment.
Rohner, Traugott and Barbakoff, Samuel	Carl Fischer Basic Method for the Violin	C. Fischer	
Rolland, Paul	Basic Principals of Violin Playing	ASTA (Presser)	
Rolland, Paul	Prelude to String Playing	Boosey & Hawkes	
Rolland, Paul and Mutschler, Marla	The Teaching of Action in String Playing	Boosey & Hawkes	See p. 123 for description.
Scheer, Leo	Scheer Violin Method	Belwin	Two books. Visual aids and tuneful technical studies.
Suzuki	Suzuki Violin School	Summy-Birchard	10 Vols. With accompaniments and demonstration records.
Wohlfahrt	Easiest Elementary Method for Beginners	Schirmer	

OTHER MATERIALS FOR THE VIOLIN
Elementary to Intermediate

Applebaum, Samuel	Building Technic with Beautiful Music	Belwin	4 Vols. Progressive through 3rd position.
Herfurth, C. Paul	A Tune A Day Scale Book	Boston Music Co.	
Hrimalyi	Scale Studies	G. Schirmer	Easy to advanced.
Keloeber, Robert	Elementary Scale and Chord Studies	Rubank	Begins simply but progresses rapidly to double-stops, chromatics, scales in thirds, etc.
Müller and Rusch	Music through the Violin	Kjos	A beginning book with a variety of musically related activities for the very young student.

AUTHOR	TITLE	PUBLISHER	DESCRIPTION OR COMMENTS
Rolland, Paul	Action Studies (Developmental and Remedial Techniques for Violin and Viola)	Boosey & Hawkes	Many of Rolland's techniques for teaching the student how to hold the instrument and how to manipulate the bow and the left hand are shown in this book through a series of pictures and explanations. At the end of the book are rhythmic exercises conceived to assist the student play and read rhythms.
Rolland, Paul	Tunes and Exercises for the String Player	Boosey & Hawkes	A recording has "practice" and "concert" versions of the tunes. The exercises are designed to develop accuracy of finger placement. The book has good finger placement charts.
Rose, Linda	Progressive Scale Studies for the Young Violinist.	Kjos	
Schloat, Warren	Introduction to the Violin	Schloat Productions	Audiovisual set of beginning lessons for young violinists. Four filmstrips with two LP records.
Sevcik, O.	Exercises in the 1st Position, Op.1, Part 1	C. Fischer	
Sitt	20 Etudes in the 1st Position, Op. 32, Book I	Schirmer	
Whistler	First Etude Album	Rubank	Includes a choice selection of 62 elementary etudes, carefully graded, fingered, and bowed by Whistler and Hummel.
Whistler	Scales in 1st Position	Rubank	
Wohlfahrt (Blay)	60 Studies in 1st Position, Op. 45, Book I	Schirmer	
Wohlfahrt	40 Elementary Studies, Op. 54	Schirmer	
Wohlfahrt	50 Easy Melodious Studies, Op. 74, Book 1, 1st Position	Schirmer	

Intermediate to Advanced

AUTHOR	TITLE	PUBLISHER	DESCRIPTION OR COMMENTS
Brown, Susan C.	Two Octave Scales and Bowings	Ludwig Music Pub. Co.	
Kayser	Elementary and Progressive Studies, Op. 20	C. Fischer	
Kayser	36 Elementary and Progressive Studies, Op. 36	C. Fischer	
Mazas	40 Selected Studies, Op. 36	Schirmer	Melodious studies.
McConnell, Albert H.	The New Dancla-Beriot Position Method	C. Fischer	
Neumann, Frederick	Violin Left Hand Technique	ASTA (Presser)	
Schradieck	School of Violin Technics, Book 1	C. Fischer or Schirmer	Exercises for promoting dexterity in the various positions.

AUTHOR	TITLE	PUBLISHER	DESCRIPTION OR COMMENTS
Schradieck	Scale Studies	C. Fischer or Schirmer	One-octave through three-octave scales, single note. Scales in thirds, sixths, octaves, tenths.
Schradieck	School of Violin Technics, Book II	C. Fischer or Schirmer	Exercises in double-stops.
Sevcik, O.	School of Violin Technics, Op. 1, Part II	C. Fischer or Schirmer	Exercises in the 2nd to 7th positions.
Sevcik, O.	School of Violin Technics, Op. 1, Part III	C. Fischer or Schirmer	Shifting exercises.
Sitt	20 Etudes with Change of Position, Op. 32, Book III	Schirmer	
Sitt	20 Etudes in the 2nd, 3rd, 4th, and 5th Positions, Op. 32, Book II	Schirmer	
Trott, Josephine	Melodious Double-Stops, Books I and II	Schirmer	Progressive melodious ètudes.
Whistler	Introducing the Positions	Rubank	Vol. I—3rd and 5th positions, Vol. II—2nd, 4th, 6th, and higher positions.
Whistler	Developing Double-Stops	Rubank	A complete course in double notes and chords from the 1st through the 5th and higher positions. Includes etudes in thirds, sixths, octaves, tenths, and chords.
Whistler	Preparing for Kreutzer	Rubank	An intermediate course of violin study based on the famous works of Kayser, Mazas, Dont, etc., Vol. I—Etudes in first through higher positions, trills, and double stops. Vol. II—Etudes in minor keys, double stops, concert caprices.
Wohlfahrt	50 Easy Melodious Studies, Op. 74, Book II	C. Fischer or Schirmer	Studies in 3rd position.
Wohlfahrt	60 Studies, Op. 45, Book II	C. Fischer or Schirmer	Studies in 3rd position.

Advanced

AUTHOR	TITLE	PUBLISHER	DESCRIPTION OR COMMENTS
Blumenstengel	Scale and Arpeggio Studies	C. Fischer	
Dont	24 Exercises Preparatory to Kreutzer and Rode, Op. 37	Schirmer	
Dont	24 Etudes and Caprices, Op. 35	Schirmer	These studies are extremely demanding in all phases of left hand and bowing techniques.
Dont	Progressive Studies with Accompaniment of 2nd violin, Op. 38	Schirmer	
Fiorillo	36 Studies or Caprices	Schirmer	
Flesch	Scale System	C. Fischer	Scale exercises in all major and minor keys, single notes, 3rds, 6ths, 8vas, 10ths, and harmonics.

AUTHOR	TITLE	PUBLISHER	DESCRIPTION OR COMMENTS
Galamian-Newmann	Contemporary Violin Techniques	Galaxy	
Gavinies	24 Studies	Schirmer	
Hrimaly	Scale Studies	Schirmer	Single notes and double-stops.
Kreutzer	42 Studies or Caprices	Schirmer	Probably the most famous of all books of studies for violin. Moderately difficult to very difficult.
Mazas	75 Melodious and Progressive Studies, Op. 36	Schirmer	
Mazas	30 Special Studies, Op. 36, Book I	Schirmer	Excellently written and very musical studies. Used as preparation for Kreutzer.
Mazas	27 Brilliant Studies, Op. 36, Book II	Schirmer	Very difficult.
Mazas	18 Artists' Studies, Op. 36, Book III	Schirmer	Extremely difficult.
Rode	12 Etudes	Schirmer	
Rode	24 Caprices	Schirmer	Difficult studies which logically follow Kreutzer.
Rovelli	12 Caprices, Op. 3 and 5	Schirmer	Difficult studies which logically follow Kreutzer.
Schradieck	Chord Studies	Schirmer	Specific studies designed to improve chord playing.
Wessely	Comprehensive Scale Studies	C. Fischer	
Wieniawski	8 Etudes-Caprices, Op. 18	Schirmer	Excellent and very musical etudes with 2nd violin accompaniment. Very difficult.

Special Study Materials

Dounis, D. C.	The Artist's Technique of Violin Playing, Op.12	C. Fischer	Technical studies designed to improve facility of the left hand and the bow.
Dounis, D. C.	The Higher Development of Thirds and Fingered Octaves, Op. 30	C. Fischer	
Flesch, Carl	Urstudien (Basic Studies)	C. Fischer	A series of scientifically designed exercises for the advanced violinist with limited time to practice.

VIOLA METHODS

Carse	Viola School, Bks. I–IV	Augener	
Fischer, Bernard	Modern Viola Fundamentals	Willis Music Co.	Easy progressive material.
Gardner, Samuel	Viola Method	Boston	2 Vols. Book I—Elementary, Book 2—Intermediate.
Laoureux-Iotti	Practical Method for Viola	Schirmer	
Sitt	Practical Viola Method	C. Fischer	
Ward, Sylvan D.	Rubank Elementary Method and Rubank Intermediate Method	Rubank	A follow-up course for individual or like-instrument class instruction. Easy to intermediate.

OTHER MATERIALS FOR VIOLA
Elementary to Intermediate

AUTHOR	TITLE	PUBLISHER	DESCRIPTION OR COMMENTS
Kayser	36 Elementary and Progressive Studies Op. 20	Schirmer	
O'Reilly, Sally	String Power	Kjos	Technical exercises.
Whistler	From Violin to Viola	Rubank	Easy studies designed to help the violinist make the change from violin to viola.
Whistler	Introducing the Positions	Rubank	2 Vols. Vol. I—3rd and half positions, Vol. II—2nd, 4th, and 5th positions.
Whistler-Hummel	Elementary Scales and Bowings	Rubank	
Wohlfahrt	Foundation Studies	Schirmer	Two books. Book I—1st position, Book II—30 studies in three positions.

OTHER MATERIALS FOR VIOLA
Intermediate

Applebaum	3rd and 5th Position String Builder	Belwin-Mills	
Carse	Viola School Bk. III	Augener	
Fischer	Selected Studies and Etudes	Belwin-Mills	
Kayser	36 Studies, Op. 20	Schirmer	
Lifschey	Daily Technical Studies	C. Fischer	
Lifschey	Scale and Arpeggio Studies, Bks. 1 and 2	Schirmer	

Advanced

Anzoletti	Dodici Studi, Op. 125	Ricordi	Extremely difficult studies and theme and variations.
Bruni	25 Melodious and Characteristic Studies	C. Fischer or Schirmer	Moderately difficult to difficult.
Campagnoli	41 Caprices	Schirmer	Difficult to very difficult.
Dont (Svecenski)	20 Progressive Studies for Viola	Schirmer	With 2nd viola.
Dont (Bailly)	24 Viola Studies, After Op. 35	Schirmer	Transcribed from the violin etudes. Difficult.
Flesch, Carl (Karman)	Scale System	C. Fischer	Adapted from the violin book.
Fuchs, Lillian	15 Characteristic Studies	Oxford	
Gavinies (Spitzner)	24 Etudes	International	Difficult. From the violin book.
Hoffmeister	12 Studies	Peters	
Kievman, Louis	Practicing the Viola, Mentally-Physically	Kelton Pub.	Programmed instruction studies for daily reference.
Kreutzer (Blumenthal)	42 Studies	Schirmer	
Kreuz, Emil	Select Studies Book IV	Augener	

AUTHOR	TITLE	PUBLISHER	DESCRIPTION OR COMMENTS
Matz, A.	Intonation Studies	Breitkopf & Härtel	Five books.
Mazas	Special Etudes, Op. 36, Bk. I and II	Schirmer	
Mogil	Scale Studies (Based on Hrimalyi)	Schirmer	
Primrose, William	The Art and Practice of Scale Playing on the Viola	Mills Music Inc.	Gives special attention to shifting with comment about the use of open strings.
Rode (Blumenau)	24 Caprices	Schirmer	Difficult. From the violin book.
Volmer	Bratschen-schule	AMP (B. Schoff)	

CELLO METHODS

AUTHOR	TITLE	PUBLISHER	DESCRIPTION OR COMMENTS
Bornschein, Franz C.	Five Lessons on the Violoncello	Oliver Ditson Co.	Goes through three octave scales.
Deak, Stephen	Modern Method for the Violoncello	Elkan-Vogel Co., Inc.	2 Vols. Vol. 1—through 7th position. Vol. 2–26 studies of medium difficulty.
Dotzauer, J. J. F.	Violoncello Method	C. Fischer	2 Vols. Vol 1—exercises and pieces in first position. Vol. 2—more advanced material.
Fuchs	Violoncello Method	Schott	3 Vols.
Kummer	Violoncello Method	Schirmer	
Langey, Otto	Otto Langey's Celebrated Tutors	C. Fischer	Moves rapidly to difficult material in one volume.
Matz and Aronson	The Complete Cellist	Broude Inc.	2 Vols. A condensation by Aronson of the extensive pedagogical work of the Yugoslavian cellist/teacher Rudolph Matz. A progressive, sequential approach. Preface by Piatagorsky.
Piatti, Alfredo	Method	Augener	
Potter, Louis, Jr.	The Art of Cello Playing	Summy-Birchard Co.	Considerable explanatory text with pictures. Moves gradually to advanced level.
Schröder, Carl	Violoncello Method	C. Fischer	3 Vols. Part I—through two octave scales. Part II—first four positions and half position. Part III—thumb position, octaves, and double-stops.
Stutschevsky, J.	The Art of Playing Violoncello	Schott	Four books.
Such, Percy	New School of Studies	Augener	Vols. 1 and 2 combined.
Suzuki/Sato	Cello School	Kjos	Vols. 3 and 4 combined.
Ward, Sylvan	Elementary Method	Rubank	
Werner, Jos.	Practical Method for Violoncello	C. Fischer	2 Vols. Vol. I—through two octave scales. Vol. II—advanced techniques.
Young, Phyllis	Playing the String Game, Strategies for Teaching Cello and Strings	University of Texas	A collection of 165 specific teaching devices designed to convey the desired concept to the student through appropriate imagery. While the "mini games" are directed primarily at the cello, the author explains how they may be used with the other strings.

OTHER MATERIALS FOR THE CELLO

AUTHOR	TITLE	PUBLISHER	DESCRIPTION OR COMMENTS
Becker	Finger and Bow Exercises (with New Scale Studies)	International	
Benoy-Sutton	Introduction to Thumb Position	Oxford Univ. Press	
Boettcher, Wolfgang	Scale System for the Violoncello	Fischer	
Cossman, B.	Cello Studies	Schott (International)	
Dotzauer	62 Select Studies	C. Fischer	2 Vols. Easy to difficult.
Dotzauer, J. J. F.	113 Etudes	Litolff (International)	3 Vols. of graded etudes.
Dotzauer	18 Exercises, Op. 120	Breitkopf & Härtel	
Duport, Jean Louis	Twenty-one Etudes	Schirmer	
Epperson, Gordon	A Manual of Essential Cello Techniques	Fox	
Feuillard, L. R.	Daily Exercises	Schott	
Francesconi, G.	Practical School for Violoncello	Suvini Zerboni	3 Vols. Vol I—1st position, Vol.II—all positions, Vol.III—advanced exercises.
Franchomme, A.	12 Caprices, Op. 7	International	With 2nd cello.
Frank, M.	Scales and Arpeggios	Schott	
Grant, Francis	Basic Thumb Position Studies for the Young Cellist	Concert Music Pub.	Studies on all four strings, pieces, and scales in thumb position.
Grant, Francis	First Position Studies	Ludwig Mu. Pub.	
Gruetzmacher	Daily Exercises, Op. 67	Schirmer	
Guerini-Silva	Thirteen Studies	Ricordi	Difficult to very advanced.
Klengel, J.	Daily Exercises	Breitkopf & Härtel	3 Vols.
Klengel, J.	Technical Studies	International	4 Vols.
Kummer, F. A.	10 Etudes Melodiques, Op. 57	Peters	Ten etudes of medium difficulty with 2nd cello accompaniment.
Kummer, F. A.	Studien für Violoncello, Op. 106	Peters	Eight etudes with second cello.
Lebell, L.	The Technique of the Lower Positions, Op. 22	Schott	2 Vols.
Lee-Rose	40 Melodic Studies	Schirmer	
Magg	Cello Exercises	Schirmer	
Merk (Klengel)	20 Studies, Op. 11	International	Moderately difficult to difficult.
O'Reilly, Sally	String Power	Kjos	Bks 1 and 2.

AUTHOR	TITLE	PUBLISHER	DESCRIPTION OR COMMENTS
Popejoy	Melodious Studies, Bks. 1 and 2	Belwin-Mills	
Popper	High School of Cello Playing	International	
Popper	15 Easy Studies	International	
Popper	Intermediate Studies, Op. 76	International	
Schroeder, Alwin	170 Foundation Studies Progressively Arranged	C. Fischer	3 Vols. Progresses to very difficult material.
Schroeder, A.	219 Technical Exercises	Leuckart	
Schulz, W.	Technical Studies for the Advanced Cellist	Schott	
Smith, G. Jean	Cellist's Guide to the Core Technique	ASTA (Presser)	
Starker	An Organized Method of String Playing	Peer-Southern Concert Music	Exercises for the left hand.
Such, Percy	New School of Cello Studies	Stainer and Bell	3 Books. Progressive difficulty.
Whistler, Harvey S.	Introducing the Positions for Cello	Rubank	2 Vols. Vol. I—4th position; Vol. 2—2nd through 3rd and a half position.

BASS METHODS

AUTHOR	TITLE	PUBLISHER	DESCRIPTION OR COMMENTS
Bille	New School for Double Bass	Ricordi	
Bottesini	Metodo Per Contrabasso	Ricordi	Begins at intermediate level and continues through advanced material.
Butler, H. J.	Progressive Method	C. Fischer	Two books.
Curtis, William	A Modern Method for String Bass	Berklee Press	Jazz oriented.
Findeisen, T. A.	Complete Method	International	4 Vols.
Green, Barry	The Fundamentals of Double Bass Playing	Piper Co.	Wide range of techniques. Many illustrations. For student, class, teacher, professional. Also one 8-inch recording.
Langey	Celebrated Tutor	C. Fischer	
Marcelli, Nino	Carl Fischer Basic Method for the String Bass	C. Fischer	2 Vols. Book I—half position through 2nd position, Book II—3rd position through 7th position.
Nanny	Complete Method for the Double Bass	Leduc	
Simandl, F.	New Method for the Double Bass	C. Fischer	2 Vols. Book I—all positions and scales. Book II—advanced studies and techniques.
Ward, Sylvan	Elementary Method for String Bass	Rubank	
Zimmerman	Elementary Double Bass Method	Schirmer	

OTHER MATERIALS FOR BASS

AUTHOR	TITLE	PUBLISHER	DESCRIPTION OR COMMENTS
Dragonetti	5 Studies	Carish	
Findeisen	25 Technical Studies	International	4 Vols.
Gardali, Douglas	Principals of Contrabass Playing	Pioneer	A treatise on playing the contrabass for already skilled, mature players.
Grodner, Murray	An Organized Method of String Playing	Lemur	
Hause	96 Etudes	Presser	
Hrabe	86 Etudes	International	
Kayser (Winsel)	36 Studies, Op. 20	International	
Kreutzer-Simandl	18 Studies	International	
Lee	Studies, Op. 31	International	
Madenski, E.	Double Bass Studies	Universal	2 Vols.
Portnoi, Henry	Creative Bass Technique	ASTA (Presser)	
Schwabe	Scale Studies	International	
Simandl	30 Etudes for the String Bass	Fischer	
Simandl	Gradus ad Parnassuma 24 Studies	International	2 Vols. Difficult to very difficult.
Slama, Anton	66 Studies in all Keys	International	
Storch-Hrabe	57 Studies	International	2 Vols.
Sturm, W.	110 Studies, Op. 20	International	2 Vols.
Turetsky, Bertram	The Contemporary Bass	University of California Press	This book is dedicated to bringing the bass into the 20th century and explaining some of the new techniques for bass employed by contemporary composers. There are many specific examples taken from a wide range of contemporary literature.

SPECIAL MATERIALS

AUTHOR	TITLE	PUBLISHER	DESCRIPTION OR COMMENTS
Green, Elizabeth A. H.	Musicianship and Repertoire for the High School Orchestra	Presser	Musical and technical problems arranged in a key-sequence.
Green, Elizabeth A. H.	Orchestral Bowings	Campus Publishers, Ann Arbor, Mich.	A compendium of typical and traditional orchestral bowings, and a guide to bowing styles required for a variety of orchestra literature.
Janowsky, Edward	Note Speller	Belwin	For violin, viola, cello, and bass. Provides exercises in writing on the staff.
Rowe, Phyllis	Music Workbook for Strings	Summy-Birchard	Worksheets dealing with the staff, clefs, note values, finger settings, musical terms, and string terms. Violin, viola, cello, bass.
Anderson, Gerald	All for Strings—Theory Workbooks 1 & 2	Kjos	

The American String Teachers Association *String Syllabus* contains graded solo lists for each of the string instruments. The *String Syllabus* may be obtained from Theodore Presser, Bryn Mawr, Pennsylvania 19010. Another source is *Prescribed Music,* published by the University Interscholastic League, Box 8028, University Station, Austin, Texas 78713–8028.

APPENDIX IV

List of Music Dealers, Instrument and Accessory Dealers

New teachers located in a community that does not have the benefit of a full-service music store often need help in finding a source for music, instruments, supplies, and repairs. The following lists are provided to give those teachers a place to start in meeting these needs.

The lists are brief. There was no attempt to make them complete. The lists include dealers who advertise widely and most of whom publish mail-order catalogs. Inclusion here does not constitute a recommendation, nor does omission imply disapproval.

MUSIC DEALERS

ASTA Publications
Theodore Presser Company
Bryn Mawr, PA 19010

Mel Bay Publications, Inc.
P.O. Box 66
#4 Industrial Drive
Pacific, MO 63069–0066

Birch Tree Group, Ltd.
180 Alexander Road
Box 2072
Princeton, NJ 08540
Includes: Summy-Birchard Suzuki Method

European American Music Distributors Corp.
P.O. Box 850
Valley Forge, PA 19482
215–648–0506

Highland/Etling Publishing
1344 Newport Ave.
Long Beach, CA 90804
213–498–5997

Byron Hoyt
2526 16th Street
San Francisco, CA 94103
800–858–8055

Edwin F. Kalmus
Music Publishers
P.O. Box 1007
Opa-Locka, FL 33054
305–681–4683

Neil A. Kjos Music Company
4382 Jutland Drive
San Diego, CA 92117–0894

Hal Leonard Publishing Corporation
P.O. Box 13819
Milwaukee, WI 53213

SHAR Products Company
2465 South Industrial
P.O. Box 1411
Ann Arbor, MI 48106

WARD Music Ltd.
412 West Hastings St.
Vancouver, B.C. V6B IL3

INSTRUMENT AND ACCESSORY DEALERS

Canapini Violin Bow Control
P.O. Box 25
Sudbury, Ontario
Canada
P3E 4N3

Concord Musical Supplies
P.O. Box 916
Maywood, NJ 07607
201–261–3871

Continental Music, Scherl and Roth
1000 Indiana Parkway
Elkhart, IN 46516

Ole Steffen Dahl
300 South Swain Avenue
Bloomington, IN 47401
812–332–84422

Domino's Discount Strings
130 S. 18th Street
Philadelphia, PA 19103
215–567–1164

Glaesel
Stringed Instruments Division
The Selmer Company
P.O. Box 310
Elkhart, IN 46515

Wm. Lewis and Son
3000 Marcus Ave.
Suite 2W7
Lake Success, NY 11042

Lyons Music Products
P.O. Box 1003
Elkhart, IN 46515
219–294–6602

Metropolitan Music Co.
Mountain Road R.R. #1
Box 1670
Stowe, VT 05672
802–253–4814

National Educational Music Company, Ltd.
1181 Route 22
Box 1130
Mountainside, NJ 07092

National Music Supply
P.O. Box 14421
St. Petersburg, FL 33733
813–321–6666

Schmitt Music Centers
88 South Tenth Street
Minneapolis, MN 55403
Continental USA 800–328–8480, Minnesota 800–292–7959

Shar Products Company
2465 South Industrial
P.O. Box 1411
Ann Arbor, MI 48106

Southwestern Stringed Instruments
and Accessories
1228 E. Prince Rd.
Tucson, AZ 85719
800–528–3430
In Arizona, 1–293–9717

Kenneth Warren
407 South Dearborn Street
Chicago, IL 60605

Philip H. Weinkrantz
Musical Supply Company, Inc.
2519 Bomar Ave.
Dallas, TX 75235
214–350–4883

Wenger Corporation
P.O. Box 448
Owatonna, MN 55060–0448
800–533–0393 X 38DJ
In Minnesota, 800–533–6774

The Wichita Violin Shop
2525 East Douglas
Wichita, KS 67211
800–835–3006
316–684–1031

The Woodwind and The Brasswind
50741 U.S. 33 North
South Bend, IN 46637
800–348–5003
In Indiana, 800–321–8391

Peter Zaret
1216 Richmond Crescent
Norfolk, VA 23508
800–222–2998
In Virginia, 804–423–3336 collect

Bibliography

ALTON, ROBERT. *Violin and Cello Building and Repairing,* Saint Clair Shores, Mich.: Scholarly, 1976.

AUER, LEOPOLD. *Violin Playing As I Teach It,* New York: Dover, 1980.

BACHMAN, ALBERTO. *An Encyclopedia of the Violin,* New York: D. Appleton-Century Co., 1937.

BARRETT, HENRY. *The Viola, Complete Guide for Teachers and Students.* University, Ala. The University of Alabama Press, 1972.

BENFIELD, WARREN, and DEAN, JAMES S., JR. *The Art of Double Bass Playing,* Princeton N.J.: Summy-Birchard Co., 1973.

BIRGE, EDWARD BAILEY. *History of Public School Music in the United States.* Washington, D.C.: Music Educators National Conference, 1966.

BOLANDER, JOHN JR. *Violin Bow Making.* San Jose, Calif.: Rosicrucian Press, 1981.

BOYDEN, DAVID. *History of Violin Playing, From Its Origins to 1761 and Its Relationship to the Violin and Violin Music.* London: Oxford University Press, 1965.

BRONSTEIN, R. *The Science of Violin Playing.* Neptune, N.J.: Paganiniana Publications, 1981.

BYTOVETZKI, PAVEL L. *How to Master the Violin: A Practical Guide for Students and Teachers.* New York: AMS Press, 1917.

COLWELL, RICHARD J. *The Teaching of Instrumental Music.* New York: Appleton-Century-Crofts, Educational Division, Meredith Corporation, 1969.

COMMON, ALFRED. *How to Repair Violins and Other Instruments.* New York: Gordon Press, 1977.

COOK, CLIFFORD. *String Teaching and Some Related Topics.* Bryn Mawr, Pa.: ASTA, Theodore Presser, 1957.

COWDEN, ROBERT L., and MUEGEL, GLENN A. *Bowing for Better Sound.* Elon, N.C.: Elon College Press, 1971.

COWLING, ELIZABETH. *The Cello.* Totowa, N.J.: Scribner, 1983.

DE RUNGS, MARIA. *Cello Syllabus.* Boston: Branden, 1973.

DILLON and KRIECHBAUM. *How to Design and Teach a Successful String and Orchestra Program.* San Diego: Kjos, 1978.

DOLEJSI, ROBERT. *Modern Viola Technique.* Chicago: The University of Chicago Press, Da Capo Press, 1939.

EDWARDS, ARTHUR C. *Beginning String Class Method.* Dubuque, Iowa: Wm. C. Brown Company Publishers, 1985.

EISENBERG, MAURICE. *Cello Playing of Today.* London: The Strad, 1957.

FARGA, FRANZ. *Violins and Violinists.* New York: Frederick A. Praeger, 1969.

FARISH, MARGARET K. *String Music In Print.* 2nd Edition. New York: R. R. Bowker Co., Xerox Education Co., 1973. *Supplement,* Musicdata, 1984.

FLESCH, CARL. *The Art of Violin Playing.* Books I and II. New York: Carl Fischer, Inc., 1939.

GALAMIAN, IVAN, and GREEN, ELIZABETH. *Principles of Violin Playing and Teaching,* 2nd Edition. Englewood Cliffs, N.J.: Prentice Hall, Inc., 1985.

GREEN, ELIZABETH A. H. *Teaching Stringed Instruments in Classes.* Englewood Cliffs, N.J.: Prentice Hall, 1966.

GREEN, ELIZABETH A. H. *Orchestral Bowings and Routines.* Ann Arbor, Mich.: Campus, 1963.

GRODNER, MURRAY. *Comprehensive Catalogue of Literature for the String Bass.* Encinitas, Calif.: Lemur, 1974.

HART, GEORGE. *The Violin: Its Famous Makers and Their Imitators.* Boston: Longwood Press, 1977.

HAVAS, KATO. *A New Approach to Violin Playing.* London: Bosworth, 1961.

HAVAS, KATO. *Stage Fright, Its Causes and Cures, with Special Reference to Violin Playing.* London: Bosworth and Co., Ltd, 1973.

HENKLE, TED. *The String Teacher's Handbook,* 5415 Reynolds St., Savannah, GA 31405.

HERON-ALLEN, EDWARD. *De Fidiculis Bibliographia; Being an Attempt towards a Bibliography of the Violin and All Other Instruments Played with the Bow in Ancient and Modern Times.* London: Holland Press, 1961.

HOFSTETTER, FRED T. *Computer Literacy for Musicians.* Englewood Cliffs, N.J.: Prentice Hall, 1988.

HORSFALL, JEAN. *Teaching the Cello to Groups.* Fair Lawn, N.J.: Oxford University Press, 1974.

HUTTON, TRUMAN. *Improving the School String Section.* New York: Carl Fischer, Inc., 1963.

JACOBY, ROBERT. *Violin Technique, A Practical Analysis for Performers.* Dobbs Ferry, N.Y.: Novello, 1985.

KENDALL, JOHN. *Suzuki Violin Method in American Music Education.* Princeton, N.J.: Birch Tree Gr., 1985.

KENNAN, KENT, and GRANTHAM, DONALD D. *The Techniques of Orchestration.* 3rd Edition. Englewood Cliffs, N.J.: Prentice Hall, Inc., 1983.

KENNESON, CLAUDE. *A Cellist's Guide to the New Approach.* Hicksville, N.Y.: Exposition Press, Inc., 1974.

KLOTMAN and HARRIS. *Learn to Teach through Playing.* Reading, Mass.: Addison-Wesley, 1976.

KLOTMAN, ROBERT H. *Scheduling Music Classes.* Washington, D.C.: Music Educators National Conference, 1968.

KRAYK, STEFAN. *The Violin Guide (For Performers, Teachers and Students).* Hollywood, Calif.: Highland Music Co., 1966.

KUHN, WOLFGANG. *Principles of String Class Teaching.* Rockville Centre, N.Y.: Belwin, 1957.

KUHN, WOLFGANG. *The Strings: Performance and Instructional Techniques.* Boston: Allyn and Bacon, 1967.

MANTEL, GERHARD. *Cello Technique.* Bloomington, Ind.: Indiana University Press, 1975.

MATESKY and WOMACK. *String Teacher Handbook for Organizing String Classes.* Sherman Oaks, Calif.: Alfred Music Co.

MATESKY, RALPH and RUSH, RALPH E. *Playing and Teaching Stringed Instruments.* Parts I and II. Englewood Cliffs, N.J.: Prentice-Hall, Inc., 1964.

MENUHIN, YEHUDI. *Violin: Six Lessons.* New York: Norton, 1981.

MENUHIN, YEHUDI, et al. *The Violin and Viola.* Riverside, N.J.: Macmillan, 1976.

NORMANN, THEODORE F. *Instrumental Music in the Public Schools.* Philadelphia, Pa.: Oliver Ditson Co., 1939.

POTTER, LOUIS ALEXANDER. *The Art of Cello Playing: A Complete Textbook Method for Private or Class Instruction.* Evanston, Ill.: Summy-Birchard Co., 1964.

PRIMROSE, WILLIAM. *Technique Is Memory: A Method for Violin and Viola Players Based on Finger Patterns.* Fair Lawn, N.J.: Oxford University Press, 1960.

RETFORD, WILLIAM CHARLES. *Bows and Bow Makers.* London: Strad., 1964.

RICHTER, CHARLES BOARDMAN. *Teaching Instrumental Music.* New York: Carl Fischer, 1959.

RILEY, MAURICE W. *The History of the Viola.* Ipsilanti, Mich.: Maurice W. Riley, 1980.

RODA, JOSEPH. *Bows for Musical Instruments of the Violin Family.* Chicago: W. Lewis, 1959.

ROLLAND, PAUL, and MUTSCHLER, MARLA. *The Teaching of Action in String Playing. Development and Remedial Techniques.* Urbana, Ill.: Illinois String Research Associates, 1974.

RUDOLPH, THOMAS E. *Music and the Apple II, Applications for Music Education, Composition and Performance.* Edited by MERRELL, RICHARD C. Drexel Hill, Pa.: Unsinn Publications, Inc., 1984.

SANDYS, WILLIAM. *The History of the Violin.* London: John Russell Smith, 1864.

SCHWARTZ, ED. The Educators' Handbook of Interactive Videodisc. Washington, D.C.: Association for Educational Communications Technology, 1986.

SHAPIRO, H. M. *The Physical Approach to Violinistic Problems.* New York: Omega Music Edition, 1954.

ST. GEORGE, HENRY. *Fiddles: Their Selection, Preservation, and Betterment.* London: The Strad Library of New York, Scribner's, 1910.

ST. GEORGE, HENRY. *The Bow: Its History, Manufacture and Use.* Boston: Longwood Press, 1977.

STARR, WILLIAM. *The Suzuki Violinist.* Knoxville, Tenn.: Kingston Ellis Press, 1976.

SUZUKI, SHINICHI, et al. *The Suzuki Concept.* San Francisco: Diablo Press, Inc., 1973.

SZENDE, OTTO, and NEMESSURI, MIHALY. *Physiology of Violin Playing.* Urbana, Ill.: American String Teachers Association, 1971.

TANGLEWOOD STRING SYMPOSIA (Louis Krasner, Chairman). *String Problems, Players and Paucity.* Berkshire Music Center with the Cooperation of the School of Music, Syracuse University, 1965.

TERTES, LIONEL. *Beauty of Tone in String Playing.* London: Oxford University Press, 1938.

TRZCINSKI, LOUIS C. *Planning the School String Program.* New York: Mills Music Co., 1963.

TURETZKY, BERTRAM. *The Contemporary Contrabass.* Berkeley, Calif.: University of California Press, 1974.

VAN DER STRAETEN, E. *The History of the Violin, Its Ancestors and Collateral Instruments.* London: Cassel, 1933.

VATELOT, ETIENNE. *Les Archets Francais.* Tome I, Paris: Sernor-M. Dufour, 1976.

WECHSBERG, J. *The Glory of the Violin.* New York: Viking, 1973.

YAMPOLSKY, I. M. *Principles of Violin Fingering.* Fair Lawn, N.J.: Oxford University Press, 1967.

You Fix Them. Cleveland, Ohio: SHERL and ROTH, Inc., 1955.

An important new publication, *The Complete String Guide: Standards, Programs, Purchase, and Maintenance,* a joint publication of the American String Teachers Association (ASTA), the National School Orchestra Association (NSOA), and Music Educators National Conference (MENC), is available from Theodore Presser, 1 Presser Place, Bryn Mawr, PA 19010 or from MENC Sales, 1902 Association Drive, Reston, VA 22091.

American String Teacher, the American String Teachers Association's official periodical on string instruments and string teaching, is the source of a great deal of current research and practice in the area of string teaching and playing. A number of the American String Teacher Association publications are handled by Theodore Presser, 1 Presser Place, Bryn Mawr, Pa., 19010. ASTA publications not already listed are listed below:

A Catalog of Contemporary American Chamber Music, by John Celentana and Creech Reynolds.

Cellist's Guide To the Core Technique, by G. Jean Smith.

Compendium of Orchestra and String Orchestra Literature, 1959–1977, edited by Ralph Matesky and G. Jean Smith.

Dictionary of Bowing Terms, by Barbara Seagrave, Joel Berman, and Kenneth Sarch.

Manual of Orchestral Bowing, by Charles Gigante.

Motion Study and Violin Bowing, by Percival Hodgson.

The Physiology of Violin Playing, by Szende and Nemessuri.

Senso-Motor Study and Its Application to Violin Playing, by Polnauer and Marks.

Sforzando Music Medicine for String Players, edited by Anne Mischakoff.

String Syllabus (revised 1986, edited by Margaret Farish).

Stringed Instrument Repair and Maintenance Manual, edited by John D. Zurfluh, Sr.

The Writings of Paul Rolland: An Annotated Bibliography by Mark Joseph Eisele.

An important new publication, *The Complete String Guide: Standards, Programs, Purchase, and Maintenance,* a joint publication of the American String Teachers Association (ASTA), the National School Orchestra Association (NSOA), and Music Educators National Conference (MENC), is available from Theodore Presser, 1 Presser Place, Bryn Mawr, PA 19010 or from MENC Sales, 1902 Association Drive, Reston, VA 22091.

Index